A good school happens where there is a personal interaction between deeply caring adults and the very special children with whom they are working. Not a ready-made program for packaged people, it is an environment responsive to the resources that both adults and children contribute to it. It is created day after day through that interaction; each one learns from and with each other as they use, build and remake the environment.

–Margaret Skutch, 1972
(To Start a School)

# Table of Contents

# The Storybook Journey

## Pathways to Learning through Story and Play

### Sue McCord

Sculpture on front cover: *The Need to Know* by Hollis Williford (1940-2007) who wrote, "It was born of a childhood reminiscence. It was at a time when a boy and his dog could relax under a shade tree and still travel to all the remote corners of the world by means of fiction, facts and fantasy. The sculpture celebrates reading as a doorway to creativity and imagination."

ISBN: 1453708308
ISBN-13: 9781453708309

To Charlie...the light of my life!

# Acknowledgments

To Sheila Goetz, Beret Strong, Cynthia Gray, and Brenda Dowell – I will be forever grateful for your endless support and expertise!

To Amy Thrasher, Kathy Stewart, Patti Sorkow, Donna Boudreau, and Kathy Krajewski – thank you, beyond words, for your valuable advice and contributions to this Journey!

To all the teachers, families, and children who have taken the Journey and made it their own in each setting…especially those at:

- The Child Learning Center at the University of Colorado
- Louisville Preschool
- Friends and Fun Children's Center
- The Acorn School for Early Childhood Development
- St. Saviors Church Nursery School
- Children's House
- Boulder Day Nursery
- The Center for Hearing Impaired Children
- The Anchor Center
- Tiny Tim Center
- Day Nursery Centers of Colorado Springs

# *Introduction*

**THE SEED FOR THE JOURNEY IS PLANTED**

The journey began when a little boy deeply touched his teachers as they observed his attempt to find meaning in the world.

In a preschool for children with developmental challenges, Dylan usually observed from a distance, expressionless, without a sound, negotiating the world in a rigid, repetitive fashion. Three years old and noticeably troubled, he would bristle when approached or invited to try something. He never spoke. The depth of his childhood depression was haunting to witness.

The school had two bus runs each day, and the small van we rode in became the extended classroom. It was a cozy space for storytelling, reading, puppeteering, and window gazing with running commentary. Dylan was the first one on the bus each day, always sitting in the same front seat. This van ultimately became a safe place for Dylan to be willing to take new risks. He started speaking in two- or three-word utterances about what he saw through the bus window but his frustration was evident, as his ideas seemed to outrun his speech.

Over time, Dylan began to speak more coherently and with greater affect. He wanted to share what he saw and to cuddle up closer to the adults to look at books on the bus, despite remaining a solitary player in school. The class was entering a period devoted to nursery rhymes, stories, and old favorites such as Little <u>Red Riding Hood</u>, <u>The Three Bears</u>, <u>Corduroy</u>, and many others. The emphasis was on the story and becoming so familiar with its plot and characters that it became a part of us, our play, and our group's common history. Familiarity with each story helped the children feel part of the social world at school – a secure world that accepted their efforts to interact with each other.

Their knowledge of the story gave them the material to become one of the characters, and as that character, the confidence to try out the social world. Dylan watched intently from the sidelines, not quite ready to join in. One morning on the bus, he discovered a Walt Disney's book version of "Peter Pan" in our permanent bus library. He chose that book thereafter, looking at every page in silent rapture. He carried it into the classroom one day and asked to have it read over and over. As time went on, he labeled all the characters and some of the events in the story. He even enjoyed Mary Martin's original recording of the Broadway musical. Other children were intermittently interested and took part, but Dylan always loved being Peter Pan. For Dylan, something was beginning to click. He was intently motivated to master the story sequence and all the characters, in a far more complex story than we would have ever imagined for him.

One morning, blue eyes sparkling, Dylan looked up at his teacher and said, "I dreamed I be Peter Pan last night!" He had finally revealed something about his world beyond school – an abstract expression of his total preoccupation with the story. The teacher suggested they play Peter Pan and asked Dylan what they would need. Dylan named the main characters and created his own narrative with much flying and returning to a makeshift Wendy house in one corner of our play yard. The song Mary Martin sings, "Let's be quiet as a mouse and build a tiny little house for Wendy, just for Wendy. Who's here to stay – a mother, a mother, at last we have a mother," became a meaningful refrain for Dylan.

The freedom of "flying" back and forth to the Wendy house seemed to release the anger and tension built up in the body of this small boy. Dylan's mother was a very young single woman who was having a difficult time being a mom, a situation reflected in Dylan's fascination with Wendy being Peter's mother. One day in a creative burst of enthusiasm, Dylan announced that the sun glittering off his seat belt was Tinkerbell! The discovery was contagious, as all the children reflected their personal Tinkerbells onto the bus ceiling. The world was responding to Dylan and Dylan to it.

Dylan began to trust his world and sense himself in relation to others. School became a safe reality in which he could depend upon consistent, supportive adults. He was curious about everything and intent upon listening to answers to his questions. He loved math concepts and reading street signs, and began to master his frustration. Teachers continued to accept his onlooker style of quiet observation, while encouraging his participation when he was ready. Peter would show up now and then in Dylan's thoughts, art, play, and sensory integration therapy. He eventually went on to try everything with the group – as Dylan! With guidance from school staff, Dylan and his mother began to find a way to relate to each other through the stories she read to him at home.

In his final months at the school, Dylan could initiate and direct sociodramatic play, often involving superheroes and storybook characters. His immersion in Peter Pan affected all areas of his development and opened a window on life that enabled him to connect with others. His personal growth went beyond our comprehension: Dylan taught us that stories hold a significant place in curricula for young children at all stages of the developmental spectrum and inspired us to take a closer look at this rich resource.

Certain conditions were necessary for Dylan to trust and grow with a fading dependence on Peter Pan. The powerful human relations he shared, the careful development of the physical and psychological environment, the thoughtful selection and organization of materials, the communication between home and school, and a keen understanding of development and the role of play were all vital parts of the process.

The Storybook Journey will share all of these aspects in separate chapters integrating the philosophy throughout in a spirit that allows children to lead the way and adults to creatively extend the children's interest.

# Chapter One

# *Chapter One: Part I*

## INTRODUCTION: WHAT IS THE STORYBOOK JOURNEY?

"It's nice to have an end to journey toward, but it's the Journey that matters in the end."
–Ursula K. Le Guin

The Storybook Journey is an approach to curriculum development that joins children, families, and teachers in the exploration of learning through children's storybooks. The journey begins by having conversations with families to identify and share their children's interests, strengths, needs, learning styles, and the priorities and dreams they have for their children. Having sought this greater understanding of the children and families in each unique classroom community, teachers observe and listen to what the children are drawn to within the classroom environment. Teachers respond to those interests by choosing a storybook to explore in depth over time. That storybook comes to life both in the classroom and through extensions to home, as teachers thoughtfully plan experiences that support children's learning and development. The environment, materials, and experiences are intentionally designed to immerse the children in a playful exploration of the story's rich literacy potential, concepts, vocabulary, sequence, and plot, as well as the sheer delight of exploring a story through their play.

Children can access this curriculum according to their individual learning styles and explore its possibilities on their own or with their peers. The shared story adventure becomes a peer conduit that supports children as they attempt to socialize. They hold the story in common. It becomes a connecting link as they learn and play together.

## WHAT MAKES THE STORYBOOK JOURNEY UNIQUE?

The unique feature of the Storybook Journey approach to curriculum is the depth of exploration of *one story over time*. Stories are a natural learning medium of childhood providing children exposure to language, early literacy, world knowledge, problem solving, emotions, and consideration of other people's point of view. Story play and reenactment provide children with the opportunity to move the ideas represented on the page into their own realm of action, pretend play, creative representation, experimentation, and social interactions. By reading and telling the story over time and exploring it in context and through a variety of modalities, children have access to rich learning opportunities inherent in each story. This occurs at a pace that allows for depth of comprehension.

Throughout the journey, teachers continue to observe children, talk with families, and document children's experiences and development to determine how to expand children's learning opportunities. The curriculum planning and the children's play become the vehicle to expand the children's experience. The Journey's holistic approach observes children's play and develops the curriculum to support not only the group endeavor, but also each child's experiences. It encourages children to lead the way and adults to creatively extend children's learning by observing their interest, ideas, and curiosity. Through responsive changes in the environment, materials, experiences, and teacher-child interactions, teachers scaffold children's learning to the next step in development. The continuity of the classroom and home experience with one story across time gives all children the possibility to absorb the richness of the language and ideas presented in each story and to truly explore the concepts in a meaningful, connected way.

**The following schematic is a simplified visual of the process:**

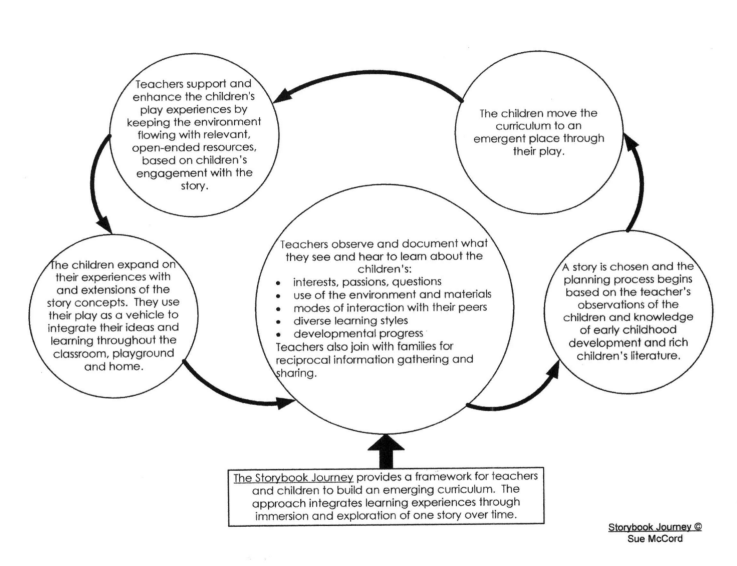

Teachers support and enhance the children's play experiences by keeping the environment flowing with relevant, open-ended resources, based on children's engagement with the story.

The children move the curriculum to an emergent place through their play.

The children expand on their experiences with and extensions of the story concepts. They use their play as a vehicle to integrate their ideas and learning throughout the classroom, playground and home.

Teachers observe and document what they see and hear to learn about the children's:
- interests, passions, questions
- use of the environment and materials
- modes of interaction with their peers
- diverse learning styles
- developmental progress

Teachers also join with families for reciprocal information gathering and sharing.

A story is chosen and the planning process begins based on the teacher's observations of the children and knowledge of early childhood development and rich children's literature.

The Storybook Journey provides a framework for teachers and children to build an emerging curriculum. The approach integrates learning experiences through immersion and exploration of one story over time.

Storybook Journey ©
Sue McCord

# Chapter One: Part *II*

## HOW ARE STORIES, PLAY, AND DEVELOPMENT INTEGRATED INTO THE JOURNEY?

The emerging curriculum touches on all of the core areas of a child's development: physical, social, emotional, cognitive, and linguistic. It is through the replay and mastering process we are able to observe how well the child has conceptualized the essence of the story and integrated it at various developmental levels. Starting with the physical, we will briefly explore the dynamics of the developmental storybook links.

<u>Physically</u> the child in the preschool years is an active agent and participant in life. The child's play is a continuous exploration with his body and senses: hearing, seeing, touching, feeling, tasting, and smelling. The child wants to physically touch all parts of his expanding world in order to internalize all of its dimensions. His mode of communication is often in the physical domain, as words are not yet his favorite means of expression. Adults need to observe a child's body language to interpret what he might be "saying." The child becomes an active participant through movement and actions to be taken in various character roles. He can also use the sensory stimulation setups in the classroom to explore his ever-changing means of expression and understanding. Burying one's arms up to the elbows in a tub filled with oobleck (a combination of water and cornstarch), or tasting homemade porridge and smelling it cook, add depth to a child's enjoyment of the related stories. For Dylan, the child in the introduction, acting out Peter Pan allowed his body and soul the freedom to fly and be relieved of tension in the safety of his story reenactment.

Educator and author John Holt has said that every child, without exception, has an innate and unquenchable drive to understand the world in which he lives and to gain freedom and competence in it. We continue to discover that stories and meaningfully linked curriculum are valuable vehicles to help a young child in this unquenchable quest to understand. <u>Cognitively</u>, the child is in Piaget's pre-operational stage of development. It is a critical time for the two- to five-year-old to gather world knowledge in a way that facilitates constructive understanding. Whatever adds to a child's understanding, capacity for growth and pleasure, sense of control, ability to relate to others' dignity and worth is the essence of cognitive learning.

The child is gathering story information that he can accommodate to modify or cope with new information or situations. A vivid example of this is the reaction one of our children had to the reading and telling of <u>Little Red Riding Hood</u> Jenny's mother died in Jenny's infancy, and she had always called her grandmother, who raised her, "Mommy." Each time we read the part where Little Red Riding Hood took the basket of goodies from "Mommy" to give to "Grandma," Jenny left the group and paced anxiously in another part of the room. Our hypothesis is that Jenny's realization that Mommy is separate from Grandma in this story was a very significant step in her attempt to assimilate her own family situation.

In the story context, the child's concept of decentering expands as a child now experiments with the idea that he can be himself, Gavard, and Peter Rabbit at the same time. As the child takes on roles and acts them out, he has a growing awareness of the separate roles as well as his evolving separate self. Transformation of self and observing transformation in other creatures is an important aspect of learning and an essential concept to master. This occurred in the children's journey with <u>The Very Hungry Caterpillar</u>. We also watched the children alternately puzzle and delight in the wondrous change of Miss Nelson as she emerged as Viola Swamp in the story <u>Miss Nelson Is Missing.</u>

Flexible thinking is enhanced by encouraging children to vary a story's content by attaching their own creative endings to a known story. The three-year-olds in our group loved making the wolf's bottom all better by pretending to put ointment on it after it was hurt in the hot water bucket of the <u>Three Little Pigs</u>. They also played out inviting the wolf to dinner in their playhouse "…if he bees good." Likewise, the four-year-olds thoroughly enjoyed adding a teenage daughter to the giant's castle in <u>Jack and the Beanstalk</u>. She had her own room and "did not have to come to dinner if she didn't want to." There was a sense of great power and satisfaction in changing and extending the plot within the story framework. The simple story lines give a child a sense of completion and predictability that allows for safe, flexible readjustments to the plot. Predictability is an important part of learning and a necessary skill for learning to read.

Children enjoy having an alternative to acting out a story scenario with others by practicing from a distance with props. Symbolic materials can be used to encourage them to play out the story within a miniature world. Three jar lids or wooden blocks in seriated sizes are transformed into billy goats and the three bears – they easily trip trap over block bridges or sleep in wooden block beds. This form of <u>externalization</u> is a supportive learning process for young children. To a child with developmental delays, the practice of communicating the replay of the story with visual cues from realistic or symbolic props and the support of an adult is extremely helpful.

A surge of developmental research on the emotional lives of children reveals the intimate interplay between the affective and cognitive aspects of a child's life. Dr. T. Berry Brazelton, a retired Harvard University researcher, pediatrician, and respected author, expressed: "It's about time we started looking at emotions more carefully. Everything we know about a child shows that healthy emotional development is the key to other kinds of growth."

<u>Emotionally</u>, the preschool child is moving through the first three stages, from trust to initiative, of Erickson's eight stages of human growth. Though trust and autonomy are being established long before a child arrives at the preschool, they need to be reestablished in the new setting away from home. The magic, escape and control over a sometimes-overwhelming world, are essential needs for a young child as he learns to manage his feelings and affective responses. Story replay can help children gain a sense of mastery as they work through the drama of the big bad wolf or the powerful troll. Playing out an emotional stress serves as a catharsis, enabling a child to begin to play out the difference between fantasy and reality. Piaget calls this compensatory play. In replay, the child has a chance to walk like a giant or to travel in someone else's shoes vicariously living the joy or resolved fear with a sense of being in control.

There can be a feeling of well-being and group camaraderie in the common knowledge of a story. Some children need long periods of watching from a distance as a story is being played out before they have the courage to risk taking part. The continuous repetition as children play with the story characters invites a shared history and shared points of reference. Given time, each child can feel, regardless of his possible delay or stage of development, "I too know what is going on; I can find a way to be a part of this story." Adults have found that by allowing for varying paces and styles, and by being keenly sensitive to the timing of their interventions, all children eventually feel safe enough to enter into some aspect of the play.

The preschool years are a time of rapid fluctuation and inconsistencies for our young children. There is so much to grapple with and to understand in their everyday experiences. What gives an experience meaning for a child is the way new information can be assimilated into what the child already understands. If the child cannot take in new information the meaning remains vague. When Jenny withdrew during the reading of <u>Little Red Riding Hood</u>, she may have been protecting herself from being overwhelmed by the new and unsettling information that "mommy" and "grand-mother" were in fact two separate people. It was a revealing factor for the staff and Jenny's family. Together they realized Jenny was now old enough to hear the story of her mother's life and passing. A small album of Jenny's mother was created, gentle stories were shared, and innocent little questions were answered. She began to understand and assimilate the new information in the warmth and security of her family.

Researchers at the National Association for the Education of Young Children reviewed recent educational research, interviewed scores of experts, and observed classrooms. They note the crucial connection between children's social and emotional life and their academic competence. Children make the biggest strides, the authors found, when they are able to cement secure, consistent relationships with responsive adults (Wilson, 2009).

The use of stories as the core of our curriculum also plays a key role in the social development and communicative competence of our young children and particularly so for the children with significant challenges. Socially, the story provides children with a central focus and common knowledge of a scenario to play out with predictable characters and sequenced situations. The storyline is a scaffold that provides each child with a support for becoming an active, playful participant at a variety of cognitive, linguistic, social, and emotional levels. Feedback from peers serves as social reinforcement. In the context of the story, the child can be encouraged to communicate. For example, in The Three Billy Goats Gruff, the group shares common knowledge of the story. The more verbal child can carry the essence of the storyline and the child with more limited verbal abilities can join in chanting "trip trap, trip trap" as he masters the words through joyful repetition, practice, and peer acceptance. Each child's sense of being a part of the interaction enhances his learning and helps him identify more closely with his peers. When Papa Bear is one of the less verbal children, he can go through the motions of being encouraged by a more verbal Mama: "Come on, Father, we're going upstairs." Papa hears the language, follows the other bears, and becomes part of the social context.

For a child to act out a part, she needs other people. Role taking in a commonly known story nudges a child to communicate and cooperate more meaningfully with another child. The child is encouraged through her interactions and role taking to try on the perspective of others. Egocentricism is still a dominant feature of this age group, and the practice of role taking helps the child to move out from self to others in the safety of the role. Repetition, meaningful imitations, turn taking, and the contagious quality of stories eventually draws nearly all children into dramatic replays during the course of their open choice and/or group times. At the simplest level, the playing out of nursery rhymes can provide a marvelous first stage for role taking and "social bumping." By acting out and being one of many Humpty Dumpty's falling off the block wall together, the children naturally land in close proximity and are in playful physical contact with each other. This social bumping is a short, spontaneous, fun "communicative" moment.

The child's cognitive abilities, his communicative competence, and his emerging sense of self directly influence the nature of social exchange and other areas of his development. Through the thoughtful interlacing of the Storybook Journey with every facet of the preschool environment and the home/school partnership, we are striving to extend and enhance the relationship between experience and the development for each individual child.

The many pressures of a high-tech, fast-paced, automated, ever-changing society influence the young child in today's world. Television, being one of the most dominating and influential factors in a child's mechanical world can be viewed as a prime inhibiter of the child's imaginative play and substitute for interactive role taking and social interaction. One appeal of the Storybook Journey is its predictable familiarity for the child and its refreshing replacement of the mecca of television's superheroes. Threads in the children's own lives weave in and out of each story. That familiarity motivates, ignites, and replenishes their ability to take part in a story and derive personal meaning.

In summary, the Storybook Journey encourages the child to be an active agent and participant in life. It provides a vehicle for the child's innate and unquenchable drive to understand the world and to gain freedom and competence in it. It entices the child to learn to manage his feelings and affective response to a sometimes overwhelming and scary world. The process of internalizing the story and joyfully participating in replay enhances the child's communication competence and social interaction. It creates the perspective that books and stories are wondrous worlds awaiting discovery.

It plants the seeds of desire to be a "reader" in the children who relive the story through play. Dylan's total involvement with Peter Pan encompassed all of these benefits and opened a window on life that allowed him to connect with the rest of the world and find personal meaning almost beyond our comprehension. Dylan opened many windows for the teachers and therapists who worked closely with him at his school. He helped us discover the potential impact of the storybook and its ability to draw even the most depressed, shy, or delayed child into the world of relationships, communication, and meaningful learning.

# *Chapter One: Part III*

**WHAT DOES THE JOURNEY LOOK LIKE FROM A BIRD'S-EYE VIEW:**
**NARRATIVE FOR CHART HEADINGS**

**FOUNDATION**

- Relationships:

If endowed with fairy tale magic, I would wish that every child had at least one human being in his life who loved, understood, and respected him enough to nurture his growth, encourage his interests, and know his dreams and fears. Ours is a very busy culture today and sustained relationships seem hard to maintain. The configuration of the family is ever changing and a child's extended family is often spread far across the country. Young children are more and more in the care of people outside the home and often in groups that would benefit from having more trained adults. My deep concern is one of human contact and the availability of enough significant others with loving arms, welcoming laps, and unhurried moments for listening...listening and really hearing the meaning behind the children's words. Communication and understanding built on a relationship comes from spending meaningful time with another, trusted human being. This kind of relationship with a teacher also builds a foundation that supports a child's ability to function comfortably in the group and to form positive relationships and interactions with peers. Our challenge is to create a classroom where all children have a genuine sense of belonging.

The Storybook *Journey*

## A BIRD'S EYE VIEW OF THE STORYBOOK JOURNEY

THE CHILD: MESS - EXPRESS - PROCESS - ASSESS       THE ADULT: OBSERVE - PREPARE - PARTICIPATE - DOCUMENT - REFLECT

| FOUNDATION | PREPARATION | PARTICIPATION | DOCUMENTATION | CONTEMPLATION |

**FOUNDATION**

PREPARE:
TO TEACH BY BUILDING:
• WELL-GROUNDED KNOWLEDGE OF CHILD DEVELOPMENT AND
• GENUINE RELATIONSHIPS

ARTICULATE:
PERSONAL BELIEFS OF HOW CHILDREN LEARN

WORK TOWARD:
CONGRUENCE BETWEEN PERSONAL BELIEFS & TEACHING PRACTICE

OBSERVE:
TO UNDERSTAND AND DOCUMENT CHILDREN'S GROWTH OVER TIME

NOTE:
GROUP DYNAMICS & CHILD IN CONTEXT OF THE GROUP

KNOW:
THE DEVELOPMENTAL SPREAD WITHIN THE GROUP

**PREPARATION**

PLAN:
WITH A KNOWLEDGE OF CHILDREN'S INTERESTS, GOALS, & DISPOSITIONS TO LEARN

WEAVE:
THE STORY MEANINGFULLY INTO THE CURRICULUM

PRIME:
FOR EXPERIENCES THROUGH A PREPARED ENVIRONMENT

BUILD ON:
DAY TO DAY EXPERIENCES WITH VARIATIONS FOR REPRESENTING AND RE-PRESENTING FOR MASTERY

**PARTICIPATION**

SUPPORT:
CHILDREN'S SKILLS TO BECOME COMFORTABLE & COMPETENT PARTICIPANTS IN LEARNING THROUGH PLAY & PRACTICE

FACILITATE:
CHILDREN'S POSITIVE RELATIONSHIPS WITH EACH OTHER IN A COMMUNITY OF LEARNERS

ENCOURAGE:
FAMILY PARTICIPATION AS TEAM MEMBERS

ADVOCATE FOR:
TEAM MEMBERS & COMMUNITY AS RECIPROCAL PARTICIPANTS

**DOCUMENTATION**

STRIVE FOR:
AUTHENTIC REPRESENTATION OF A CHILD'S CAPACITIES

REVISIT:
GROWTH OVER TIME IN ALL DEVELOPMENTAL AREAS THROUGH:
OBSERVATION NOTES, VIDEO JOURNAL, AUDIO TAPES, PHOTOGRAPHS & SLIDES, PORTFOLIOS, CHILD/FAMILY INPUT, PATHWAYS

**CONTEMPLATION**

PAUSE:
TO INTERPRET COLLECTIONS & OBSERVATIONS

COMPREHEND
HOW EACH CHILD IS LEARNING

ENCOURAGE:
CHILD TO REFLECT ON OWN LEARNING WITH TEACHERS AND FAMILY

THINK:
TOGETHER WITH THE FAMILY ABOUT GUIDING THE CHILD'S NEXT STEPS & SUPPORTING POTENTIAL LEARNING

SUE McCORD
THE STORYBOOK JOURNEY©

We are talking about the most important aspect of preparation for all teachers, but especially for teachers of young children. It is the ability to form and sustain trusting and genuine relationships not only with children but also with their families. Equally important to a healthy classroom atmosphere is the development of authentic relationships with our teaching staff. This preparation before setting foot in a classroom, involves devoting serious time to discovering our own voice and to honestly facing ourselves and reflecting upon: what we believe about our own abilities, how our childhood influenced our lives, and why we have chosen teaching young children as our profession.

- <u>Beliefs</u>: Our beliefs about how children learn are extremely important. Sue Vartuli wrote, "Teachers' beliefs are often implicit and unarticulated, yet they influence teacher perceptions, judgments, and decisions and direct teachers to act in certain ways." This being the case, it is important for us to explore not only our beliefs about <u>how</u> children learn, but also whether we believe <u>all</u> children have the capacity to learn. Making sure that our personal beliefs and our teaching practices are congruent will help the children hone learning experiences that are more positive. It's important to revisit our beliefs in order to interpret and clarify them. Many members of teaching teams, having established a mutual trust, find it helpful to share what they believe with one another. Listening to each other and probing for meaning often helps team members to reflect and articulate more clearly their personal beliefs and philosophies as well as those of the center. It also supports building more solid relationships within the team and a better understanding of each other.

- <u>Observation</u>: In order to truly know the children in our care, we must become keen observers who are well grounded in understanding child development as well as becoming reciprocal information partners with families. Being well grounded in child development helps guide our observations; and our observations truly teach us important information about the uniqueness of each child's development. It is a dance between our background knowledge and what we see and hear happening in the classroom. We learn to use our observations to document how each child is navigating the territory…exploring the joys and frustrations of forming social relationships with their peers, playing out their everyday experiences and fantasies, moving, touching, and transforming. We observe to learn more about each child's unique learning style, emotional development, and physical well-being, and to understand how our teaching should respond to the developmental spread within the group. Our gift and challenge will be to capture these meaningful moments of learning in ways that will authentically represent each child's growth over time.

## PREPARATION

Thoughtful preparation time allows teachers to ready themselves to be present and available for the children as well as to create engaging environments and materials for children's diverse interests and challenges.

Observations generally guide the Storybook Journey planning process and classroom preparation. Fortified by observing children's play and conversations, teachers gather topics and ideas for what story they might launch for a Journey. Teachers have chosen stories based on their beautiful use of language, introduction of new vocabulary, child humor, familiarity, a parent or child suggestion, or because they wanted to share a story that might inspire a particular classroom project, or sometimes they just want to share a story they love. Other plans may emerge from different starting points, such as a story that children frequently request or seek in the story nook, or one that the staff feels is relevant to what has happened in the classroom. For example, one center had some old gaudy jewelry donated to them with big chunky, shiny glass "jewels." The children loved the jewelry! The teacher thought it would be fun to introduce the story: The Bremen Town Musicians because the robbers in the story steal some jewels. It was a hugely engaging and successful three-week Journey.

Once a story is chosen, the staff gathers to read it together, brainstorm the concepts that could be introduced from the story, and begin to plan how to meaningfully weave the concepts into the classroom centers. All centers of the classroom are prepared or primed in terms of what can be set up in the environment to make the story come alive. The concepts are explored through materials, various environmental setups, group times, and children's spontaneous play (inside and outside), which often extends all the way home to be enjoyed with their families. Teachers enrich the play by building on the children's day-to-day experiences. Many relevant open-ended, hands-on resources enhance the environment. Open-ended refers to materials that do not have a specific "correct" use and thus inspire the child's impact on them; sand, water, clay, paints, mud, and wire are a few examples. They are multipurpose materials that allow random experimentation and a means to extend children's imaginations and learning.

In our sincere attempt to teach, we can sometimes rob children of their own discoveries. "We ignore what children have to learn and instead impose what we want to teach thus putting children at risk for no purpose" (Elkind, 1987). It is therefore extremely important to prime the learning situation with experiences that children can relate to and explore over time. An example of this might be to bring caterpillars into the classroom before reading The Hungry Caterpillar to the children. Watching the caterpillars devour all the dill in the jar each day before spinning their cocoons is a real-life experience that primes the children for a more whimsical adventure with the storybook rendition.

## PARTICIPATION

"It takes a village to raise a child"…it takes the building of trusting relationships to raise a community of learners and participants. Years ago, Urie Bronfenbrenner, a former professor at the College for Human Ecology at Cornell University, proposed an ecological system to demonstrate the interrelated world of child, family, and neighborhood/community. It is a more complex system than we will discuss here, but he identified the first three components as:

<u>microsystem</u>: looking at the child as the center of the system

<u>mesosystem</u>: looking at the child as surrounded by his immediate and extended family and

<u>macrosystem</u>: looking at the child as a member of the community/ neighborhood/school

Perhaps it would be helpful to borrow from Dr. Bronfenbrenner's idea and translate it into a "community of learners" that would look at how the learners interrelate and how important it is for all learners to be active participants.

<u>Participants as a community of learners</u>:

child to child & child to family & child and family to teacher & all three related to the community

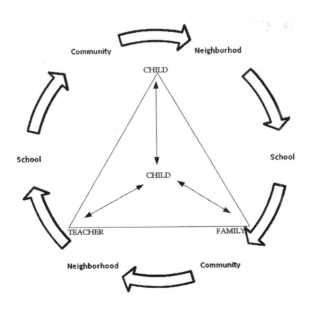

Participation is a vital part of the Storybook Journey as well. Stories become an important vehicle in the school experience for children, teachers, and families to participate in their shared connection with the story experience. Families are invited to join their children in natural and unique ways, bringing what happens in the classroom home through newsletters, videos of the class in action, a traveling wonderbook (scrapbook documenting the "life" of a Journey), reading and acting out the story at home, and many other possibilities. The degree of participation by families depends on the time, energy, and circumstances of each family and each teacher. Meaningful participation is something to hope for from everyone involved.

Some centers have been very clever in extending the story experience into the community. One center had the children's pressed clay renditions of the "Wild Things" (from <u>Where the Wild Things Are</u>, Maurice Sendak) displayed on the walls of their local bank, accompanied by a write-up about their school being part of the neighborhood. Another center baked "gingerbread people" and the teachers arranged with the chief of police to hide the children's cookies at the police department. The next morning the children discovered their cookies missing! The class explored the school – no cookies! The teachers suggested they all walk downtown and stop at various stores to see if anyone had seen the runaway "gingerbread people." Eventually, they found them…you know where. It was a great way to remind the community that children need all of us to care about them and for the children to have a positive and fun encounter with their immediate community… especially the police.

## DOCUMENTATION

"Documentation is the process of reciprocal learning. Through documentation we can leave traces that make it possible to share the ways children learn." Carlina Rinaldi

The Storybook Journey's approach to documentation strives to leave "traces" by authentically representing children's capacities in all areas of their development. Information is gathered over time through observation, listening, recording, reflecting, and sharing. Meaningful documentation is time consuming. It is imperative, however, that we find a way to document what is happening in a child's life in all domains. The tools we use to make children's learning visible to them, to their families, and to us as their teachers are many and varied, including observation notes, audio tapes, photographs, portfolios, child-family-Teacher Input, Pathways, and the requirements of the State Standards. Each of these will be discussed in chapters seven and eight.

**CONTEMPLATION**

When we share the responsibility of learning and teaching with a family, our understanding of each other's dreams, hopes, and goals for a child must be clear and honest. What is our intention in meeting together, and how can we reflect and share our observations and interpretations of the information and materials we've all gathered? We not only want to confer about "academics" but, equally important at this stage in a child's life, we want to understand on a profound level the child's social, emotional, cognitive, and physical development. We also want to recognize and honor all of the ways a child has of expressing himself in what Loris Malaguzzi calls the "hundred languages of children." Building this partnership with parents creates a unified effort and meaning for a more positive school and home experience for the child.

Reflecting with children on their own play and work is a marvelous and revealing practice. If we see children as active agents in their own learning and documentation, we find that they feel more respected and empowered. Revisiting and reflecting with each child in a quiet, private place deepens and broadens their knowledge and understanding of the concepts that are embedded in their work and learning. Some schools build in a scheduled time to join child, teacher, and family in a brief conference to encourage the child to share from one section of the portfolio what she has learned at school.

Sometime before the end of the year, most families (especially those who have children with particular learning challenges) appreciate an opportunity to confer with the teacher and other staff about guiding their child's next steps. For many families, the preschool staff members are the first advocates outside of their immediate family. We need to be especially sensitive to what help and support they may need from us in the transition from room to room or school to school. For all families a conference is an important way to determine the best placement to meet their child's future developmental needs and educational experiences.

In closing this introduction to The Storybook Journey, I'd like to share a very poignant quote from Professor T. Ripaldi in John Taylor's Notes on an Unhurried Journey.

When we adults think of children, there is a simple truth that we ignore; childhood is not preparation for life; childhood is life.

A child isn't getting ready to live; a child is living. The child is constantly confronted with the nagging question: "What are you going to be?" Courageous would be the youngster who, looking the adult squarely in the face, would say, "I'm not going to be anything; I already am." We adults would be shocked by such an insolent remark, for we have forgotten, if indeed we ever knew, that a child is an active, participating, and contributing member of society from the time he is born.

Childhood isn't a time when he is molded into a human who will then live life; he is a human who *is* living life. No child will miss the zest and joy of living unless these are denied him by adults who have convinced themselves that childhood is a period of preparation.

How much heartache we would save ourselves if we would recognize the child as a partner with adults in the process of living, rather than always viewing him as an apprentice. How much we would teach each other…Adults with the experience and children with the freshness; how full both our lives could be. A little child may not lead us, but at least we ought to discuss the trip with him; for, after all, life is his journey too.

# REFERENCES AND RELATED READING

Almy, M. (1966). *Young Children's Thinking: Studies of Some Aspects of Piaget's Theory.* New York, NY: Teachers College Press.

Ayer, J. A. (1982). *Sensory Integration and the Child* (5th edition). Western Psychological Services.

Beck, L. E. and Winsler, A. (1995). *Scaffolding Children's Learning: Vygotsky and Early Childhood Education.*Washington, DC: National Association for the Education of Young Children

Bettelheim, B. (1979). *The Uses of Enchantment: The Meaning and Importance of Fairy Tales.* New York, NY: Alfred A. Knopf.

Biehler, R. (1976). Child Development: An Introduction. *Erikson: Stages of Psychosocial Development.* Boston, MA: Houghton Mifflin Company.

Bodrova, E. and Leong, D. (1996). *Tools of the Mind: The Vygotskian Approach to Early Childhood Education.* Englewood Cliffs, NJ: Prentice Hall.

Bredekamp, S. and Copple, C. (1997). *Developmentally Appropriate Practices in Early Childhood Programs* (revised edition). Washington, DC: National Association for the Education of Young Children.

Bronfenbrenner, U. (Ed.) (2005). *Making Human Beings Human: Bioecological Perspectives on Human Development.* London: Sage Publications.

Cohen, D., Stern, V., and Balaban, N. (1997). *Observing and Recording the Behavior of Young Children* (4th edition). New York, NY: Teachers College Press.

Coleman, D. (October 1984). Emotions Enter Child's Repertory like Clockwork, *New York Times* (Quoted by T. Berry Brazelton).

Culkin, M. L. (Ed.) (2000). *Quality in Young Children's Programs: The Leader's Role.* New York, NY: Teachers College Press.

Curtis, D. and Carter, M. (2000). *The Art of Awareness: How Observation Can Transform Your Teaching.* St. Paul, MN: Redleaf Press.

Duckworth, E. (1987). *The Having of Wonderful Ideas.* New York, NY: Teachers College Press.

Edwards, C. (Ed.) (1998). *The Hundred Languages of Children: The Reggio Emilia Approach – Advanced Reflections.* Greenwich, CT: Ablex Publishing Corporation.

Elkind, D. (1987). *Miseducation: Preschoolers at Risk.* New York, NY: Knopf.

Gronlund, G. and Engel, B. (2001). *Focused Portfolios: A Complete Assessment for the Young Child.* St. Paul, MN: Redleaf Press.

Hawkins, F. P. (1974). *Journey with Children: The Autobiography of a Teacher.* Niwot, CO: University Press of Colorado.

Holt, J. (1967). *How Children Learn.* New York, NY: Dell Publishing Co. Inc.

Hyson, M. (2003). *The Emotional Development of Young Children: Building an Emotion-Centered Curriculum.* 2nd Edition. New York, NY: Teachers College Press.

Isenberg, J. (1990). Teachers Thinking and Beliefs and Classroom Practices. *Childhood Education,* 66 (5).

Kessler, R. (2000). *The Soul of Education: Helping Students Find Connection, Compassion, and Character at School.* Alexandria, VA: Association for Supervision and Curriculum Development.

Lindfers, J. W. (1999). *Children's Inquiry: Using Language to Make Sense of the World.* New York, NY: Teachers College Press.

Koplon, L. (2008). *Unsmiling Faces: How Preschools can heal.* New York, NY: Teachers College Press.

Mc Mullen, M.B. and Alat, K. (2002). Education Matters in Nurturing of the Beliefs of Preschool Caregivers and Teachers. *Early Childhood Research and Practice,* 4(2).

Paley, V. G. (1992). You Can't Say you Can't Play. Cambridge, MA: Harvard University Press.

Paley, V. G. (1991). *Bad Guys Don't Have Birthdays: Fantasy Play at Four.* Chicago, IL: The University Press.

Peterson, R. and Felton-Collins, V. (1986). *The Piaget Handbook for Teachers and Parents: Children in the Age of Discovery, Preschool-3rd Grade.* New York, NY: Teachers College Press.

Sandall, S. Schwartz, I. S., and Wolery, R. A. (2002). *Widening the Circle: Including Children with Disabilities in Preschool Programs.* New York, NY: Teachers College Press.

Schickendenz, J. (1999). *Much More than the ABCs: Early Stages of Reading and Writing.* Washington, DC: National Association for the Education of Young Children.

Shore, R. (1997). *Rethinking the Brain: New Insights into Early Devel*opment, New York, NY: Family and Work Institute.

Stone, J. (2001). *Building Classroom Community: The Early Childhood Teachers* Role. Washington, DC: National Association for the Education of Young Children.

Ripaldi, T. (1993). In Taylor, John, *Notes on an Unhurried Journey* New York, NY: Four Walls Eight Windows

Vartuli, S. and Marcon, R. (2005). The Heart of Teaching. Washington, DC: National *Association for the Education of Young Children,* 60(5).

Wilson, D. M. (May/June 2009). Developmentally Appropriate Practice in the Age of Testing. *Harvard Education Letter,* p. 2.

Yelland, N. J. (Ed.) (2000). *Promoting Meaningful Learning: Innovations in Educating Early Childhood Professionals.* Washington, DC: National Association for the Education of Young Children.

Zigler, E. F. (Ed.) (2004). *Children's Play: The Roots to Reading.* Washington, DC: Zero to Three Press

# Chapter Two

## Trekking Into the Land of Literature:
### Selecting, Presenting, and Extending Stories with Young Children

# Trekking Into The Land Of Literature:

**SELECTING, PRESENTING, AND EXTENDING STORIES WITH YOUNG CHILDREN**

> It's important, especially with younger children, to repeat the same lively stories over and over again, so book language loses its strangeness and becomes familiar. The language of books sounds different. It looks different. It _is_ different.
>
> —Mem Fox

Stories have a powerfully enriching and magnetizing effect on the lives of children. Children listen to them with more than their ears; they absorb them through their souls, and through a closeness and shared enjoyment with other human beings. The very young snuggle up close, making the parent's lap one of the first and warmest literacy environments. They listen with an ever-expanding notion of what is possible through sharing the world of storybook characters.

Storybooks become a way for children to relate their lives to the lives of the characters and a means of matching some of their feelings with the characters' feelings and experiences. Stories do not give answers, but instead allow children to extrapolate meanings that are relevant to them. A child who knows the story of The Three Billy Goats Gruff might be having a "troll-like" day and wish to be "under that bridge" in a private space away from others or perhaps identify with Max in <u>Where the Wild Things Are</u>. Maurice Sendak has the magical ability to remember what it is like to be a child. He gets right inside children's thoughts and, in a special way, elaborates their fantasies. All of us know how <u>Where the Wild Things Are</u> touches young children, as they ask to hear it over and over again. It reveals a world where feeling in control is hard and a warm dinner following an episode of bruised pride is very welcome. For some children, however, that warm dinner may not appear and the fantasy of the story is their only relief from difficult circumstances.

Stories have been a part of the human experience since man has inhabited the earth. They teach lessons, explain natural phenomena in the world, and pass along traditions from one generation to the next. Long ago, people shared them orally and later chiseled or burned them into rock walls and caves. Children could join their families for story gatherings, embedding them in their own social experiences, though the stories were often intended for adult ears.

Fast-forward to today's world, and stories have exploded into books, newspapers, magazines, films, videos, CDs, DVDs, computers. Who knows what will evolve in the future. Our young children today are exposed to a media frenzy. They often hear and see things way before they can sort out the meanings. As teachers and caregivers, the greatest gift we can bring to young children is to join with their families in ensuring that there is meaningful, delicious early childhood literature in their lives. When we are reading a story, we can pause to check on children's understanding or insert an explanation as we're going along. Many interesting ideas, words, and illustrations can be discussed together. Some children may want to revisit and explore the book on their own following such a discussion.

Some early childhood professionals believe that storytelling should precede reading stories with young children, as it fosters the ability of children to listen carefully and create their own mental images before being exposed to images created by artists. Other professionals believe it is important for children not only to listen to a story, but also to see that print conveys meaning and that illustrations support what children are hearing.

The Storybook Journey believes that print, illustrations, and storytelling are important, and relishes the idea of exploring many different modalities for bringing rich children's literature to life. We all want to engage children's minds. We want to capture their sense of wonder, to stimulate their imagination, and encourage their passion to investigate and learn. Imagination is perhaps the most powerful human ability, letting us create simulated realities we can explore without abandoning the real world (Brown, 2009). Children conceptualize, organize, and construct meaning from what they feel, see, and hear in unique ways. Therefore, it is important for us to provide repeated exposure – in a variety of ways – to the story concepts, characters, rich language (that we also use in spontaneous conversation), and a healthy exposure to the plot. In this way, we can meet the abilities of all children. The Storybook Journey does this through repeated reading aloud of one story over time and the thoughtful use of puppets, mini-worlds, flannel boards, music, movement, and other creative ways that teachers and children have made story replay come alive.

Teale, Junko, Yokota, and Martinez (2008) have stated that "reading aloud can also significantly enhance young children's background knowledge, vocabulary, concepts about print, familiarity with different text structures, and even their phonological awareness, letter knowledge, and sight word knowledge. It serves as the foundation for developing a lifelong joy of reading. But the degree to which reading aloud succeeds in accomplishing any of these goals, we believe, begins with the books the teacher selects to read aloud." Teachers using the Storybook Journey would add to this statement that the repeated readings and play with one story for as long as the children are engaged has a substantial effect on the children's retention and use of these literacy skills.

## I. Selecting Stories for the Journey

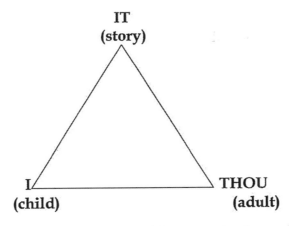

"Thou" could also include other children in the class who share the journey

David Hawkins (1970), a well-known philosopher and advocate of sound early childhood learning, wrote an article entitled "I, Thou, It." The article speaks of the valuable relationship between the teacher ("I") and the child ("Thou"). In it, Hawkins states that the first goal of teaching is to encourage engrossment and engagement in learning. When that happens, "the child becomes alive for the teacher as well as the teacher for the child. They have a common theme for discussion; they are involved together in the world." He goes on to say it is important that "there be some third thing of interest to the child *and* to the adult, in which they can join in outward projection. Only this creates a possible stable bond of communication, of shared concern."

The article must be read in its entirety to fully appreciate Hawkins' keen ability to articulate the essence of early learning. The point I want to borrow from the article is the value of having "some third thing" to share that creates a common bond of communication and interaction. The "it" part of the triangular configuration for the Journey is the story. The story is a very important part of the school and home experience and the connection between them. The story is interesting and enjoyable for both the child and the adult. It creates a common focus and a communication link with the adult. It eventually joins children interactively with their peers through meaningful story replay. They have a shared experience that creates a space for discussion and reenactment. They become involved together in their extended story world.

A.  Ideas that support storybook selection:

- Observe:

  One of the most successful ways teachers have chosen books to share with children is through observing the children in their classrooms. They watch and listen to the children's play and daily experiences to gain an understanding of the children's interests, questions, prior experiences, humor, fears, and other aspects of their lives. Many excellent books today can match and expand on the children's experiences and enhance their comprehension and play.

- Notice:

  What storybooks do the children gravitate to in the book corner or in any other area of the classroom? If looking at books is a way for children to transition between activities, which books do they choose most frequently?

- Confer:

  Parents are a very helpful resource. Ask them to keep you posted on stories that appeal to their children at home. Perhaps their children will want to share one of their favorite books with the class. This can give you a chance to see if the stories they bring in are interesting to the other children and perhaps possible candidates for a journey.

- Consider:

  Stories don't always have to come from adults observing children. You may want to share journeys from storybooks and authors you have loved over the years. Remember the classic fairytales too, as some children may not have been exposed to them. It would also be fun to see what parents would like to share from their childhood favorites.

Sometimes there will be classroom situations or events (e.g., the death of an animal, struggles with friendships, a visiting veterinarian) where you choose a story to address an issue or upcoming event. Storybooks can encourage discussion as well as be a resource for children who want to revisit a book on their own. Storybooks can also set the stage for an upcoming field trip or classroom visitor. Some of these stories will serve as "reference" books in the classroom, while others can be developed into a full-blown journey. The children's response will guide your choices.

- Share:

Discuss and share books with colleagues, as they have often experienced using certain stories with children and have developed unique and creative experiences and extensions. When Where the Wild Things Are was first published, I was just returning to teaching after a maternity leave. A colleague told me she was reading the book to her class of three-year-olds. It mesmerized them. I remember being shocked, as I found the illustrations to be rather scary – with all those sharp teeth and claws! She invited me to observe one morning while she read it to these little ones. Scared they were not! This story spoke deeply to them. They were totally engrossed, and each time she closed the book, they'd say, "Read it again." How could I have been so mistaken? It eventually became one of my absolute favorites to read to children. I loved seeing how they relished hearing it and acting it out over and over again.

With the first reading of a storybook, children will become familiar with the storyline, the characters, the words, and the illustrations. As children "read" books again and again, they gradually take a more active role in telling the story and predicting what will happen. This outcome is a desirable one, as it provides children with valuable practice using language and emerging print concepts (Ezell & Justice, 2005).

- Consult:

Librarians and bookstores that specialize in children's literature are an outstanding resource. They are able to keep abreast of the ever-growing world of new and "revived" storybooks.

In summary, the following short checklist can provide helpful reference criteria when selecting books for young children. Look for:

- Repetition:   of a word, phrase, incident, sound (alliteration) (e.g., Caps for Sale, Chicka Chicka Boom Boom, Little Red Hen)
- Sequence:   the order of a series of events that occur (e.g., The Three Pigs, The Hungry Caterpillar, The Three Billy Goats Gruff)

- <u>Simple Plot</u>: the plan of action in a story that can be easily understood (e.g., <u>Owl Babies</u>, <u>The Mitten</u>, <u>Corduroy</u>)

- <u>Small Number of Speaking Characters</u>: a small number of characters makes it less complicated for most preschoolers (e.g., <u>Yo! Yes?</u>, <u>Little Bear</u> series, <u>Frog and Toad</u> series)

- <u>Story Length and Subject Matter</u>: are important criteria for our youngest children (e.g., nursery rhymes, <u>Good Night, Gorilla</u>, <u>Goodnight Moon</u>, <u>Owl Babies</u>, and <u>Whose Shoes?</u>)

- <u>Vocabulary</u>: exposing and introducing children to new words, and then using them spontaneously in conversation (e.g., <u>Tough Boris</u>, <u>Where the Wild Things Are</u>, <u>Six Crows</u>)

- <u>Rich Language</u>: a new way to experience words or metaphors we don't often use in everyday speech (e.g., <u>Scarecrow</u>, <u>Mrs. Biddlebox</u>, <u>Frederick</u>)

- <u>Illustrations</u>: vary what children are exposed to: colorful/black and white, simple to complex, realistic/imaginative, use of different media (e.g., <u>Swimmy</u>, <u>Water Dance</u>, <u>Gingerbread Baby</u>)

- <u>Be Daring</u>: sometimes you or the children will come across a book that might have very little to do with this list of criteria, but you believe your group will enjoy it. Journey with it and see where it goes. Interesting lessons can come from a spontaneous choice.

- <u>Other Aspects to Look for:</u>
  - ➢ humor (<u>Mean Soup</u>)
  - ➢ rhythm of the words (<u>We're Going on a Bear Hunt</u>)
  - ➢ common experiences such as birthdays, bedtime, friendships (<u>Two Cool Coyotes</u>)

- <u>Picture and Reference Books:</u>

  Personal connections will steer the children's interests.

  Provide books that will support their curiosity and fascination.

  | | |
  |---|---|
  | animals | insects |
  | vehicles | snakes |
  | nature | sea life |
  | space | babies |
  | doctors | other cultures |

<u>Fairy tales:</u>

Fairy tales are an important part of childhood. In his book, <u>The Uses of Enchantment</u>, Bruno Bettelheim explains the core message he believes fairy tales convey to children. That message is that there are difficulties in life that are unavoidable…and that this is part of being human.

The characters in fairy tales are usually stereotyped. This makes it easier for our youngest children to identify with them. Folktale characters are portrayed as powerful or weak, foolish or wise. The children can identify with different characters at different times: the good little goat or the mean ugly troll, the beautiful Cinderella or the wicked stepmother, the mean pirates or little Tinkerbell. Children are experimenting with roles they choose to try on. What does it feel like to be the powerful troll, the wicked witch, or the blond intruder facing three bears at once? Fairy tales provide a chance for children to try to make sense of life through their make-believe play. They try on various roles in their dramatic replay and perhaps begin to work out some of the emotional and life issues with which they identify.

Fairytales evoke many different feelings in parents and teachers alike. It's wise to have a discussion about introducing them in your class. Two references for help in understanding the pros and cons of using fairy tales are:

- Bettelheim, B. (1976) <u>The Uses of Enchantment: The Meaning and Importance of Fairytales</u>, New York, NY: Alfred A. Knopf;
- Howarth, M. (1989), "Rediscovering the Power of Fairytales: They Help Children Understand Their Lives," <u>Young Children</u>, 45(1) 58-65, National Association for the Education of Young Children, Washington, DC.

## II. Presenting Stories for the Journey

Central to presenting the Storybook Journey is bringing stories to life and introducing scripts and concepts into the children's play and knowledge of the world. A unique aspect of storybooks is how they offer an opportunity to decontextualize language. This means that the events and concepts in storybooks are not restricted to the here and now. Rather, the events may reflect actions, and ideas that exist beyond the present – potentially in the past, in the future, or in another world altogether (Curenton & Justice, 2004; Greenhalgh & Strong, 2001). The ages of the children and their unique development will reveal which stories to start with for the first few journeys. It is best to begin with simple scripts, and then encourage and move to greater complexity. Nursery rhymes, for example, offer the ingredients young children so enjoy – brevity, nonsense, and the repetitive rhythm of the words.

Two versions of the children retelling Humpty Dumpty:
the child decorated egg and the Play-doh puppet egg

Beginning stories such as <u>Goodnight Moon</u>, <u>The Carrot Seed</u>, <u>Caps for Sale</u>, and <u>Goldilocks and the Three Bears</u> also have these vital characteristics, especially repetition and a simple story line. This is particularly important in an inclusive setting, as we want all children to be able to re-enact the less complicated rhymes or tales. Simple stories give all beginners a certain security in attempting to replay stories with peers and an opportunity to practice with feelings of confidence.

Children who quickly grasp the meaning of a story will be given many opportunities to expand their own learning by choosing from an array of materials and prepared classroom environments. It is not the simplicity of a story that "holds children back." Rather, it is how a story is offered and what choices are available for children as they use the story as a base from which to explore and expand. Matt, a very bright and socially comfortable four-year-old, had been listening intently to the <u>Three Billy Goats Gruff</u> being read, sung, and acted out at various times all week. He wanted to explore and expand the story in his own way. Knowing the classroom supplies very well, he went over to the "Trash-to-Treasure" section and started hunting for the materials he wanted to create his own miniature world. He found three plastic lids of seriated sizes for the goats, two square pieces of scrap wood and a tongue depressor for the bridge, and created a troll with a triangular piece of wood and yellow frizzy wool for "wild hair." At our group time, with his project completed, he told the story to the other children using three different voices for the goats. The children were glued to his every word. He then brought the treasures home to tell the story to his younger brother.

<u>Reading the Storybook</u>

The ideal way to present a story for a journey is to read it to the children. We do this primarily so the children can hear the "book language" and vocabulary in the story. Words are essential in building the thought connections in the brain. The more language children experience, through books and conversations with others, the more advantaged socially, educationally, and in every way they will be for the rest of their lives (Fox, 2001). At the same time, children are being exposed to the idea that what they are hearing is coming from written words. The illustrations in the book can delight and support children in their comprehension of what they are hearing. For some children, illustrations bolster their ability to attend, especially if they are not used to listening to stories with a group of peers.

Another benefit of starting a journey with the storybook is that children then have a tangible means to revisit the story on their own or share it with their peers. They can check the illustrations to visually prompt the story sequence for retelling, or they can use their imaginations – referring to the illustrations as needed – to inspire their own version. It is very important that children connect the stories they are hearing to the books being read. They will look at these books now and learn to read them in the future.

Think of people in the children's lives who can make an impact in terms of reading a story. For example, if a firefighter visits the classroom, extend the time with the children by having this "hero figure" read a story of his or her choice or the story you're taking on a journey. Invite other guest readers such as siblings, parents, grandparents, directors, principals, or the teachers they might have the following year. We had a janitor in our school who became a vital part of our classroom. We would invent problems so he could come to our room for a few minutes. He would lay out his tools on the floor so the children could help him decide which one would be best to fix the sink, chair, or whatever we pretended needed his attention. One day we asked Clint if he would like to read our Storybook Journey story, <u>The Little Engine That Could</u>, to the group. He was thrilled to be asked and the children gladly joined him for the "I think I can, I think I can" refrain. It was hard to tell who enjoyed it more…the children or Clint!

## Telling the Story

Telling a story can be absolutely magical once we develop the confidence to try it and the willingness to practice and refine our skill. It frees us to give our visual attention to the children and be fully aware of their reactions. We can ad lib, embellish, personalize, lengthen, or shorten the story according to the children's interest and attention span. It is fun to develop dramatic voices and expressions for each character. Our telling a story can stimulate the children's mental images of the characters and the environments they inhabit. One of the greatest gifts is the model we can provide for encouraging them to tell their own creative stories.

Child dictating story to the teacher

Vivian Paley, a former kindergarten teacher and well-known author, has developed a wonderful extension of the children's original dictated stories. She writes down a child's story verbatim and then asks the child if she or he would like to have it acted out. If the answer is yes, she asks if the child would like to act out one of the parts or be the director. She then reads the story as the chosen characters act it out. The story instantly becomes a play. Just think of the power and incentive to tell a story this process invites!

To get started, most of us feel it best to retell a simple story with only one or two characters who speak with distinctly different voices, a plot that has a sequence of events that are easy to keep in order, and repetition of an incident or phrase. Good examples include Caps for Sale – "You monkeys, you! Give me back my caps!" – or Good Night, Gorilla, when all of the animals have their cages unlocked by the Gorilla and escape one at a time.

If you're feeling a little uncertain about how to start storytelling, you may want to have a puppet tell the story. I did this one time as a student teacher with the school puppet we called "Safety Dog." He always came out before a field trip to go over things to remember before we were on our way, like waiting at the corner and holding on to the rope with the class before crossing the street. This time the class was going on a field trip that required driving to our destination. I wanted to tell the group a simple story that would remind them of the importance of buckling their car seat belts. I put Safety Dog on my hand and told a rather dramatic adventure of Safety Dog falling out of his car seat because he forgot to buckle up. I really dramatized his bouncing around in the seat, his fall, and the bump he got on his head. I assured Safety Dog that the ice pack would make him feel all better soon and that I was sure he would never forget to buckle up after that.

After I told this story, we gathered at the snack table. Absolutely wide-eyed, Latisha turned to me and said, "Did you *hear* what happened to Safety Dog? He falled out of his car set and hurted his head." She had no idea that I had told the story – she was so mesmerized by the puppet that she never saw the puppeteer. That was a great confidence builder for me. I could "hide" behind Safety Dog until I felt I could swing it on my own. A puppet can certainly be a support for beginners!

If there is a wide spread in the children's developmental abilities, storytelling can be a bit of a challenge. Some children may need a condensed version, your familiar voice, and the tangible storybook and illustrations to be able to stay focused. In this case, see if you can form two smaller groups and tell the story to each group according to their ability to understand and attend.

Smaller groups for storybook reading are nice for any group, as children can more readily see the illustrations, sit closer to the reader, and have fewer distractions. Group size is a personal and perhaps philosophical decision that is worth talking about with one's team and colleagues. Some preschools have found that senior members of the community really enjoy coming into classrooms for story time, especially if they can read to a small group.

## III. Extending Stories on a Journey

Years ago, a graduate student shared a definition from The Joy of Cooking (1946) that provides a unique analogy to what the Storybook Journey is doing with stories. It reads, "Never underestimate the power of a marinade…Marinades are a means of spreading flavor by immersion…the soaking period may vary from only a few minutes to many hours." Obviously, the stories are our marinade. We immerse the children in stories and related meaningful experiences. Some children soak up the meaning quickly, while others need to soak it up for weeks, repeating it for mastery, for love of the story, or for deeper comprehension. Children, when given a choice, will opt for their favorite forms of immersion. It is our task to offer them a variety of experiences and materials so they can self-select the form and timing of that "marination."

The Storybook Journey probes new routes through a story by developing environments, selecting and extending the use of materials, and exploring unique ways to link the story concepts to the various curriculum areas or centers in a classroom. It is a rich mingling of dramatic play, sensory materials, blocks, art, science, math, manipulatives, books, and many other experiences. Story props, extensions, and reenactment setups are available throughout the classroom environment as a resource or framework for story replay. They are usually novel arrangements of the available equipment that present children with invitations to relive the story through play, exploration, discovery, and their unfolding connections to one another.

In the previous sections, we talked about selecting and presenting stories. In this section, we will discuss extending the stories through props set up to engage the children in replaying story scripts with their peers. The props we set up in the environment are the same props we have used in presenting the story to the children at group time. After reading the book and exploring it together for a few days, the story can be sung or told on the flannel board or told with puppets, miniature worlds, or dramatic play. We can do all of these over time or explore the possibilities of one particular prop, depending on the group's engagement and the children's and teachers' creative extensions. There's a lovely, fluid process between adults and children as they relive the story together.

After a prop is used in telling the story at group time, it moves into the classroom environment. In some classrooms, it is placed in a storybook area or in with the blocks, sand table, or wherever it might summon children to retell the story or create their own adventure.

For example, one story extension of <u>The Three Little Pigs</u> was set up on a low platform placed near the block area. (It was actually an old bookcase that had been emptied out and tipped over so the back of the bookcase was the top of the platform. This created a solid surface for manipulating props and a perfect height for sitting or kneeling for play.) Three little rubber pigs and one big mama pig, three houses made out of small boxes, and a plastic wolf were set on top of the platform. One child even built a small house of blocks for the wolf. This setup remained as long as the children's interest lasted. Sometimes one child would take all the parts; other times five children would gather and they'd each have a part. To add variety, one day the teachers substituted four pinecones for the pigs, a rock for the wolf, and grass, twigs, and small blocks for the various houses.

As the children's interest waned, the teacher put the twigs and grass away and encouraged the children to build houses for all the pigs she had added to the block area. Along with unit blocks, she also put out a variety of other materials, including Lego pieces, Cuisenaire rods, small baskets of assorted wood scraps, wooden Popsicle sticks, tongue depressors, and jar lids. The children added other things they found in the trash-to-treasure corner. The pigs' houses now became elaborate works of architecture. They catalyzed a long adventure with building, as the three pigs faded into history. At this point, the teacher realized the story was over for this group. The construction of buildings was now the focus of their attention.

The teacher very cleverly moved into the story of <u>Roxaboxen</u> by Barbara Cooney. This is a delightful story about some neighborhood children who build a small village out of boxes and mark off each person's property with rock borders. The teacher's choice was such a sensitive way of offering the other children in the class a way to join the building project and the replay of a new story. She also introduced the inspiring book, <u>Block Building for Children</u> by Lester Walker.

Story extensions are limitless if you are comfortable with the collection and storage of "stuff" that children and teachers can turn into props for story retelling. It is wise to use a mixture of concrete and abstract props to inspire the children's imaginative and creative replay. Providing props for the various stories is a shared endeavor. The more variety, the more options everyone has to tell and retell a given story. Repetition invites comfort and familiarity with the story. It builds a collective memory bank that encourages children to replay and reenact the story with one other. This can be a real social boost, especially in groups of children with a significant variance in abilities.

I. <u>Providing Materials for Story Exploration</u>:

- <u>Puppets</u>:

  Anything can become a puppet if children have been encouraged to create and use their ingenuity. Having organized and treasured trash available will inspire creative heads, features, bodies, limbs, and outfits (e.g., a lunch-size paper bag is easy for a child to fit over one hand while the other hand glues on the various features; this works well for a short-lived puppet). There are also excellent commercial puppets that are readily available in stores, school supply catalogs, and garage sales.

- <u>Miniature Worlds</u>:

  Miniature worlds are just what the words suggest. They are small versions of the story props that adults and children can use to retell a story.

Children can create their own or use those created or gathered by adults. For example, a miniature world was created for <u>The Three Bears</u> using the bears from a puzzle, three detergent bottle tops in seriated sizes for the bowls, chairs from a dollhouse, and beds made out of blocks. Goldilocks was a small blond doll rescued from a gumball machine. It's interesting to see how children assign new meaning to the materials available.

A miniature world set up for retelling <u>The Secret Birthday Message</u> by Eric Carle

Miniature world set up for playing out <u>The Three Little Pigs</u>

- <u>Maxi Worlds</u>:

  Sometimes a story will lend itself to a large figure for replay. One class of four-year-olds wanted to keep retelling <u>Jack and the Beanstalk</u>. The teacher suggested making a giant out of some huge clothes she borrowed from a parent. The children spent two days stuffing the giant and making his head from a pillowcase. There was a discussion and practice drawings of the expression he should have on his face. *Mean* was the winner. The children took turns manipulating this "maxi world" like a huge puppet – two at a time they'd hold him up under his arms and one would be his loud voice!

- <u>Flannel/Felt Boards</u>:

  There are commercial felt boards and characters available in catalogs. Boards can also be made from a stiff square of cardboard covered with flannel or felt. The story characters can be copied from the storybook, cut out of a coloring book or magazine, or drawn freehand. To preserve them, cover them with clear contact paper and back them with strips of rough sandpaper. The sandpaper can be glued on or attached with double-stick scotch tape. The sandpaper keeps the characters upright and makes them adhere to the flannel or felt.

- Magnetic Boards:

  Anything that holds a magnet can become a storyboard: a refrigerator, file cabinet, or hospital bed bars. Portable versions can be fashioned from cookie tins, old large reel film canisters, baking sheets, stove mats, metal shelves, and so on. This metal base can be propped on your lap, up against a sturdy pile of books on a chair, or leaned against the back of a chair with something on the lower front to keep it from sliding around.

  Magnetic tape that has an adhesive backing can attach to any character you want to use on the metal surface. This tape is available at fabric, hardware, and novelty stores.

- Stories on Tape or CDs:

  Setting up a tape recorder or CD player with earphones in a quiet place in the room gives children a new way to hear a familiar story retold. Multiple copies of the storybook can be added so that all of the children listening to the recording can follow along with the story in the book. It's a good idea to expose the children to both kinds of retellings: one with listening only and one with a copy of the book while listening.

- Paint or Draw a Story:

  Whether you're comfortable with drawing stick figures or capable of drawing realistic characters, children seem to really enjoy watching stories come alive on the paper. They are also very accepting of our various attempts at drawing!

In one classroom, children painted a large mural in tones of green, blue, and yellow. The teacher stretched the mural across a wall and used it as the backdrop for telling the story of Swimmy. On separate pieces of tagboard, the teacher drew pictures of the lobster, eel, and other characters. As Swimmy swam along and met each character, the characters were placed on the backdrop with a small piece of tic tac (the sticky stuff – easily removed – used to attach pictures to walls). Each child had made her or his own red fish to stick up at random. When it was time to form the big fish with Swimmy as the eye, the teacher created the image with the children's red fish. If these props remain available, children can use them at their leisure to retell the story of Swimmy on their own or with the group. They can also do all of the drawings and place them up on the mural when their sea creature "swims" into the story.

- Overhead Projector Story:

  Place a blank overhead plastic sheet on the glass of the projector. Use two small pools of cooking oil on the sheet as a means to hold food-coloring drops. This works particularly well for the story of Little Blue and Little Yellow by Leo Lionni. Drip the food coloring from an eyedropper into one of the pools of oil as you introduce yellow, blue, and then add their friends, red, purple, and the rest of the gang to the other pool. Of course, when yellow and blue "hug" each other, you stir the two colors together and little green emerges. It is really quite magical and makes the "blob characters" seem real.

- Play-Doh Characters:

  Using the story of <u>Little Blue and Little Yellow</u> again, the teacher can make Play-Doh balls in both yellow and blue. A bit of each color of Play-Doh should be reserved to use later in the story. As she tells the story, the teacher combines the blue and yellow balls, kneading them until they turn green (as they do in the story when they hug). The reserved yellow and blue balls are then used to tell the part of the story where the "blobs" cry because their families don't understand whom these "green" children could be. When they cry, yellow cries yellow Play-Doh tears and blue cries blue Play-Doh tears. The "blobs" pull themselves back together (the teacher collects the yellow tears she made back into little yellow, likewise little blue) and they run home to their respective families.

  The possibilities for Play-Doh are endless. A blob of green Play-Doh molded around a finger on one hand and a blob of brown Play-Doh molded around a finger on the other hand can become instant "puppets" to retell the stories in the series <u>Frog and Toad Are Friends</u>.

- Character Dress-up:

  Dress up as one of the characters from the book you are taking on a journey. You might, for example, don overalls, a straw hat, big boots, and neckerchief when you do <u>Old MacDonald Had a Farm</u>. You can wear green clothes and big swim flippers when you do <u>Frog and Toad Are Friends</u>. Greet the children at the door and enjoy the range of reactions you'll elicit from the children, their families, and even the bus driver! It's a fun way to weave the story into your day, right from the first "good mornings."


- Use of Nature:

  In the story <u>Mousekin and the Golden House</u>, a discarded Halloween pumpkin becomes a mouse's wonderful winter home. When we had pet mice in our classroom one year, we took our used jack-o'-lantern and put it in our mouse's cage. It made the story come alive when our mouse did exactly what Mousekin did: she ran inside, ate the seeds, and pulled in everything she could to make her winter nest.

We also brought in a big spider to see if he'd spin a web as the spider had done in one of our favorite stories, The Busy Spider. For two days we watched our aquarium, but no web. On the third day, the spider had escaped. On the fourth day, hanging from wall to water pipe was an exquisite web with a fat spider perched right in the center. What excitement! So many things on the journey happen spontaneously. The *real* curriculum often happens while you're busy planning something else!

- Musical Instruments or Voice Participation:

It is fun to experiment with various ways to involve the children in story replay. A teacher in Colorado, whose class just didn't want to stop playing with Jack and the Beanstalk, decided to try a new twist. She gave the children various instruments to represent the characters or sounds from the story. As the teacher told the story, the children added sound effects.

> Jack was the xylophone (up the scale to ascend the beanstalk and down the scale to descend)
> Beans – maracas or rice in shakers
> Cow – cowbells
> Giant – loud drums
> Giant's wife – tone blocks (lightly tapped for the footsteps)
> Harp (autoharp or any stringed instrument), coins to drop, and crowing sounds (for the giant's treasures)

The teacher later varied the replay with simple words and sounds. For example, Jack would say: "Look, Mother, magic beans!" The rest followed: Cow (moo, moo, moo), Giant (Fi Fie Fo Fum), Jack's mother (Jack, Jack, Jack), Giant's wife (Sh! Sh! Sh!), etc. Of course, all of this can vary according to the creativity of everyone involved.

Reenactment of <u>caps for sale</u>

- <u>Child and Adult Reenactments</u>:

  For children, acting out a story with adults is a delightful first step to acting out a story with peers. For many children with varying abilities, the support of an adult is comforting as they take on character roles for the first time. Offering an invitation to join in by extending a hand or wheeling a child in a wheelchair through the pretend forest may be the modest beginning. When we acted out <u>Where the Wild Things Are</u> with our faces painted, it was hard to tell the children from the adults during the wild rumpus. Even the most reluctant actor became caught up in the fun of it!

- <u>Act Out the Story</u>:

  Dramatic replay of a story gives children the opportunity to identify with the characters in the story they've heard. They learn the nature of a "wolf" by becoming one. Reenacting trolls, giants, mean witches, and fairy godmothers requires that a child begin to identify with a character, moving and acting in such a way that it communicates how that character might feel. It reveals the child's observation skills, attention to detail, experiences, and ability to integrate and act upon a wealth of information.

For children to act out parts in a replay of a story, they need other people. Role taking in a commonly known story becomes an effective nudge toward communicating and cooperating with another person. Interactions and role taking encourage children to "try on" the perspectives of others. The practice of taking parts also helps a child to expand beyond self and move closer to others within the safety of a role.

Creating a space in the environment with some things that children can use for spontaneous reenactments serves as an inspiration for many children. Go to garage sales, thrift shops, families, and bargain sales for things like scarves, hats, boots, wigs (or string mops you can dye different colors), sunglasses, frilly nightgowns, jewelry, and whatever else you can muster up. The problem is always display and storage! Brainstorm with colleagues and families to find simple ways to display and hang things for use as well as provide for easy cleanup and storage when items are not being used.

- Slides From a Book:

Using one of the classic books your children enjoy, photograph every page with slide film. (This can also be done commercially, but it is very costly!) A darkened part of the room can become your "theater" with children bringing their chairs, rugs, and pillows to watch the book up on the screen. As you show the slides of each page, the group can tell, read, or share the story together. This is a particularly effective way to "read" a story to a larger group of children. It is also a way to enlarge pictures from a small book so the group can experience the pictures and story together without frustration. In this world of modern technology you could also do this with a digital camera, PowerPoint, *and* a large wallet.

- Real Connections:

"Pickety Fence" is a wonderful poem by David McCord in his book entitled Every Time I Climb a Tree (1980). He has captured in words the sound of a fence when a stick is run across its surface. One day while out on the playground, a teacher ran a stick along the fence saying: "pickety fence, pickety fence, give it a lick, it's a lickety fence…lickety lick, lickety lick…" The children delighted in joining in the activity by creating their own sound words. When they went in for group time and the teacher read the poem, one child picked up on the real-life connection: "Hey, that's just what *our* fence said!" This simple illustration demonstrates the subtlety and power of meaning-making for children.

Other ideas and directions for simple replay props are in
Chapter Five, Props for the Pilgrimage

Storybooks have the potential to touch every aspect of human development and can be an integral part of a young child's life. Whether told through nursery rhymes, songs, poems, books, or a child's growing imagination, stories provide a meaningful avenue for children who are exploring ways to orient themselves in the world.

Threads that exist in children's own lives weave in and out of each story. Familiarity with elements of a story appears to motivate, ignite, and replenish their ability to take part in and derive personal meaning from the story. It creates a way for children to become connected to the special people in their lives. Through the wondrous exploration of storybooks, the Storybook Journey provides one approach among many for children and adults to learn about each other, the world, and themselves.

Regardless of language, cultural, social ability, experience, or familial differences, the enjoyment of living with stories can bring us together in significant ways. Stories themselves can play a prominent role. Their universal appeal joins us through the magic of transforming us to another place. From this storybook world, perhaps we can more comfortably view our lives at a distance and in a different form. Perhaps through the characters and the episodes we become aware of the many joys, fears, feelings, and struggles we share in learning to live together comfortably as caring human beings. Sharing stories not only shows us pathways to literacy, but pathways that connect us to each other.

**Suggested Books for a Storybook Journey**

(There are thousands more to be explored!)

(T) in front of a book title suggests it is particularly enjoyable for toddlers.

- <u>Nursery Rhymes and Poetry for the Journey</u>:
  The simplicity of many of these rhymes and poems makes them excellent selections for beginning journeys and reenactments.

  (T) <u>Mother Goose Rhymes</u> – Colin and Moira Maclean

  (T) <u>Nursery Rhymes</u> – Father Gander (Dr. Douglas W. Larche)

  <u>Positively Mother Goose</u> – Loomans, Kolberg, and Loomans

  (T) <u>The Real Mother Goose</u> – Blanche F. Wright

  <u>The New Adventures of Mother Goose</u> – Bruce Lansky

  <u>When We Were Very Young</u> – A.A. Milne

  <u>Hailstones and Halibut Bones</u> – Mary O'Neill

  <u>Where the Sidewalk Ends</u> – Shel Silverstein

  <u>A Child's Garden of Verses</u> – Robert Louis Stevenson

  <u>The Owl and the Pussycat</u> – Edward Lear

  <u>Take Me Out of the Bathtub</u> – Alan Katz

  (T) <u>Chicken Soup with Rice</u> – Maurice Sendak

  <u>Adventure on Klickitat Island</u> – Hilary H. Hippely

  <u>Every Time I Climb a Tree</u> – David McCord

  <u>My Favorite Things</u> – Richard Rodgers and Renee Graef

  (T) <u>Who is Tapping at My Window?</u> – A.G. Deming

  <u>Mouse Mess</u> – Linnea Riley

  <u>Five Little Monkeys Wash the Car</u> – Eileen Christelow

  <u>When Mama Comes Home Tonight</u> – Eileen Spinelli

  (T) <u>Time for Bed</u> – Mem Fox

  <u>Hush!</u> (A Thai Lullaby) – Minfong Ho

  <u>Mrs. Biddlebox</u> – Linda Smith

- <u>Songs and Chants for the Journey</u>:

  Songs and chants are very appealing, especially for our youngest children. Their brevity and simple tunes make them a good choice for beginning journeys.

  <u>The Teddy Bears' Picnic</u> – Jimmy Kennedy and Michael Hague

  (T) <u>Five Little Ducks</u> – Pamela Paparone

  (T) <u>Over in the Meadow</u> – Ezra Jack Keats

  (T) <u>Over on the Farm</u> – Christopher Gunson

  <u>Five Little Monkeys Sitting in a Tree</u> – Eileen Christelow

  <u>Peanut Butter and Jelly</u> – Nadine B. Westcott

  (T) <u>Old MacDonald Had a Farm</u> – Glen Rounds

  <u>Old MacDonald Had a Workshop</u> – Lisa Shulman

  (T) <u>The Wheels on the Bus</u> – Maryann Kovalski

  <u>Row, Row, Row Your Boat</u> – Iza Trapani

  (T) <u>The Itsy Bitsy Spider</u> – Iza Trapani

  <u>Down by the Bay</u> – Raffi and Nadine B. Westcott

  <u>Catch a Little Fox</u> – Fortunata

  (T) <u>Little Green Frog</u> – Rozanne L. Williams

  <u>The Fox Went Out on a Chilly Night</u> – Peter Spier

  (T) <u>Hush Little Baby</u> – Sylvia Long

  <u>Down by the Station</u> – Will Hillenbrand

  <u>Who Took the Cookies from the Cookie Jar?</u> – Bonnie Lass and Philemon Sturges

  <u>Take Me Out of the Bathtub</u> – Alan Katz

  <u>There Was an Old Lady Who Swallowed a Fly</u> – Pam Adams

  <u>I Know an Old Lady Who Swallowed a Fly</u> – Colin and Jacqui Hawkins

  <u>There Was an Ol' Cajun</u> – Deborah O. Kadair

  <u>There Was an Old Lady Who Swallowed a Trout!</u> – Teri Sloat

- <u>Favorite Stories for a Journey</u>:

  (T) indicates particularly good for toddlers, but not limited to them.

  <u>King Bidgood's in the Bathtub</u> – Audrey and Don Wood

  <u>Roxaboxen</u> – Alice McLerran and Barbara Cooney

The Squiggle – Carole L. Schaefer

The Frog and Toad series – Arnold Lobel

(T) Blueberries for Sal – Robert McCloskey

The Snowy Day – Ezra Jack Keats

Flat Stanley – Jeff Brown

The Sweet Patootie Doll – Mary Calhoun

Dandelion – Don Freeman

Heckedy Peg – Audrey and Don Wood

Stone Soup – Marcia Brown

Miss Tizzy – Libba M. Gray

Charlie Needs a Cloak – Tomie dePaola

Something from Nothing – Phoebe Gilman

The Goat in the Rug – Charles L. Blood and Martin Link

Tops and Bottoms – Janet Stevens

The Tortoise and the Hare – Janet Stevens

Miss Nelson is Missing! – Harry G. Allard and James Marshall

Little Blue and Little Yellow – Leo Lionni

(T) Good Night, Gorilla – Peggy Rathmann

A Chair for My Mother – Vera Williams

Leo the Late Bloomer – Robert Kraus

The Rainbabies – Laura K. Melmed and Jim LaMarche

(T) The Great Big Enormous Turnip – Helen Oxenbury

Swimmy – Leo Lionni

The Doorbell Rang – Pat Hutchins

Frederick – Leo Lionni

Strega Nona – Tomie dePaola

Gilberto and the Wind – Marie Hall Ets

Tough Boris – Mem Fox

(T) Caps for Sale – Esphyr Slobodkina

The Hatseller and the Monkeys (A West African Folk Tale) – Baba Wagué Diakité

Yo! Yes? – Chris Raschka

Next Please – Ernst Jandl and Norman Junge

The Little Mouse, the Red Ripe Strawberry, and the Big Hungry Bear – Don and Audrey Wood

Scarecrow – Cynthia Rylant

Martha – Gennady Spirin

The Raft – Jim LaMarche

Owl Moon – Jane Yolen

Grandpa Bear's Fantastic Scarf – Gillian Heal

I Know a Lady – Charlotte Zolotow

The Legend of the Indian Paintbrush – Tomie dePaola

Six Crows – Leo Lionni

Abiyoyo – Pete Seeger and Michael Hays

The Gunniwolf – Wilhelmina Harper

Sitting in My Box – Dee Lillegard

Flap Your Wings – P.D. Eastman

Edward and the Pirates – David McPhail

Parts and More Parts – Tedd Arnold

Bark, George – Jules Feiffer

Song and Dance Man – Karen Ackerman

Everybody Needs a Rock – Byrd Baylor

(T) The Wide-Mouthed Frog – Keith Faulkner

How I Became a Pirate – Melinda Long

Three Pebbles and a Song – Eileen Spinelli

Mean Soup – Betsy Everitt

Wilfrid Gordon McDonald Partridge – Mem Fox

One Dark Night – Lisa Wheeler

Corduroy – Don Freeman

Mousekin's Golden House – Edna Miller

The Case of the Hungry Stranger – Crosby Bonsall

The Secret Birthday Message – Eric Carle

(T) The Very Hungry Caterpillar – Eric Carle

We're Going on a Bear Hunt – Michael Rosen

Umbrella – Taro Yashima

Barn Dance! – Bill Martin, Jr.

Froggy Gets Dressed – Jonathan London

The Carrot Seed – Ruth Krauss

Anansi and the Moss-Covered Rock – Eric Kimmel

The Bremen-Town Musicians – Ruth B. Gross

Harold and the Purple Crayon – Crockett Johnson

Thunder Cake – Patricia Polacco

Little Lumpty – Miko Imai

Make Way for Ducklings – Robert McCloskey

Katy No-Pocket – Emmy Payne

Chopsticks – Jon Berkeley

The Ticky-Tacky Doll – Cynthia Rylant

Little Bear series – Else Holmelund Minarik

Where the Wild Things Are – Maurice Sendak

Cook-a-Doodle-Doo! – Janet Stevens and Susan S. Crummel

One Dark Night – Hazel Hutchins

John Brown, Rose, and the Midnight Cat – Jenny Wagner

Why Cowboys Sleep with Their Boots On – Laurie L. Knowlton

The Walking Coat – Pauline Watson and Tomie dePaola

The Snowmen at Night – Caralyn Buehner

Tacky the Penguin – Helen Lester

(T) Olivia – Ian Falconer

Hedgie's Surprise – Jan Brett

The Mitten – Jan Brett

The Magic Boots – Scott Emerson

Grandfather Twilight – Barbara Berger

Monsters Are Knocking – Alison Lester

Goodnight Moon – Margaret Wise Brown

Dreams – Ezra Keats

Watch Out for the Chicken Feet in Your Soup – Tomie dePaola

When I Was Young in the Mountains – Cynthia Rylant

Tikki Tikki Tembo – Arlene Mosel

Anansi and the Spider (A Tale from the Ashanti) – Gerald McDermott

Mooncake – Frank Asch

Bear Shadow – Frank Asch

Bear's Bargain – Frank Asch

Lizard's Song – George Shannon

Dance Away – George Shannon

(T) Each Peach Pear Plum – Janet and Allan Ahlberg

(T) Polar Bear, Polar Bear, What Do You Hear? - Bill Martin, Jr.

(T) Brown Bear, Brown Bear, What Do You See? – Bill Martin, Jr.

(T) The Very Busy Spider – Eric Carle

Bear and Mrs. Duck – Elizabeth Winthrop

(T) Rosie's Walk – Pat Hutchins

Just Me and My Dad – Mercer Mayer

(T) You and Me, Little Bear – Martin Waddell

(T) Whose Shoes? – Anna G. Hines

Lisa Can't Sleep – Kaj Beckman

(T) When I'm Sleepy – Jane Howard

Red Leaf, Yellow Leaf – Lois Ehlert

Play with Me – Marie Hall Ets

(T) Three Little Kittens – Paul Galdone

(T) Who Hops? – Katie Davis

Some Smug Slug – Pamela D. Edwards

Sheep in a Jeep – Nancy Shaw

Amazing Anthony Ant – Lorna and Graham Philpot

(T) What Did You Put in Your Pocket? – Beatrice Schenk de Regniers

Franklin's Blanket – Paulette Bourgeois

Amos and Boris – William Steig

The Kissing Hand – Audrey Penn

(T) Owl Babies – Martin Waddell

Clyde Monster – Robert L. Crowe

There's an Alligator under My Bed – Mercer Mayer

There's a Nightmare in My Closet – Mercer Mayer

(T) Go Away, Big Green Monster! – Ed Emberley

Brave Bear – Kathy Mallat

Alexander and the Terrible, Horrible, No Good, Very Bad Day – Judith Viorst

Mrs. Biddlebox – Linda Smith

Don't Fidget a Feather – Erica Silverman

It's Mine! – Leo Lionni

The Relatives Came – Cynthia Rylant

Koala Lou – Mem Fox

A Squash and a Squeeze – Julia Donaldson

Butterfly House – Eve Bunting

I Am an Artist – Pat Collins

(T) Feathers for Lunch – Lois Ehlert

Owen – Kevin Henkes

Water Dance – Thomas Locker

(T) Fox Makes Friends – Adam Relf

Two Cool Coyotes – Jillian Lund

(T) Bear Snores On – Karma Wilson

Johnny Appleseed – Rosemary and Stephen Vincent Benét

(T) Here Are My Hands – Bill Martin, Jr. and John Archambault

(T) The Jacket I Wear in the Snow – Shirley Neitzel

Millions of Cats – Wanda Gag

(T) Golden Bear – Ruth Young

(T) In the Night Kitchen – Maurice Sendak

Five Ugly Monsters – Tedd Arnold

(T) Jessie Bear, What Will You Wear? – Nancy W. Carlstrom

(T) Ask Mr. Bear – Marjorie Flack

Turtle Tale – Frank Asch

What Baby Wants – Phyllis Root

Papa's Bedtime Story – Mary Lee Donovan

(T) Hattie and the Fox – Mem Fox

(T) A Hat for Minerva Louise – Janet Morgan Stoeke

(T) The Napping House – Audrey and Don Wood

- Books to Explore with Small Groups and Individual Children
  **Wordless**:

  These books invite children's creative ideas as they look at the pictures and venture to tell what they see or think is happening. Such books can also be the beginning of children's dabbling in and experimenting with telling a story using visual prompts.

Goodnight Max – Hanne Türk

Moonlight – Jan Ormerod

Sunshine – Jan Ormerod

Tuesday – David Wiesner

The Snowman – Raymond Brigges

Good Dog, Carl – Alexandra Day

The Red String – Margot Blair

One Frog Too Many – Mercer Mayer

If… – Sarah Perry

**Alphabet:**

The following books present the alphabet in unique ways. Encourage playfulness with letters by putting these books out with alphabet puzzles, magnetic letters, old typewriters, alphabet beads and blocks. An extension could be to place file cards with the children's names on them in this same area so the children could find the letters of their names and match them to their cards.

The Butterfly Alphabet – Kjell B. Sandved

The Alphabet – Monique Felix

Dr. Seuss's ABC – Dr. Seuss

The Alphazeds – Shirley Glaser

Tomorrow's Alphabet – George Shannon

ABC The Wild West – Florence Cassen Mayers

A My Name Is… – Alice Lyne

Grandmother's Alphabet – Eve Shaw

Chicka Chicka Boom Boom – Bill Martin, Jr. and John Archambault

I Unpacked My Grandmother's Trunk – Susan R. Hoguet

Animalia – Graeme Base

Old Black Fly – Jim Aylesworth

A You're Adorable – Martha Alexander

Q is for Duck – Mary Elting and Michael Folsom

The Handmade Alphabet – Laura Rankin

Alphabet City – Stephen T. Johnson

The Alphabet Tree – Leo Lionni

<u>Arf! Beg! Catch!</u> – Henry Horenstein

<u>Pignic</u> – Anne Miranda

- <u>Books for Reflecting on Diversity</u>
  The following books offer avenues to explore diversity in all aspects of life. They invite exploration, reflection, and discussion among the staff and children as well as within the families. For example, in the story of <u>Stellaluna</u> by Janelle Cannon, a bat lands in a nest with "strange" birds who eat and sleep very differently from bats. Just think of how you can address this with the children so the meaning becomes relevant and they can relate to Stellaluna's situation.

<u>This Land is Your Land</u> – Woody Guthrie and Kathy Jakobsen

<u>Hats, Hats, Hats</u> – Ann Morris

<u>Bread, Bread, Bread</u> – Ann Morris

<u>Houses and Homes</u> – Ann Morris

<u>We'll Paint the Octopus Red</u> – Stephanie Stuve-Bodeen

<u>You Don't Need Words!</u> – Ruth B. Gross

<u>No Mirrors in My Nana's House</u> – Ysaye M. Barnwell and Synthia S. James

<u>Mice Squeak, We Speak</u> – Arnold Shapiro and Tomie dePaola

<u>All the Colors of the Earth</u> – Sheila Hamanaka

<u>I Love My Hair!</u> – Natasha A. Tarpley

<u>Snowballs</u> – Lois Ehlert

<u>Amazing Grace</u> – Mary Hoffman

<u>Sophie</u> – Mem Fox

<u>Dandelion</u> – Don Freeman

<u>Say Hola to Spanish</u> – Susan M. Elya

<u>Big Moon Tortilla</u> – Joy Cowley

<u>Gramma's Walk</u> – Anna G. Hines

<u>William's Doll</u> – Charlotte Zolotow

<u>Who's in a Family?</u> – Robert Skutch

<u>All the Colors We Are</u> – Katie Kissinger

<u>The Tortilla Factory</u> – Gary and Ruth W. Paulsen

<u>Alejandro's Gift</u> – Richard Albert

<u>Bein' with You This Way</u> – W. Nikola-Lisa

The Crayon Box That Talked – Shane Derolf

Now One Foot, Now the Other – Tomie dePaola

A Special Trade – Sally Wittman

This is Our House – Michael Rosen

Crow Boy – Taro Yashima

The Big Orange Splot – Daniel M. Pinkwater

Arthur's Nose – Marc Brown

Friends at School – Rochelle Bunnett

One Hundred Is a Family – Pam M. Ryan

Whoever You Are – Mem Fox

Hooway for Wodney Wat – Helen Lester

Elmer – David McKee

Stellaluna – Janell Cannon

Frida – Jonah Winter

Owen and Mzee: The True Story of a Remarkable Friendship – Isabelle Hatkoff, Craig Hatkoff, and Dr. Kahumba

My Friend Isabella – Eliza Woloson

To be a Kid – Maya Ajmera and John D. Ivanko

**Books to Grow On: Latino Literature for Young Children** – Isobel Schon
Describes appealing books for young children – in English and in Spanish - with a joyous view of Latino peoples and cultures. The books suggested are exquisitely written to resonate with the symmetry and rhythm of the Spanish language. #581 (in Spanish #581S)

**Dije que el lenguaje marque el rumbo a la alfabelización (Let Language Lead the way to Literacy)**
Order: The Teacher Talk Series from the Hanen Center #7465 (NAEYC)

**Books to Grow On: African American Literature for Young Children** – Jessie C. Brown and Lee A. Oates, eds.
Introducing young children to books they find appealing is crucial in developing their literacy skills and love of reading. Organized by reading level, this annotated book list gathers outstanding children's literature that interests African-American children and other young readers. #568
Order materials on line: www.naeyc.org/shoppingcart

Ordering address: NAEYC Resource Sales

P.O. Box 96261

Washington, DC 20090-6261

Ordering materials toll free: 1-866-623-9248

Organization address: NAEYC (National Association for the Education of Young Children)

1509 16th Street NW

Washington, DC 20036-1426

Toll free: 1-800-424-2460

Excellent References on Diversity for Teachers:

Derman-Sparks and Ramsey, Patricia, G. (2006). *What If All the Kids Are White?: Anti-bias Multicultural Education with Young Children* and Families. New York, NY: Teachers College Press.

Derman-Sparks, Louise (1989). *Anti-bias Curriculum: Tools for Empowering Young Children*. New York, NY: Teachers College Press.

Gurian, Michael (2001). *Boys and Girls Learn Differently: A Guide for Teachers and Parents*. San Francisco, CA: Jossey-Bass A Wiley Company.

Hoffman, Eric (2004). *Magic Capes, Amazing Powers: Transferring Superhero play in the Classroom.* St. Paul, MN: Redleaf Press.

Nieto, Sonia (1999). *The Light in Their Eyes: Creating Multicultural Learning Communities.* New York, NY: Teachers College Press.

Odom, Samuel (Ed.) (2002). *Widening the Circle: Including Children with Disabilities in Preschool Programs.* New York, NY: Teachers College Press.

Paley, Vivian Gussin (1995). *Kwanzaa and Me: A Teacher's Story.* Cambridge, MA: Harvard University Press.

Paley, Vivian Gussin (1997). *The Girl with the Brown Crayon: How Children use Stories to Shape their Lives.* Cambridge, MA: Harvard University Press.

Paley, Vivian Gussin (1989). *White Teachers.* Cambridge, MA: Harvard University Press.

Paley, Vivian Gussin (1984). *Boys and Girls: Superheroes in the Doll Corner.* Chicago, IL: The University of Chicago Press.

Wolpert, Ellen (2005). *Start Seeing Diversity: The Basic Guide to an Anti-bias Classroom.* St. Paul, MN: Redleaf Press.

**Chinaberry**
www.chinaberry.com
1-800-776-2242
2780 Via Orange Way
Spring Valley, CA 91978

**Daedalus Books**
www.salebooks.com
1-800-395-2265
P.O. Box 6000
Columbia, MD 21045-6000

www.tepress.com
1-800-575-6566
Children's Book Committee of Bank Street College of Education (2007). <u>The Best Children's Books of the Year</u>. New York, NY: Teachers College Press.

**Classic Stories and Variations**

The Gingerbread Man – Jim Aylesworth

The Gingerbread Boy – Scott Cook

**Variation:**

Gingerbread Baby – Jan Brett

Jack and the Beanstalk – Lorinda B. Cauley

Jack and the Beanstalk – John Howe

Jack and the Beanstalk – Sindy McKay

**Variation:**

Jim and the Beanstalk – Raymond Briggs

The Mitten – Jan Brett

**Variations**

The Mystery of the Missing Red Mitten – Steven Kellogg

The Woodcutter's Mitten (An Old Ukranian Tale) – Loek Koopmans

Little Red Riding Hood – Tina Schart Hyman

Little Red Riding Hood – Della Rowland

**Variations:**

Little Red Riding Hood: A Newfangled Prairie Tale – Lisa C. Ernst

Look Out, He's Behind You – Tony Bradman and Margaret Chamberlain

Little Critter's Little Red Riding Hood – Mercer Mayer

Lon Po Po – Ed Young

Little Red Cowboy Hat – Susan Lowell

Little Red Riding Hood / The Wolf's Tale – Della Rowland

The Three Billy Goats Gruff – Janet Stevens

The Three Billy Goats Gruff – Graham Percy

**Variations:**

The Three Silly Billies – Margie Palatini

The Toll-bridge Troll – Patricia R. Wolff

Three Cool Kids – Rebecca Emberley

The Goat Lady – Jane Bregoli

Peter and the Wolf – Selina Hastings

Peter and the Wolf – Sergei Prokofiev (translated by

Maria Carlson)

**No Variations**

Goldilocks and the Three Bears – Janet Stevens

Goldilocks and the Three Bears – James Marshall

Goldilocks and the Three Bears – Prue Theobalds

The Three Bears – Byron Barton

**Variations:**

Goldilocks – Dom Deluise

Deep in the Forest – Brinton Turkle

A Bad Week for the Three Bears – Tony Bradman and Jenny Williams

Tackylocks and the Three Bears – Helen Lester

Rolling Along with Goldilocks and the Three Bears – Cindy Meyers (baby bear uses a
wheelchair)

Rumpelstiltskin - Paul Zelinsky

**No Variations**

The Three Little Pigs – Margot Zemach

The Three Little Pigs – James Marshall

The Three Little Pigs – Steven Kellogg

**Variations:**

The Three Little Javelinas – Susan Lowell

The Three Little Wolves and the Big Bad Pig – Eugene Trivizas

Who's Afraid of the Big Bad Wolf? – Tony Bradman

The Three Little Pigs and the Fox – William H. Hooks

Who's at the Door? – Jonathan Allen

Ziggy Piggy and the Three Little Pigs – Frank Asch

The Fourth Little Pig – Teresa Celsi

Wait! No Paint! – Bruce Whatley

The True Story of the Three Little Pigs! – Jon Scieszka

The Three Little Rigs – David Gordon

The Little Red Hen – Paul Galdone

**Variations:**

The Little Red Hen (Makes a Pizza) – Philemon Sturges

The Little Red Hen – Jerry Pinkney

# REFERENCES AND RELATED READING

Bettelheim, B. (1976). *The Uses of Enchantment: The Meaning and Importance of Using Fairytales.* New York, NY: Alfred A. Knopf.

Brown, S. (2009). *Play: How it Shapes the Brain, Opens the Imagination, and invigorates the Soul.* New York, NY: Avery.

Curenton, S. and Justice, L. M. (2004). Low-Income Preschoolers' Use of Decontextualized Discourse Features Spoken Narratives. *Language, Speech, and Hearing Services in Schools, 35,* 241-255.

DeBruin-Parecki, A. (2008). *Effective Early Literacy Practice: Here's How, Here's Why.* Ypsilanti, MI: High Scope Educational Research Foundation and Baltimore, MD: Paul H. Brookes Publishing Co. (p. 102).

Ezell, H. K. and Justice, L. M. (2005). *Shared Storybook Reading.* Baltimore, MD: Paul H. Brookes Publishing Co., 28.

Fox, M. (2001). *Reading Magic: Why Reading Aloud to our Children will Change their Lives Forever.* New York, NY: A Harvest Original Harcourt, Inc., 17-18.

Hawkins, D. (1970). *ESS Reader.* Newton, MA: Elementary Science Study Education Center, 45-50.

Howarth, M. (1989). Rediscovering the Power of Fairytales: They Help Children Understand Their Lives. *Young Children, 45*(1), 56-58. Washington, DC: National Association for the Education of Young Children.

Schickendanz, J. (1986) *More than the ABCs: The Early Stages of Reading and Writing.* Washington, DC: National Association for the Education of Young Children.

Schickendanz, J. (1999). *Much More than the ABCs: The Early Stages of Reading and Writing.* Washington, DC: National Association for the Education of Young Children.

Snow, C.E.; Burns, M.S.; and Griffin, P. (Eds.) (1998). *Preventing Reading Difficulties in Young Children.* Washington, DC: National Academic Press.

Walker, L. (1995). *Block Building for Children.* Woodstock, New York, NY: The Overlook Press.

# Chapter Three

## An Expedition with Storybooks:
### Bringing Stories to Life through Thoughtful Planning

# An Expedition With Storybooks:

## BRINGING STORIES TO LIFE THROUGH THOUGHTFUL PLANNING

"Principles and developmentally appropriate practice are derived from the belief that children's developmental needs and interests should provide direction for educational planning and teaching. " –Sue Bredekamp

Developing a program that gives children both the security of a plan and the freedom to make constructive choices is essential! When children feel in control of their lives, it greatly enhances their energy for learning and potential for developing positive human relationships. Children's learning should be at the very core of planning for such a program. This is in contrast to planning the "things" that children "must learn." In other words, one philosophy looks to the curriculum for the core of its planning, while the other looks to the children. One measures success through prescribed formats and statistics the other through human contact, personal pursuits, and an individual's developmental growth over time.

An old version of *Webster's New Collegiate Dictionary* defines the word "curriculum" as "[L, a running racecourse, fr. currere to run.] a course of study." Based on my observations in schools over the years, the racecourse analysis for many seems appropriate. The pace and academic demands set by some administrators and parents for our youngest children have all the pressure of a race and leave many of our children in a cloud of dust along the sidelines. On a racecourse one must follow the pack, go in one direction, and be judged against "the best" or the *first* one to reach the finish line. For many, to reach the "finish line" is to have had the experience but missed the meaning. The question to explore is: who in the field of education decides what the finish line means and where the finish line is to be placed?

How often we rush children through the paces! So intent are we to cover certain materials that we leave little time for children to assimilate the meaning or to demonstrate their unique approach and understanding. Many curricula seem to favor breadth over depth. An interesting fable illustrates what happens when a curriculum is so intent on *teaching* the material to be covered that it overlooks the originality and uniqueness of each "child." This curriculum fable seems less fable each time I read it. It describes a curriculum that requires the same level of participation in the same course of study regardless of the individual's talents, interests, or special challenges.

### *A Curriculum Fable*
### *Author Unknown*

*One time the animals had a school. The curriculum consisted of running, climbing, flying, and swimming, and all the animals took all the subjects.*

*The Duck was good in swimming, better, in fact, than his instructor, and he made passing grades in flying, but he was practically hopeless in running. Because he was low in this subject, he was made to stay in after school and drop his swimming class in order to practice running. He kept this up until he was only average in swimming. But average is acceptable, so nobody worried except the Duck.*

*The Eagle was considered a problem pupil and was disciplined severely. He beat all the others to the top of the tree in climbing class, but he used his own way of getting there.*

*The Rabbit started out at the top of the class in running, but he had a nervous breakdown and had to drop out of school on account of so much make-up work in swimming.*

*The Squirrel led the climbing class, but his flying teacher made him start his flying lesson from the ground up instead of the top of the tree down, and he developed charley horses from over-exertion at the takeoff and began getting C's in climbing and D's in running.*

*The practiced Prairie Dogs apprenticed their offspring to a Badger when the school authorities refused to add digging to the curriculum.*

*At the end of the year, an abnormal eel, that could swim fairly well, run, climb, and fly a little, was made valedictorian.*

Perhaps too many children are going to schools where the curriculum reads much like this dramatic fable! A colleague of mine explored the word *curriculum* in a number of different sources and learned that the English word, derived from Latin, meant "to journey." That wonderful discovery opened up a whole new path for this project, for the journey means finding pathways and avenues to learning, individual routes to mastery, and passages into places unknown! It also means we can all venture into the same territory via different roads and discover its wonders with our own style of gathering and using information. As more of our schools move toward including all children in regular classrooms, planning for diverse learning strategies and for children's individual needs will become even more crucial to each child's success. The role of adults in education will change. Parents, support staff, and teachers will be much more involved in teaming, consulting, and seeking each other's advice and expertise.

Storybook Journey planning provides a framework for drawing on the talents of all those who work with children in a particular group or classroom. It is a planning process that invites everyone's input, interests, and expertise. The success of constructing and implementing such a planning process depends on our ability:

1. To invest our energy as much in the learning process as we do in the teaching.
2. To learn about each child in the context of the family as well as in the context of the classroom.
3. To look honestly at what we value and begin to understand how that is actualized in the classroom.
4. To be aware of the full developmental spectrum of our children and to match their individual needs and interests with the plans.
5. To trust children's ability to select their mode of learning with support, guidance, intentional facilitation, and modeling from adults.
6. To advocate and implement peer modeling and cooperative learning.
7. To encourage the meaningful interactions of the team. The team includes all of the people in the children's lives: families, teachers, support staff, directors, principals, peers, volunteers, and others.
8. To create a learning-rich environment with appropriate choices in materials and various strategies for practicing their skills.

## MAPPING THE JOURNEY:

In the Storybook Journey, the program plans serve as a guide sheet or reference map for traveling with a story. They record the ideas generated and gathered by the staff during the planning session. Most of the plans specifically invite the children's engagement with the story through many different modalities. Other experiences that are provided in the classroom are offerings that respond to the children's individual interests and pursuits. Teachers vary the materials in the classroom to support the children's exploration of: blocks, art materials, math, science, sensory materials, dramatic play props, manipulatives, and the like.

An important part of the Journey planning process is to gather everyone who interacts with the children in the classroom and has a stake in developing ideas on a particular story. Input from each individual enriches the planning dynamics and story development. If you are fortunate to have support staff members (occupational therapists, speech-language specialists, paraprofessionals, practicum students, interested parents), invite them to participate in the planning process. This will stretch everyone's thinking to focus on and include all aspects of the children's development in the planning process. Ideally, this type of collaborative planning also serves to give each team member a deeper sense of what is being developed in the class. It also gives everyone certain ownership in setting up the environment and becoming more intimately involved in all aspects of the program. Naturally this will depend on the time availability of all involved!

The written plan provides a means for us to track where we are headed and whether we are arriving as planned or have ventured off on other routes. The plan documents the organization of ideas around a story, the children's interests, and individualized suggestions for children who may need extra support. Briefly summarizing the events of the completed week on the back of the plans or in a designated space gives the team a chance to review the plans, expand certain experiences, change others, and share observations on the children's involvement before going on to the next week. This is an informed way to evaluate the process and to document highlights, pitfalls, and new approaches and extensions for further development of the story.

## PLANNING STARTS WITH BRAINSTORMING

The planning process is a dynamic part of each journey. It starts with gathering your classroom staff to brainstorm and discuss ideas that are present in the chosen storybook. Many programs struggle with finding a time when classroom staff members can get together. Schedules, other commitments, coverage of rooms, and endless other circumstances can prevent the team from scheduling a planning session. Because this process is such a vital part of the Journey teaching, the team is encouraged to make it a <u>high priority</u>! Work toward setting up a specific time each week when all persons involved can be on hand for at least an hour. Notice that the statement is "work toward" a weekly session together with the team. If this seems impossible at the moment, try to find a way to <u>make it</u> happen. It is very hard for a teaching team to "own" what is going on in a classroom when they have not played a part in the planning process.

If you teach alone, gather with other teachers in your center or school and brainstorm a story together. Though you may take the story in different directions with the children in your classroom, this gives you a chance to share each other's experiences, expertise, and ideas for environmental setups and use of materials, and to develop engaging story extensions.

## BRAINSTORMING FOR A STORYBOOK JOURNEY

Brainstorming can be defined as an unrestricted offering of ideas by all members of a group. For the Journey, it is an enjoyable and productive way to explore and share ideas. It engages the teaching team in the magic and learning within each story. Teachers have found that there is an ideal order for the brainstorming-to-implementation process.

1.  It is helpful to start a planning session with a <u>brief</u> statement of what led to the selection of the story being explored: observation of the children's interests and experiences; teachers' interest in developing a particular story; a child, family, or team member's suggestion; or an event in the class that could be enhanced by a related story; and the like.

2.  The story, song, poem, or nursery rhyme to be explored is then read aloud. The purpose of this is for all the brainstormers to see the illustrations, hear the version of the story being used, and take note of all the concepts.

3.  Next the group generates a list of concepts that have the potential to develop the curriculum around the chosen story.

4.  The ideas and concepts can simply be listed on a chalkboard or a sheet of easel-size paper. If you have limited time, you may need to remind people to focus on just the listing of concepts first and not all of the possible extensions at this point. This way the group does not get caught up in discussing only one concept in detail at this time. The nitty-gritty of planning and developing the concepts and ideas into experiences for the children is where you should devote the bulk of your time.

5.  Once the list of concepts has been created from everyone's brilliant thinking, the next step is to organize the concepts to make planning a fluid and meaningful process. The most efficient way for many teachers has been the method of webbing. This involves categorizing concepts into a web that links concepts and ideas in preparation for writing the plan. For a simple example, let's take the nursery rhyme of <u>Wee Willie Winkie</u> and follow how one group of teachers worked out their ideas from observing the children to writing the plans. You will see how a simple rhyme can be woven into meaningful explorations for the children.

Two teachers and a parent volunteer met for an hour after school to brainstorm ideas for starting their first Journey. They chose <u>Wee Willie Winkie</u> for a number of reasons. First, they were new to teaching and to the journey, and so they wanted to start simply. Second, they had observed a small group in the dramatic play area who were looking through the baby clothes to find pajamas for their dolls. The children chattered about what they wore to bed – pajamas, nightgowns, and T-shirts. Javier, overhearing all of this, yelled over from the block corner that he had Sponge Bob all over his pajamasAt snack time that day, the teacher said she heard some children talking about their pajamas. She asked Javier if he wanted to share what he had on his pajamas. He sure did…and the chatter was rekindled. Little snippets of the group's sleepwear, bedtime rituals, and fears trickled out.

The teachers wanted to try the process of moving from what they observed and heard in the children's play to the suggested steps for taking a Journey. The following is their adventure.

### READ ALOUD AND THINK ABOUT CONCEPTS FOR:

**Wee Willie Winkie**

Wee Willie Winkie rungs through the town
Upstairs, downstairs in his nightgown
Rapping at the window, crying through the lock
Are all the children in their beds?
Now it's eight o'clock

### BRAINSTORM AND LIST CONCEPTS FROM WEE WILLIE WINKIE:

| | | |
|---|---|---|
| Rhyming words | up and down | beds |
| Running | nightgown | clocks |
| Crying | rapping | eight |
| Town | windows | night/day |
| Stairs | locks | going "through" |
| | | Something |

**Note:** You may choose at this pint to take the listed concepts and discuss ideas for working one or two of them into your plans for the first week. For those who prefer to organize the concepts into categories before developing the plans, webbing is one way to progress. In the following example, the teachers did both the webbing of Wee Willie Winkie and the listing of idea before writing out their plans. It is really a matter of trying out what works best for each brainstorming group. There is not right way to do this part of the Journey. You want to flesh out the ideas together and develop a plan than moves with the children's interests and engagement in learning.

## WEBBING THE LIST OF CONCEPTS INTO CATEGORIES

The "Incubation Web"
(Hatching Ideas for the Duration of the Journey)

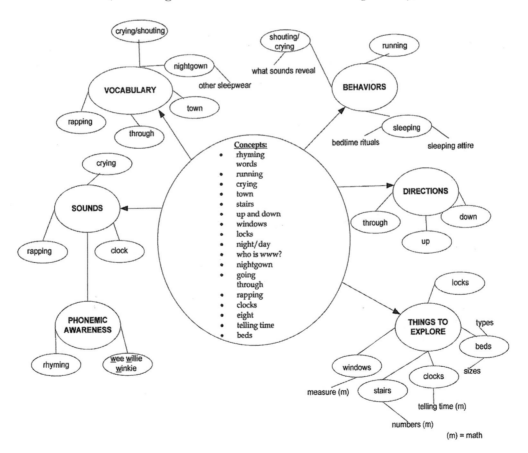

The webbing piece is our guide to discuss extensions
that can be put into a plan for week one.

Let's look at one of the categories and see how a discussion flowed and developed into a plan for this class of three-year-olds.

- **Listing of possible ideas to use in the plan:**

The team chose the idea of sleeping from the webbing, with an emphasis on bedtime rituals and sleeping attire. The teachers listed all of the possible ideas they anticipated might be of interest to the children in their group. Included in the list were some possible ideas the teachers wanted to probe and explore with the children. Where the probes lead the journey depends on the children's investigation and interest.

Bedtime Rituals:

bath/shower time

game playing

TV/video/DVD

music

story: read/told/CD/tape

blankies

sleeping buddies: dogs, cats, stuffed animals, dolls, siblings

blankets, sheets, sleeping bags, quilts, comforters

bedtime snacks

How do they like to sleep: back, side, stomach?

Does anyone want to share their dreams?

What do they like about going to bed?

How do they wake up in the morning?

Sleep Attire:

pajamas

nightgowns

other: t-shirts, underwear, tank tops

2-piece/1-piece with feet

long sleeve, short sleeve, sleeveless

designs: patterns, stripes polka dots, characters, flowers, animals

materials,: flannel, cotton, soft, fluffy, itchy

closure: snaps, buttons, zipper, velcro

**STORYBOOK JOURNEY PLANNING SHEET** ©
Sue McCord

Story: Wee Willie Winkie
Dates: 9/25-29/06

### SCIENCE

Continue with rock explorations. Add water and magnifying glasses.

### SENSORY

-put 8 plastic bottles, 8 funnels and 8 pitchers in water table – add 8 other things to table all week:
-tubes, straws, eye droppers.
Try "rapping" on various things while children hid their eyes and guess what they hear.

### MOTOR (INDOOR/OUTDOOR)

-Bring out see saw (for up and down)
-Turn rocking boat over for the stairs
-Explore all the stairs in our school

### GROUP STORY EXPERIENCE

-Read poem dressed up like Wee Willie
-Act out Wee Willie with children
-Tell poem with a puppet dressed in nightgown and night cap
-Tap out poem with rhythm sticks and triangle for striking 8 o'clock

### MATH

-Do various things around the room with series of 8 (i.e., water table)
-Put real clocks in dramatic play area (and around the room). Add play clocks they can manipulate

### CONCEPTS

- rhyming words
- stairs
- sleeping attire
- rapping
- eight
- locks
- night
- clocks
- beds

STORY: Wee Willie Winkie

### DRAMATIC PLAY/ ENVIRONMENTAL SET-UP

-Add nightgowns and p.j.s to dress up rack
-Night cap, candle, stairs
-If possible make a cardboard door with keyhole

Pam will dress up as Wee Willie Winkie – nightgown, nightcap, candle and slippers and greet the children in the morning.

### ART EXPLORATION

-Redo paint jars with new colors
-Add materials and wallpaper samples with patterns and different textures to collage box (cut paper in shape of pajamas so they can design their own p.j.s)

### FAMILY CONNECTIONS

-Send home a copy of Wee Willie Winkie
-Plan a family night at the library (6:30 – 7:30) for stories in their pajamas or "nightgowns"
-Maybe get library cards

### UNDERSTANDING DIVERSITY

-All the different patterns and characters on p.j.s
-Different time pieces – clocks, watches, timers
-Types of sleepwear

### COOKING/SNACKS

-Cheerios (eat them with a toothpick) and apple juice
-Parent snack day
-Celery, apples, grapes, water
-8 raisins, 8 Wheat Chex, grape juice. They count out seconds.
-8 cheese cubes and pretzels

### MUSIC/MOVEMENT

-Sing songs we learned last week and add When you're up, you're up
-Use rhythm sticks to tap out poem. Use triangle for striking 8 o'clock

- **Plan for one week:**

This plan was created by two teachers and a parent volunteer. You may have noticed that each section of the planning sheet indicates that some things are planned around Wee Willie and some are extensions or additions from the previous week (i.e., science). It is important not to "force" the story concepts into the plans. The point is to keep all areas of the room alive with interesting and engaging open-ended experiences. By watching how the children are using the various areas of the room and the materials provided, we learn how to extend, introduce additional concepts, and/or change the environment.

Children often take the plans in unanticipated directions that give us new insights and challenges. The ability to go with the spontaneity of children's ideas takes courage and a willingness to accept that you'll be traveling uncharted territory for a while. This is where observation is so valuable! Keep observing and listening to gain a sense of where the children's interests lead. Weave their ideas into a revision or extension of the plans. Provide the props that will support their attempts to find meaning. Just remember that life is a series of adjustments and so is our teaching. For example, in the classroom we are following, one child brought in her stuffed rabbit from home and said he needed a nightgown. Her nightgowns were too big for him! The teacher said, "I wonder if he won't get too hot, because most rabbits have enough fur to stay warm." A group gathered around them and the conversation switched to other animals. The teacher had a number of books about animals in the wild and brought them out to explore. For this smaller group, the journey went off into a whole new adventure. Other children floated in and out of the original group over the next week. The teacher made a special space in the science area with books that showed animals in the winter and some fur pelts she had borrowed from a friend. (She also brought in some materials for Olivia to make a nightgown for her rabbit, as she was still convinced her rabbit was cold.)

Various other concept "nudges" can be woven into the environment or fan out into the playground, neighborhood, and homes. In this way, the children can explore other tangible parts of the Wee Willie Winkie story. For instance, there were math, motor, and snack ideas in the plans that were not part of the original concept of pajamas.

Other possibilities to explore (if the children show an interest or if you would like to encourage exploration with one of the other brainstormed concepts):

Clocks

Place various timepieces around the room or in the math center. Beg or borrow such things as alarm clocks, digital clocks, clocks with hands, regular watches, stopwatches, and timers. They come with different rings, alarms, chimes, gongs, and ticks. Children are particularly fascinated if they can see the inner workings. This can become an ongoing project if you collect watches and old clocks that they can take apart. It exposes the children to written numbers from 1 to 12 and may spark an interest in playing with "time telling." There is also the difference of digital clocks and numerical. Some children, during their explorations, might be curious to know what the lines between each number on a clock represent. Counting all of the lines aloud together will give them a sense of "60." Setting a timer for an hour might help them become aware of how long it takes to get to 60 minutes.

### Locks

Locks are fascinating and working with them becomes an engaging investigation. Start begging for door locks, padlocks, bicycle locks, those on suitcases and diaries, combination locks, locks with a variety of keys, old locks, new locks and on it goes.

### Stairs

Search for stairs in the school building, on the playground, on a walk through the neighborhood, at home…Explore what they are made of (cement, wood, rocks, steel). How are they held together? How big is each step (measure with various rulers, tape measures, string, how many "hands" long or high?)…How many different ways can you go up and down stairs?

Explore how else one can get to higher places: ladders, ramps, ropes, elevators, chairlifts, and pulleys.

The only limit to the length and depth of the journey is our willingness to imagine and wonder like a child. Remember to observe carefully. The children will guide us to where they want to go with the extensions. These are <u>just</u> examples of what can evolve once you start a journey.

You can see how the simplest of stories, poems, or songs can spin off and lead into ever-expanding experiences. <u>Remember</u>, however, <u>not</u> to use <u>all</u> the concepts or ideas you brainstormed at one time. Choose what you think will involve the children in meaningful play, observations, and a deeper knowledge of the things they hear about in a story. Be open to moving in the direction the children take the plans. We are aiming for depth of investigation and expanding on the <u>children's</u> curiosity, ideas, and engagement with learning. Children need time to reflect on the story to make personal connections to the content and to play with new ideas and information as their interests are sparked. The discussion that surrounds the storybook reading and the extended experiences are what give the story meaning. As much as possible we want to bridge the story content to the children's lives.

"Meaningful connections are another priority in the curriculum planning of good teachers. Young children learn best when the concepts, vocabulary, and skills they encounter are related to something they already know and care about when the new learnings are themselves interconnected in meaningful, coherent ways. Children do not learn as readily when information and experiences are presented in isolated, unrelated chunks. Learning experiences are integrated and meaningful when children work on projects and other studies in which they can see the connections between concepts and skills they encounter" (Copple, C. and Bredekamp, S. [Eds.], 2009).

Reflection

Let's pause for a moment and consider your own circumstances when it comes to planning.

- What is required in your child-care setting or school in terms of tangible evidence of plans and how are they to be written?
- Are there any scheduling issues involving shared spaces (e.g., playground or eating spaces) that require a specific time schedule and present a challenge to your plans?
- What is your comfort level in moving from observing the children's interests and involvement, to selecting a story, and finally to creating your plans based on those observations?

Some teachers and administrators feel more secure knowing what is planned in detail for each day of the week. They prefer that learning centers and "activities" be clearly laid out ahead of time so everyone knows exactly what is to be set up in the environment each day. The plans are posted and carefully followed. This form of planning may hamper following the children's interests and extending their experiences because the <u>plan</u> becomes the focus. It can also change the pace and length of children's explorations and engagement.

For a **<u>fictional</u>** example, take one section of a planning sheet for Wee Willie Winkie that reads: **<u>Monday</u>** explore keys and locks, **<u>Tuesday</u>** cut out pictures of sleeping attire, **<u>Wednesday</u>** explore clocks. What happens to the children who were really interested in the locks on Monday? They wanted to try the keys on other locks, take the locks apart, explore the insides, compare the gears, create new projects with the parts, and so on. When they came into the room on Tuesday, the clocks were gone and the workspaces had magazines and catalogs for a pajama search! This is like one of us almost figuring out the plot in a mystery novel before going to bed, then discovering the next morning that the rest of the pages have been torn out of the book!

The same is true with spending longer periods with one story. Read it frequently during a journey so the children can really hear the story language, comprehend on different levels, revisit the illustrations, and discuss their thoughts and ideas. As Eleanor Duckworth said, "Too many experiences are like looking out the tour bus window." One reading of a favorite story can't begin to be enough. How often have we heard…"Read it again!…Read it again!"

Some teachers feel comfortable with a "flowing" emergent plan that has a general direction to pursue in the first week of the new journey story. The environmental setups relate to one or more of the concepts discussed during the "webbing incubation" process. These setups tend to serve as probes or nudges during the first week. The teachers observe how the children are interacting with the available materials to learn what extensions will encourage further investigations, research, genuine learning opportunities, and self-expression. They listen to the children's thoughts and serve as intentional learning partners to help them make connections to the story, their prior experiences and offer challenges to deepen their knowledge.

Fred Rogers, of Mister Rogers fame, had a teacher who called this approach a "guided drift." This was such a great term that I borrowed it to make an analogy. You have a plan, which is "the boat." You are the rudder. The rudder guides the drift of the plan to the places where the children are focusing their attention. We could continue this idea by sharing the rudder with the children as they help us continue to steer the plans into the deeper meanings they want to explore.

Some teachers go between both the structured plan and the emerging plan. It really has much to do with experience, what we believe about how children learn, comfort levels, trust, and what the administrators of the school require. If one wishes to move into a more fluid form of planning and implementation, it takes courage, confidence, and an ability to articulate why this is beneficial in order to negotiate changes in the requirements. Focusing on what engages children's interests is a fascinating and alive way to teach and learn. I hope you will feel supported in your efforts if you would like to try sharing "the rudder" with the children.

NAEYC researchers, in a recent report, say that being a responsive classroom teacher means being able to adapt the curriculum to address students' needs and interests and allow children to discuss their experiences, feelings, and ideas (Wilson, 2009).

Research has also long indicated (especially that written by Vygotsky) that children do best when they are supported to achieve their goal just beyond their current level of mastery. He called this the zone of Proximal Development (Bodrova & Leong, 1996, pp. 35-47).

Many of us who have taught young children over the years know that it is critical to address children's needs and interests and support children to achieve their goals for mastery! This can happen only when teachers observe children's thinking and play, listen, intentionally interact, gain a real understanding of the children in their class, and create plans for those children. Strict adherence to a regimented curriculum with lesson plans written on subject matter out of context puts children, whom we know learn and develop at different rates, at a tremendous disadvantage and under unnecessary stress.

"Play and experiential learning have been shown to bring lasting benefits to children, while the effectiveness of didactic instruction and scripted teaching are not supported by valid long-term studies. Children need kindergartens (and preschools) that emphasize child-initiated play and well-designed experiential learning rather than didactic instruction or its opposite, a laissez-faire approach where play disintegrates into chaos" (Miller & Almon, 2009).

The following chart is a pictorial review of the Storybook Journey planning pathway. Some teachers have found this chart a "quick study" that reminds them there are a series of steps that make the Journey meaningful and engaging for the children. It is another way of looking at the process if you prefer a diagram to the words.

**PLANNING THE JOURNEY**
A web of learning events that involve children, staff and families

To know when to end a Journey and transition into a new story

To know the children

Children's engagement and learning in all areas of development

OBSERVE

SELECT STORY

DOCUMENT

Based on observations of children's interests

The story concepts are the center of the web. Experiences you wish to foster for each Journey spin from that center. The experiences the children create may take you down new pathways. Follow them for engaging and sustained involvement.

Materials and environment to match interests

EXPAND

BRAINSTORM IDEAS

List ideas

Web categories or use Emerging Idea Gathering Sheet

OBSERVE

PLAN

Set ideas into motion one week at a time

What is sustaining the children's interest and involvement

IMPLEMENT CURRICULUM

Involve families

Gather materials

Integrate story into centers

Create environment

Build rich learning opportunities

**Sample Planning Sheets for the Storybook Journey**

<u>Selection</u>

This section is devoted to a number of different planning sheets. Look them over and see if they will be of any help in writing out your plans each week. The way a staff decides to create their plans is highly individualized. The sheets are merely suggestions. If any of them work for you, please copy them and adjust them to fit your needs.

The plan sheets include:

➢ <u>The Infant's Journey</u> (p. )

➢ <u>The Toddler's Journey</u> (p.)

➢ Two preschool <u>Planning Sheets</u> (pp.) have the same categories on each sheet, but formatting differences give you some choices.

➢ <u>The Individual Planning Sheet</u> (p.) was developed for speech-language therapists, but it can also be used by occupational therapists, if you are fortunate enough to have either one working with children in your room! In our fast-paced lives, it is usually difficult to find the time to meet with those who come into our classroom for short periods. The Individual Planning Sheet might serve as a support link. The therapists could suggest ideas for story connections that would further support the children's development in either therapy. Many teachers have found that what therapists suggest is interesting for <u>all</u> children. This is especially true with equipment for occupational therapy. This sheet can also be used by therapists to connect what you are doing in class to their individual sessions with various children.

This section also has a few planning sheets filled out for your review. They are <u>only</u> examples to be used as "inspiration" and not "cheat sheets"!

## THE INFANT'S JOURNEY
## CREATING INVITATIONS TO PLAY ©

FAMILY/CAREGIVER OBSERVATIONS & THOUGHTS
ABOUT INDIVIDUAL INTERESTS & CHALLENGES

SENSORY PLAY

MUSIC

BOOKS

NURSERY RHYMES, SONGS, POEMS

VARIATIONS IN THE ENVIRONMENTAL SET-UPS

HOME PARTNERSHIPS

Concepts · Vocabulary

STORY:

DATE:

## THE INFANT'S JOURNEY
## CREATING INVITATIONS TO PLAY ©

FAMILY/CAREGIVER OBSERVATIONS & THOUGHTS
ABOUT INDIVIDUAL INTERESTS & CHALLENGES

### SENSORY PLAY

- soft stuffed mice made from different textures and patterns
- listen to tick of big toy clock
- make ticking sounds with tone block and stick
- creep fingers up and down babies leg or back when saying the rhyme

concepts · Vocabulary
- mice
- clocks
- sound of chime for one o'clock
- up down

### MUSIC

- sing Hickory Dickory Dock – make up any tune (while changing diapers, rocking infant to sleep, while feeding child)
- play gentle music with soft beat or gentle instruments – harp, flute and the like

### BOOKS

Mouse Paint (colorful)
Goodnight Max
Mouse Mess
Give a Mouse a Cookie

### NURSERY RHYMES, SONGS, POEMS

- sing, read or make up little rhymes or poems whenever possible. Infants need to hear our voice and the cadence of speech
- just say mouse, mouse, mouse... mice, mice, mice in different tones, rhythms and pitch. Say it, sing it, slowly, faster, softer, louder.

### VARIATIONS IN THE ENVIRONMENTAL SET-UPS

- enlarge pictures of mice from books or magazines – put them around the room
- find a few large size clocks with good sounding ticks
- vary the pictures and toys

### HOME PARTNERSHIPS

A parent might be wiling to make a soft mouse out of a soft material for the class

STORY:

Hickory Dickory Dock

DATE:

## THE TODDLER'S JOURNEY
## "FUN JUST WAITING TO HAPPEN"

LITERACY FOCUS:

SENSORY PLAY:

RUG PLAY AND MANIPULATIVES:

NATURE:

MOTOR (INSIDE/OUTSIDE):

DRAMATIC PLAY:

MUSIC:

EXPLORATION OF ART MATERIALS:

EXPLORING DIVERSITY:

STORY:

DATE:

Story Concepts

A Book About Me
Where's Spot
Once Upon A Lullaby
Good Night Moon
Nursery Rhymes

NOTES ON INDIVIDUAL CHILD'S INTERESTS AND CHALLENGES

FAMILY CONNECTIONS

Storybook Journey © Sue McCord

# THE TODDLER'S JOURNEY
## "FUN JUST WAITING TO HAPPEN"

**LITERACY FOCUS:**
- wonderful words to play with
  - heaping
  - plop
  - melting
  - crunch
  - smack
  - sinking
- other books with winter, snow, animals they see in winter, dressing for winter, fun in the snow, etc.

**SENSORY PLAY:**
- snow in the water table
- experiences with cold, warm, wet, dry

**RUG PLAY AND MANIPULATIVES:**
- winter puzzles
- miniature world set up with real snow

**NATURE:**
- tracks in the snow
- wet
- melting
- winter
- snow
- winter animals

**MOTOR (INSIDE/OUTSIDE):**
- dressing -- mittens, zippers, boots, etc
- climbing drifts
- shoveling snow
- angel making
- throwing snowballs

**DRAMATIC PLAY:**
- all kinds of winter clothes to try on: scarves, boots, ski boots, galoshes, mittens, gloves, etc.

**ART:**
- white paint on black paper at easel
- paint the snow outside with tempera paint and fat brushes
- make snowballs and roll them in paint across a big piece of paper

**MUSIC/MOVEMENT:**
- making sounds for plop, smack, crunch with found materials
- pretend making snowman

**EXPLORATION OF ART MATERIALS:**
- painting snow outside with easel paint
- finger paint on a mirror
- finger paint on a table or paper

**EXPLORING DIVERSITY:**
- skin color
- night/day
- different snow tracks

**Story Concepts**
- winter
- snow
- snow suit
- high
- path
- crunch
- ways of
- walking
- plop
- slowly
- tracks
- smack
- snowballs
- snowman
- angels
- climber
- melting
- sinking
- heaping
- up/down
- pack
- warm
- pocket
- wet
- empty
- breakfast
- deep
- dream
- sad
- falling
- tall

A BOOK ABOUT ME
WHERE'S SPOT
ONCE UPON A LULLABY
GOOD NIGHT MOON
NURSERY RHYMES

**STORY:** The Snowy Day

**DATE:**

**NOTES ON INDIVIDUAL CHILD'S INTERESTS AND CHALLENGES**

**FAMILY CONNECTIONS**

Storybook Journey © Sue McCord

91

## STORYBOOK JOURNEY PLANNING SHEET ©

Sue McCord

Story:
Dates:

SCIENCE

SENSORY

MOTOR
(INDOOR/OUTDOOR)

GROUP STORY EXPERIENCE

MATH

CONCEPTS

DRAMATIC PLAY/
ENVIRONMENTAL SET-UP

ART EXPLORATION

STORY:

BLOCKS & MANIPULATIVES

COOKING/SNACKS

FAMILY CONNECTIONS

UNDERSTANDING
DIVERSITY

MUSIC/MOVEMENT

# STORYBOOK JOURNEY PLANNING SHEET ©

Sue McCord

Story: Wee Willie Winkie
Dates: 9/25-29/06

## SCIENCE

Continue with rock explorations. Add water and magnifying glasses.

## SENSORY

-put 8 plastic bottles, 8 funnels and 8 pitchers in water table -- add 8 other things to table all week:
-tubes, straws, eye droppers. Try "rapping" on various things while children hid their eyes and guess what they hear.

## MOTOR (INDOOR/OUTDOOR)

-Bring out see saw (for up and down)
-Turn rocking boat over for the stairs
-Explore all the stairs in our school

## GROUP STORY EXPERIENCE

-Read poem dressed up like Wee Willie
-Act out Wee Willie with children
-Tell poem with a puppet dressed in nightgown and night cap
-Tap out poem with rhythm sticks and triangle for striking 8 o'clock

## MATH

-Do various things around the room with series of 8 (i.e., water table)
-Put real clocks in dramatic play area (and around the room). Add play clocks they can manipulate

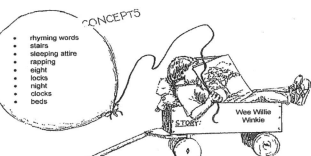

CONCEPTS
- rhyming words
- stairs
- sleeping attire
- rapping
- eight
- locks
- night
- clocks
- beds

STORY: Wee Willie Winkie

## DRAMATIC PLAY/ ENVIRONMENTAL SET-UP

-Add nightgowns and p.j.s to dress up rack
-Night cap, candle, stairs
-If possible make a cardboard door with keyhole

## ART EXPLORATION

-Redo paint jars with new colors
-Add materials and wallpaper samples with patterns and different textures to collage box (cut paper in shape of pajamas so they can design their own p.j.s)

## BLOCKS & MANIPULATIVES

Have children explore various ways to build stairs.

## FAMILY CONNECTIONS

-Send home a copy of Wee Willie Winkie
-Plan a family night at the library (6:30 – 7:30) for stories in their pajamas or "nightgowns"
-Maybe get library cards

## UNDERSTANDING DIVERSITY

-All the different patterns and characters on p.j.s
-Different time pieces -- clocks, watches, timers
-Types of sleepwear

## COOKING/SNACKS

-Cheerios (eat them with a toothpick) and apple juice
-Parent snack day
-Celery, apples, grapes, water
-8 raisins, 8 Wheat Chex, grape juice. They count out seconds.
-8 cheese cubes and pretzels

## MUSIC/MOVEMENT

-Sing songs we learned last week and add When you're up, you're up
-Use rhythm sticks to tap out poem. Use triangle for striking 8 o'clock

STORYBOOK JOURNEY PLANNING SHEET ©
Sue McCord

STORY:

DATE:

| | |
|---|---|
| MOTOR (INDOOR/ OUTDOOR) | |
| SCIENCE | |
| MATH | |
| SENSORY | |
| COOKING/SNACKS | |
| ART EXPLORATION | |
| BLOCKS & MANIPULATIVES | |
| DRAMATIC PLAY (SET-UP) | |
| MUSIC & MOVEMENT | |
| GROUP TIME | |

| FAMILY CONNECTIONS | UNDERSTANDING DIVERSITY |
|---|---|
| | |

FEATURED CONCEPTS:

STORYBOOK JOURNEY PLANNING SHEET ©
Sue McCord

STORY:
DATE:

| | |
|---|---|
| **MOTOR (INDOOR/ OUTDOOR)** | Have ladder against tree or lying down so they can step over each rung.   Clean shed so they can carry and move heavy things!   Play hide and seek on playground ——————————————————————————→ |
| **SCIENCE** | Save all the seeds and pits – experiment with planting them. Bring in literacy with having them create labels so they will know what they've planted. ————————————————→   Learn about where bears and mice really live. ————————————————→ |
| **MATH** | • Make chains with various things (paper clips, paper straws) (measure them with various things and record length and number of "links")   • If pits start to grow, record growth and which ones are growing the fastest and highest   • Weigh "heavy and light" objects.   • Work on understanding and demonstrating what is half of something. |
| **SENSORY** | Smell, taste, eat strawberries – add new fruits each day.   Listen t. "fferent kinds of footsteps and guess who they represent – mouse, bear, others. |
| **COOKING/SNACKS** | • Strawberries (out their own with plastic knives)   Strawberry smoothie   Other fruits and make our own fruit juices – serve with crackers and cheese   • Yogurt |
| **ART EXPLORATION** | Put only red on easel – add white, black, green, etc. One each day so children can experiment with what colors they can make starting with red. Display different shades of red. |
| **BLOCKS & MANIPULATIVES** | Have children build structures on trays and then try to lift them to judge what is heavy? Light? |
| **DRAMATIC PLAY (SET-UP)** | See what places in the room they can find to hide (create new ones) ——————————→   Setup ideas for sharing, e.g., 1 box of crayons to share at art table, 2 children sharing one book, etc.   Explore locks and keys adding new challenges to explore each day ——————————→ |
| **MUSIC & MOVEMENT** | Tromping like the bear, tiptoeing like the mouse with drum and triangle |
| **GROUP TIME** | Read story (See if they know who is telling the story)   Create disguises with group ——————————→ Write up their hiding stories |

| FAMILY CONNECTIONS | UNDERSTANDING DIVERSITY |
|---|---|
| • Send story home   • Have families create disguises – if they have a camera send in a picture for children to share. If not, we'll take some in school. | other bear stories: Corduroy, Pooh, Paddington mice stories: Mouse Paint, Give a Mouse a Cookie, etc. t sizes, habitats, bodies of mice and bears; also different skin, pits, etc. |

FEATURED CONCEPTS:

**Making Story Connections through Hands-On Experiences**

**(An Explanation of the Planning Sheet Categories)**

**Story Concepts:**

The balloon portion of the brainstorming sheet is reserved for listing the concepts and ideas elicited from the stories. (Story connection example: For Red Riding Hood, the list might include such things as red, head coverings, talking to strangers, real wolves, aging, caring for someone who is ill, and forests/woodlands)

**Cooking/snacks:**

Cooking can be an engaging learning experience for children. The setup needs to be carefully planned to maximize the children's participation and learning. The idea is to relate the snack and cooking activity to the story whenever feasible. Create a calm, accepting atmosphere at snack time that encourages children to socialize. Plan a unique "focus" in the middle of the table now and then to encourage conversation, i.e., a live gold fish in a glass bowl, a spider or bug in a jar, a bird's egg found on the playground. (Story connection example: Humpty Dumpty was an egg so anything related to eggs would be appropriate—boiled eggs, trying different kinds of eggs, making "egg boats," peeling eggs, etc.)

**Construction: manipulatives, blocks, Legos, puzzles, etc.:**

Using a variety of manipulatives provides children with alternative ways to see relationships, patterns, represent their world, and to learn about balance, symmetry, classification, and shapes through trial and error. (Story connection example: Children make Lincoln Log, block, or Lego houses for three pigs or use hollow blocks to build a home big enough for three bears to enter.)

**Art experiences related to the story:**

Art in the Storybook Journey is a child's personal and visual statement. It is the child's original use of paints, clay, crayons, pencils, markers, and collage materials. If there is a material link to the story, that will be set up in addition to the other art offerings that are always available. (Story connection example: Making masks for acting out Sendak's <u>Where the Wild Things Are</u>. Choices are offered for the mask's base, plaster gauze, paper plates, etc. Everything possible is available for eyes, nose, mouth, teeth, and hair. There are no models or preconceived ideas. The children plan and draw a sketch of ideas if they choose or just freely create an original. (One child asked for face paint and that was his mask.)

## Family connections:

Meaningfully involving families in their children's lives at school helps to establish a partnership in learning. Newsletters, meetings, slide or video sharing of the children's day in school, and a personal note, phone call or e-mail all help to make a connection to the family. Keeping families involved with the Storybook Journey specifically can be done in a number of ways: A copy of the story can be attached to the newsletter; families can read or act out the story at home; props can be shared both ways; and any member of the family can come and read, sing, or tell a story, help with material gathering, or borrow the story suitcase (a small kit with a taped version of the story in the language spoken at home, a book, and a miniature world. This is particularly helpful if a family is not literate or needs to have the story translated into another language.)

## Sensory

The information we receive about the world comes to us through our sensory systems: touch, taste, smell, sight, and sound. Providing experiences that stimulate and satisfy a child's sensory needs is an important part of our daily setup. Water, sand, snow, bird seed, shaving cream, and the like are all rotated in turn through our standing water table or provided in large plastic bins set up on the floor. (Story connection example: Are You My Mother? provides an obvious chance to experience many kinds of bird seed in the water table to dump and fill, sort, bury, hide objects, or watch them slide through tilted plastic tubes, and listen to the sounds they create.) When you're finished, stuff peanut butter into pine cones, roll them in bird seed and hang them on trees as natural birdfeeders. (Be aware of allergies to peanuts!)

## Outdoor play

The outside environment provides an excellent arena for story play or reenactment. A certain spontaneity is unleashed when children play outside. Sandboxes, bushes, stones, twigs, snow, water, leaves, rocks, trees, gardens, hills, logs, and walls are all potential props. (Story connection examples: sand becomes porridge for *The Three Bears*; trees are Red Riding Hood's forest; bushes are haystacks for hiding Boy Blue or a makeshift stick house for one of the Three Pigs.)

## Science

Young children are naturally curious and eager to understand their world through self-exploration and discovery over time. The challenge is to set up appropriate areas inside and outside for hands-on experiences. They must hold meaning to the children and allow for extensions to their growing knowledge of plants, animals, and changes through such things as cooking, awareness of weather, moon cycles, seasons, death, and so on. (Story connection example: The Little Red Hen provides a simple story that progresses from the planting of grain to bread making. There are many science-related extensions such as growing seeds and tending the plants, harvesting wheat, grinding the grain, changes that occur during the cooking process, watching the bread rise, smelling it cooking, and so on. All kinds of grain in its plant and refined forms would be fascinating to explore.)

## Math:

Math offers a concrete way to make order of things and experiences. As adults we can provide many varied opportunities for children to meaningfully count, see numbers on the calendars, book pages, phones, clocks, scales, measuring tapes and rulers, on score boards, TV remote and the like. (Story connection example: One summer a group grew "bean stalks" for *Jack and the Bean Stalk*. They found all kinds of ways to measure them: with hands, shoes, their own bodies, string marks on a paper strip, a ruler, and a yardstick. They documented growth over time once a week and recorded it.

## Understanding diversity:

Highlighting diversity as a part of the planning sheet helps us search through the story ideas and concepts for valuable ways to include the broadest understanding of diversity. The primary aim is to sensitively incorporate diversity into the curriculum in a way that is meaningful to the children. Become aware of different sizes, colors and ways of solving problems, etc. in each story. Discuss these together at group time. Pose questions that will help children probe these differences. (Story connection example: In *Swimmy*, a little fish that looks and thinks differently from the other fish develops a peaceful strategy to save himself and his friends from an intruder. Through acting this out the children can experience the feeling of working together to cleverly solve a problem.

**Group/circle time:**

> One of the most important kinds of developmental progress that children can make is their ability to represent their knowledge of the world in many different modalities and media. - David Weikart

Group time with The Journey is a gathering of the children and teachers for enjoyment, learning, and sharing common knowledge of the story being explored. Reading, telling, listening, singing, acting out, placing the character on a mural, dancing, and manipulating puppets or miniature worlds all add new dimensions to a child's involvement and comprehension of the story. It isn't just repeated readings and telling of the story that matters, but <u>how</u> it is read and told. For the experience to be meaningful and effective, it must be an interpersonal event of shared engagement, shaped by those who participate in the experience.

After a story has been shared at group time, any props that have been used move out into the classroom. They may show up on a special table, in the block area, book corner, or wherever the teachers feel the props will invite children to engage in replay. Children – through their repetitive play with story characters and plot – rehearse, practice, and master the joys and vital aspects of the story.

It is important to know that group times can vary according to the interests and ideas of the children and/or teachers. The plan may indicate one thing, but if the children have an exciting project, event, or their own stories to share – that becomes the focus of one part of group time.

The repetitive use of the story in many different modalities at group time is key to the Storybook Journey. Other experiences are certainly introduced as they become relevant during the course of a Journey, but the emphasis is on the story.

**Repetition of stories through various modalities for:**

- <u>Active exploration of story language & vocabulary</u>
- <u>Story structure: sequence, plot, characters</u>
- <u>Developing listening skills</u>

- <u>Meaning making</u>
- <u>Increased quality for reenactment and socialization</u>
- <u>Time to explore, practice, master</u>
- <u>Concept development</u>

**<u>Dramatic play/prop building/environmental set-ups:</u>**

This section of the planning sheet is meant to focus attention on what materials need to be gathered so the children and team can develop props and set up a space to encourage story replay. What is available and what needs to be borrowed or made that will help to create an environment that invites story-related play? For many children, available props provide the means for them to play out their own interests with the overlay of the story. (Story connection examples: All kinds of cardboard tubes can be gathered for horns or tails for the three billy goats; old sheets (or scarves) can be used to tie-dye butterfly wings for *The Very Hungry Caterpillar's* metamorphosis or to use as tents for *Just Me and My Dad* or capes for Peter Pan. Boxes can be the houses for the three pigs. Simple "furniture" can be used to represent a bed, table, chair, and so on for Little Red Riding Hood's grandmother's apartment or house.) Open-ended props allow for spontaneous role playing and the creation of imaginative characters.

**<u>Extensions beyond the classroom:</u>**

Where can the class go or who can come visit to help extend story concepts, knowledge, and enjoyment? (Story connection example: Visiting the planetarium as an expansion of reading *Moon Cake*; observing pasta being made in a pasta carry-out to go with the story *Strega Nona*; or inviting musicians from high school or elsewhere to come with selected instruments for replay of *Peter and the Wolf* or a harp for *Jack and the Beanstalk*.)

**<u>Related books, poems, and stories:</u>**

A wide variety of books is available for children to peruse. A special part of the reading nook might feature different versions of the same story (e.g., there are about 10 or 11 versions of *The Three Bears*, or you may want to just emphasize "bearness" and display books about real bears or story bears: Corduroy, Paddington, Pooh, etc.).

**<u>Literacy links to story:</u>**

Reading, writing, listening, and "the hundred languages of children" (Loris Malaguzzi) are all a part of literacy. Think about *how* literacy can be brought into all areas of the curriculum and the story replay; for instance, there could be a miniature world setup available with an audiotape so a nonverbal child can "act" out the story with the miniatures while hearing the story on tape; children writing (or dictating) their own stories and acting them out or developing cozy places in the room that encourage children to look through all kinds of books. (Story connections or "additions": Mama Bear reads a paper, Papa Bear writes a shopping list or reads a recipe for porridge, all of the bowls are labeled (Mama Bear, Baby Bear, etc.); children can make signs and post them in the woods for *Little Red Riding Hood,* such as: "This is the way to grandma's," "one way," "stop to pick the flowers," "knock before entering," etc. Grannie's house can also have the address written on the mailbox — (Grandma Hood, 1 Forest Lane. It's a way of nudging awareness of environmental print and emphasizing that letters, words, and numbers hold meaning.)

## Ongoing Program Essentials for Young Children: A Checklist

The purpose of this section is to provide a quick check and explanation of all of the other important activities available to the children on a daily basis. These activities are set up as an ever-present choice for the children whether they are linked to the story plans or not.

### Art Center

A separate setup for the children's independent use and exploration. The presentation and offerings vary according to children's interests and the teacher's desire to introduce new materials.

- paints (tempera, water color, finger paint)
- variety of utensils to paint with: brushes for house painting, watercolor brushes, toothbrushes, etc. also cotton swabs, pieces of sponge, or rags.
- trash-to-treasure items for collages, sculptures, free forms (beads, wood scraps, fabric, paper scraps, telephone wire, jar lids, small boxes, etc.)
- markers, colored pencils, regular pencils, ballpoint pens, crayons
- glue, staples, masking tape, adhesive tape
- scissors, protractors, rulers
- Play-doh, clay, and tools to use with both assorted paper, cardboard, wood scraps

### Block Area

Blocks are a valuable tool for constructing representations of the world, studying relationships, patterns, designs, balance, and for experimenting, planning, and playing! They need as much space as possible, free from traffic pathways. Blocks are a marvelous means of joining individuals in a group project or social endeavor. Organize blocks for visual cues and organized, independent clean up.

- check unit blocks to see if you have at least one complete set
- blocks come in all forms: large hollow blocks, unit blocks, cardboard bricks, large and small Legos, waffle construction blocks, and more. The most important ones are made of unpainted, finished wood, but if you cannot afford them, find substitutes as children need to build!

### Woodworking and Take-Apart

Create a place for construction with wood and real tools. This area must be safe and supervised. It may need to be a special feature area, closed on days when supervision is low, but try to find a space for it. Safety glasses are highly recommended.

- various sizes of soft wood scraps (pine, poplar)
- screwdrivers (regular and Phillips), pliers, hammers
- hand drill with varying bits
- screws, nails, tacks
- hinges, corners, washers, C-clamps
- wire, spools, wheels, machine parts
- dowels
- old vacuum, typewriters, record players, clocks, hair dryer, windshield wiper motors, and more (all with plugs removed) are great for children to take apart and to use for construction projects

### Animals, Plants and Other Living Things

Learning to care for something that cannot survive in captivity without our taking the responsibility to feed, water, change cage, and so on is essential. There is also the learning value of coping with the realities of death and dying as a process of life when children see fish and plants die.

- rotating classroom pets is a valuable experience. Being exposed to a number of species as well as caring for particular needs can teach priceless lessons. Many pet shops are willing to help you with this experience (for a price) if they trust of your care practices.
- pets that seem to do well on a permanent basis are fish in aerated tanks, guinea pigs, newts, hermit crabs, and snails. Worm and ant "villages" also do well if carefully maintained.
- plants, bulbs, bean seeds, vegetable tops, cuttings, and pits are fun to experiment with and add great warmth to in a room when healthy.
- Be aware of allergies to animals or their bedding. State Health Departments also have regulations on amphibians that vary across state lines.

## Sensory

"Messing about" with a variety of sensory experiences is both stimulating and meaningful to young children. It involves touching, hearing, seeing, smelling, and tasting. Setups and materials will dictate what to do. Many programs keep their water table or large bins in use at all times with a rotating variety of materials. Some of the most popular are:

- water, mud, sand, dirt, snow
- bird seed, pebbles, egg shells (washed)
- cornstarch (dry and with water)
- shaving cream, soap flakes (with water)
- accessories such as scoops, spoons, cups, sifters, detergent bottles, funnels, strainers, colanders, tubes, siphons

★Sensory experiences are important in helping to organize key areas of the brain!

## Cooking

Preparing food with children can be a very satisfying experience. In today's hurried world of fast foods and fast paces of living, many children do not have a chance to prepare food with their families. Observing changes, textures, processes, smells, recipe reading, and tasting are all very valuable ways of gaining and mastering new information (always check for food allergies first!)

- shell peanuts and make peanut butter with a food grinder
- break eggs, explore shells, beat own egg with egg beater and scramble for snack
- wash, peel, and chop veggies for soups and salads
- cook a whole chicken, peel meat off the bones and make chicken tortillas. Clean bones and dry them on paper towels. Surprise children and bury them in the sandbox for a "dinosaur" dig.
- expose children to a variety of tools: peelers, scrapers, nutcrackers, blenders, toasters, food processors, grinders, strainers, foley food mills, graters, and more.

## Dramatic Play

Children want to try on the world of others as a way of mastering meaning. Setting up an area of the room that encourages a variety of role-taking possibilities requires planning and careful attention to storage, display, and clean up. Rotating props for the following will invite interesting play:

- doctor, dentist, or veterinarian office— include waiting room, magazines, nurse's station, secretary, receptionist
- firehouse: hats, slickers, boots, old hose
- barber/hair dresser/beautician (*Dandelion*) supermarket (*Mexicale Soup*) toy shop (*Corduroy*)
- office: phones, pads, old computer, pencils, pens, adding machine
- home replications (*Three Bears*, *Three Pigs*)
- shoe store (*Cinderella*)
- restaurants
- police station: badges, same props as office
- post office (*Jolly Postman*, *A Letter for Amy*)
- car, airplane, bus (*Wheels on the Bus*)
- spaceship (*Moon Cake*)
- open-ended props: scarves, jewels and wood scraps

## Gross Motor

Young children are creatures of action. No matter how small your space, provide some way for children to move their bodies in a variety of unstructured events. Have some of the following available:

- slides
- swings
- sawhorses
- tree stumps
- planks
- ramps
- scooter boards
- wheel toys
- parachutes
- tunnels (create or buy)
- balls (large and small)
- barrels
- hoops
- large wooden blocks
- large boxes
- roller skates
- bikes/trikes
- scarves & music
- bridges
- things to crawl over, around, through
- ropes (<u>only</u> with adult involvement) a rope tied to the top of a slide makes a wonderful climbing experience for the children. They walk <u>up</u> the slide hand over hand with the rope and go <u>down</u> the stairs

103

## III. A Summary and Collective Thoughts on Journey Planning

**Included in this section:**

- Observation: a critical aspect of meaningful planning
- Reflection: "R" words for the Journey
- Transition: an option for a week between Journeys
- Progression: quick review of planning steps
- Selection: examples of various planning sheets
- Suggestions: ideas to share for story extensions
- Inspiration: a bibliography of those who influenced the development of the Journey over the years

### Observation

A critical aspect of meaningful planning

Through our observations and reflections we are invited to learn more about how best to expand the children's ideas and interests. Each time we observe a child's experience with the Journey, it brings up new questions or provides new insights into the uniqueness of the child. These observations reveal how children navigate and connect with what has been provided in the environment. Our observations guide our planning and inspire a vital, flowing curriculum.

### Reflection

Using "R" words to remind us how important it is to pause frequently and:

**R**eflect – where have we been with a story and where are we going?

**R**eview _what interests are being revealed by the children?

**R**efine ➢

**R**ethink ➢ How are we developing the plans, experiences materials, and the environment to support children's learning?

<u>R</u>efocus    ➤

<u>R</u>econceptualize  ➤

<u>R</u>ework    ➤

<u>R</u>epresent and Re-present ➤

<u>R</u>eenact    ➤

<u>R</u>ehearse (practice)  ➤ Through exploration of stories over time and in different modalities, the child selects, models and demon-strates the most comfortable means of

<u>R</u>etell    ➤ internalizing and mastering elements of a story.

<u>R</u>elive    ➤

<u>R</u>espond – as active listeners

<u>R</u>evisit – experience the children have shared through the creation of tangible items are also helpful for families and visitor to see and better understand the progression of a Journey including:

- Photo albums of classroom journeys
- Wall displays
- Videotapes of children's experiences with the story
- Project exhibits
- Documentation panels

<u>R</u>elish - the meaning of living with stories together and weaving a common thread of shared experiences and understanding of self, each other, and the world of storybooks.

## Transitions

An option for a week between Journeys

Children have a way of letting us know when their interest in a story begins to wane. It helps at this point to pause for a moment and ask ourselves: will a change in the environment or materials spark a new direction with the Journey or is it really time to venture on a transition week? Some teachers prefer to move right into another story at this point while others choose to have an open transitional week without a Journey. It is a week set aside to explore a variety of storybooks, poetry, projects, and other experiences that are not tethered to a particular story. It is also a chance to wrap up any extended projects and prepare children for the following week's experience.

One preschool staff believes a transitional week is an opportunity for the staff to read a variety of stories and poetry that has always been available around the room, but usually read to a small group or individuals. It gives the staff an opportunity to think carefully about the experiences for the next Journey. Staff members also feel that this week provides some time for rituals to end the last Journey. The walls are stripped of all the former story-related projects and certain props are packed away. The room gets a good "house cleaning." A photo album documenting the children's Journey and the storybook they just finished remain in the room for the children's reflection and revisits.

The transition week is spent reading many different books at group time and in small groups. This provides an excellent opportunity for teachers to see what stories appeal and whether they might be ones to pursue for a future Journey. The emphasis can also be on areas of the room or materials that haven't been used very much. It might be a time to add new materials for woodworking, feature work with real clay, weave, have parents come in to read their favorite storybooks in small groups, bring out board games that have been hanging out in the storage closet, and the like.

When a staff prefers to go right on to a new Storybook Journey, they usually have a way of giving closure to the past story while introducing the new one. The teachers set aside the final Friday at group time for the closure of a long Journey and the introduction to the next story the children will explore. The book just finished, the miniature world, and the puppets or other popular props are moved to a shelf that is set up for revisiting past stories. All story props are put into separate see-through boxes and labeled by story. The new storybook is introduced and read to the group. It is placed on a low table by the door to await their arrival on Monday morning. The new story is introduced to the families in the Friday newsletter.

## Progression

### A quick review of the planning steps

- ➢ It is essential to plan for at least one hour every week!
- ➢ Plan for one week at a time.
- ➢ Assess what took place during that week.
- ➢ Plan for extensions, follow-up, and new experiences.
- ➢ Write out evolving plans with the team and share with families.
- ➢ Make provisions for individual interests as well as for the group.
- ➢ Adapt to meet all children's abilities.
- ➢ Use a variety of visuals:

  - ➢ for children to revisit their experiences

  - ➢ for parents to understand the learning that is involved in a Journey

  - ➢ for visitors to learn about the children's in-depth engagement with a story over time

### Suggestions

There are three points to be mentioned that don't quite fit into the other categories. They are intended to be helpful hints for story extension and revisits.

Children as story planners: As preschool children reach the age of four and five, many of them are capable of planning with an adult mentor. This can be a fun experience for all involved. The process of getting it started can vary according to how you want to introduce the idea. One teacher approached the subject at group time one day. She said she was wondering if anyone would like to help plan a Journey for the class. Two children not only wanted to do it, they had the story they wanted to do! They had chosen Thunder Cake by Patricia Polacco. Their interests were in the storm and making cakes.

The next day, the teacher met with the two children and they read and discussed the story together. They chose the storm, cakes, and added grandmother to the concepts they wanted to explore. The teacher helped them organize their ideas into a list of possible experiences. She took their ideas to the rest of the staff. They discussed them during their usual planning meeting and worked them into a simple plan for the following week. The teacher shared the finished schedule with the two children on Monday morning and together they made final adjustments.

This is an interesting experience, especially if you are in an all-day child-care setting where you have more time in the course of a day to pursue children's ideas. It has also been successful in half-day settings, though they are usually more modest in scope.

Introducing multiple versions of a story: So many stories today have spin-offs from the original version. (For example, there are over twelve variations of The Three Little Pigs!) When introducing new versions to young children, make sure the children are well grounded and understand the original version before going into the variations! The children will gain much more from the plot's "twist" if they have a clear understanding of the original story.

Sometimes it is helpful to encourage children to make up a different ending to give them a sense of manipulating a known plot. A group of three-year-olds were reenacting The Three Pigs outside one day when a sympathetic little girl called to the wolf (who had been "blown" out of the chimney) to come back. She wanted to put Vaseline on his sore bottom.

Book covers as extensions: Some classrooms post the paper cover (or a copy of the cover) on a wall outside their classroom when the Journey is completed. That wall then records all of the books they have taken on an adventure. This often sparks some wonderful chatter about their favorite story, the characters, or experiences they had during a particular Journey. These conversations have been with families, peers, and even visitors. It's an effective way for the children to remember what stories they've traveled with and to see what aspects of each story they recall.

## Inspiration

### "An Eclectic Gathering"

The Journey has been inspired and influenced by many different philosophies, authors, children, university students, talented teachers, colleagues, speech-language pathologists, occupational therapists, and committed families. The following bibliography is a selection of books I cherish. You would notice them the minute you saw my bookshelves. They have tattered covers, bent over pages, paper clips, or stickies marking essential passages, and yellow highlighter dancing across oh so many wonderful thoughts. Look up any of them you haven't read and be likewise inspired!

### An Eclectic Gathering of Suggested Reading

Ayers, J. (1982). *Sensory Integration and the Child.* Los Angeles, CA: Western Psychological Services.

Berk, L. and Winsler, A. (1995). *Scaffolding Children's Learning: Vygotsky and Early Childhood Education.* Washington, DC: National Association for the Education of Young Children.

Bodrova, E. and Leong, D. (1996). *Tools of the Mind: The Vygotskian Approach to Early Childhood Education.* Columbus, OH: Merrill.

Bronfenbrenner, U. (Ed.) (2005). *Making Human Beings Human.* Thousand Oaks, CA: Sage Publications.

Burns, M.S., Griffin, P., and Snow, C. (1999). *Starting Out Right.* Washington, DC: National Academy Press.

Carson, R. (1965). *A Sense of Wonder.* New York, NY: Harper and Row Publishers.

Cohen, D. and Stern, V. (1978). *Observing and Recording the Behavior of Young Children.* New York, NY: Teachers College Press.

Copple, C. and Bredekamp, S. (Eds.) (2009). *Developmentally Appropriate Practice in Early Childhood Programs Serving Children from Birth through Age 8.* Rev. Ed. Washington, DC: National Association for the Education of Young Children.

Culkin, M. (Ed.) (2000). *Managing Quality in Young Children's Programs.* New York, NY: Teachers College Press.

Curtis, D. and Carter, M. (2000). *The Art of Awareness: How Observation Can Transform Your Teaching.* St. Paul, MN: Redleaf Press.

Denham, S. (1998). *Emotional Development in Young Children.* New York, NY: The Guilford Press.

Derman-Sparks, L. (1989). *Anti-bias Curriculum: Tools for Empowering Young Children.* Washington, DC: National Association for the Education of Young Children.

Duckworth, E. (1992). *The Having of Wonderful Ideas.* New York, NY: Teachers College Press.

Edwards, C., Gandini, L., Forman, G. (1998). *The Hundred Languages of Children: The Reggio Emilia Approach.* London: Ablex Publishing Corporation.

Epstein, A. S. (2007). *The Intentional Teacher: Choosing the Best Strategies for Young Children's Learning.* Washington, DC: National Association for the Education of Young Children.

Epstein, A. S. (2009). *Me, You, Us: Social-Emotional Learning in Preschool.* Ypsilanti, MI: High Scope Press, and Washington, DC: National Association for the Education of Young Children.

Forman, G. and Kuschner, D. (1977). *The Child's Construction of Knowledge: Piaget for Teaching Children.* Monterey, CA, Brooks & Cole

Fox, M. (2001). *Reading Magic.* New York, NY: Harcourt, Inc.

Gerber, M. (Ed.) (1979). *The RIE Manual: For Parents and Professionals.* Los Angeles, CA: Resources for Infant Educators.

Hatton, S.D. (2005). *Teaching by Heart.* New York, NY: Teachers College Press.

Hawkins, F.P. (1974). The Logic of Action. New York, NY: Pantheon Books.

Healy, J. (1987). *Your Child's Growing Mind.* New York, NY: Doubleday.

Himley, M. and Carini, P. (2000). *From Another Angle: Children's Strengths and School Standards.* New York, NY: Teachers College Press.

Hohmann, M. and Weikart, D. (1995). *Educating Young Children.* Ypsilanti, MI: High Scope Press.

Isbell, R. and Exelby, B. (2001). *Early Learning Environments that Work.* Beltsville, MD: Gryphon House, Inc.

Jones, E. R., G. (1992). *The Play's the Thing.* New York, NY: Teachers College Press.

Kessler, R. (2000). *The Soul of Education: Helping Students find Connection, Compassion, and Character at School.* Alexandria, VA: Association for Curriculum Development.

Louv, R. (2008). *Last Child in the Woods.* Chapel Hill, NC: Algonquin Books of Chapel Hill.

Martin, W. (1999). *The Parents' Tao Te Ching Ancient Advice for Modern Parents.* New York, NY: Marlowe & Company.

Maxwell, K.D., Ritchie, S., and Bredekamp, S. (2009). *Issues in Pre-K – 3rd Education: Using Developmental Science to Transform Children's Early School Experiences* (#4). Chapel Hill, NC: University of North Carolina, Frank Porter Graham Child Development Institute, First School (available online at www.allianceforchildren.org).

Miller, E. and Almon, J. (2009). *Crisis in the Kindergarten: Why children need to play in school.* College Park, MD: Alliance for Children. www.allianceforchildren.org in PDF format for downloading or P.O. Box 444, College Park, MD 20741.

Owocki, G. (1999). *Literacy Through Play.* Portsmouth, NH: Heinemann.

Paley, V. G. (1990). *The Boy Who Would be a Helicopter: The uses of storytelling in the classroom.* Cambridge, MA: Harvard University Press.

Paley, V. G. (1997). *The Girl with the Brown Crayon: How children use stories to shape their lives.* Cambridge, MA: Harvard University Press.

Paley, Vivien, G. (2004). *A Child's Work: The Importance of Fantasy Play.* Chicago, IL: The University of Chicago Press.

Pink, D. H. (2006). *A Whole New Mind: Why Right-Brainers Will Rule the Future.* New York, NY: Riverhead Books.

Reynolds, G. and Jones, E. (1997). *Learning From Children's Play.* New York, NY: Teachers College Press.

Schickendanz, J. (1999). *Much More than The ABCs.* Washington, DC: National Association for the Education of Young Children.

Shore, R. (1997). *Rethinking the Brain: New Insights into Early Development.* NY: Family and Work Institute.

Walker, L. (1995). *Blockbuilding for Children.* Woodstock, New York, NY: The Overlook Press.

Warren, R.( 1979). *Caring: Supporting Children's Growth.* Washington, DC: National Association for the Education of Young Children.

Wilson, D. M. (May/June 2009). *Developmentally Appropriate Practice in the Age of Testing.* Cambridge, MA: Harvard Education Letter, p. 2.

Zigler, E., Singer, D.; Bishop, J. (2004). *Children's Play: The Roots of Reading.* Washington, DC: Zero to Three Press.

# IV. In-depth Examples of One Storybook Journey over Time

<u>Corduroy</u> by Don Freeman

Included in this Section

- Brief write-up of story for parent newsletter
- Journey "Emerging Idea" Gathering: ideas accumulated during brainstorming session and in the course of the Journey
- Planning sheets from the first two weeks of the Journey
- Individual Planning Sheet to enhance communication among therapists, family, and classroom teacher
- Highlights on other extensions from final weeks of the Journey with Corduroy
- Photos of <u>Corduroy</u> experience

<u>Corduroy</u> – Don Freeman

1968, Scholastic Book Services, New York

<u>Corduroy</u> is an endearing story about a toy bear that lives in a department store. He is discovered by Lisa, a little girl who wants to take him home. Her mother explains that she has already spent too much money and that the bear looks used. He is missing a button on his overalls.

Undaunted, Lisa returns the next day with her piggy bank in hand. She buys Corduroy and takes him home to the special bed she has made for him right beside her own!

<u>Journey Idea Gathering and Corduroy Planning Sheets</u>

The following page is a small-size representation of what you can set up on a spare wall in your classroom. The purpose of this sheet is to document the ideas you gathered in the beginning brainstorming and add new ideas that you have gleaned from your observations of the children's play. This can either be on a large sheet of mural or easel paper, a chalkboard, or whatever works best for you.

This note-taking suggestion will move the planning process along for the duration of the Journey, as you will accumulate so many new ideas from your observations of the children's engagement, interests, and conversations. Crossing off what you've used each week and circling what is left to try, if relevant, helps simplify the process.

Two planning sheets on <u>Corduroy</u> show the progression from week I to week II. Our Journey with <u>Corduroy</u> actually went on for four weeks. Included are a few highlights and thoughts from those final two weeks.

One school posted this Idea Gathering on a wall outside the classroom with a colored pencil and encouraged families and visitors to add their ideas. It is a great way to involve families in the process. A copy of the story was also set up close to the chart for a reference.

Journey "Emerging Idea" Gathering
Story:_____

Targeted Concepts & Vocabulary

Featured Experiences

Group Story Experiences

Concepts:

Science

Dramatic Play

Music/Movement

Art Exploration

Cooking/Snacks          Family Connections          Understanding Diversity

## Journey "Emerging Idea" Gathering
### Story: Corduroy

### Featured Experiences
- Make own Corduroys
- Make Corduroy's bed
- Walk to Salvation Army with donated toys

### Sensory
- Various materials used for bedding
- Feeling the bear skins on loan
- Recording of bear sounds
- Small plastic bears in water table with snow or cup caves
- Use flashlights to find toys in the dark
- Pick up mini bears with bare feet

### Motor
- Climbing stairs, ladders
- **Using pulleys with various weights**
- **Balance with stepping over rungs of ladder on floor**
- Jumping on mini tramp (like Corduroy on mattress)
- Sewing buttons on burlap and on Corduroy's overalls

### Targeted Concepts & Vocabulary
- real bears
- toys
- toy store
- emotions
- money
- escalator
- night
- watchman
- flight of stairs
- apartment

### Science
- Bears
  - Habitats
  - Food
  - Coverings
  - Behavior
- Visit zoo if possible (?)
- Show tape or DVD of various bears

### Story Concepts
- bears (real/pretend)
- **toys**
- **toy store**
- shoppers
- overalls
- buttons
- **emotions**
- evening
- **escalator**
- mountain
- sales person
- delayed gratification
- friendship
- curious
- furniture
- mattress
- yanked
- toppled
- **night watchman**
- dashing
- hiding
- beds
- chest of drawers
- enormous
- **flight of stairs**
- **apartment**
- **money**
- buying
- savings

### Group Story Experiences
- **Read & discuss story**
- **List of toys to gather**
- **Flannel board**
- Mini world
- Read to their bears brought from home
- Read to Corduroy they will make
- Act out story (videotape it)
- Act out using their own Corduroys
- Move like toys in toy shop
- DVD of polar bears
- Call Dan about showing bear skins

### Dramatic Play
- **Set up Lisa's bedroom**
- Have shoe boxes and cut up cloth so they can use them for bed and blankets for own Corduroys they'll make
- Collect scarves, wigs, purses, wallets, play money, sunglasses, hats
- Small bears in block area

### Art Exploration
- Cut paper on easel in shape of Corduroy
- Use cookie bear cutters with playdoh
- Make brown playdoh (white for polar bears)
- **Toy catalogs for collage**
- Collect boxes, mailing envelopes, cloth scraps, etc. for making Corduroy's bed

### Cooking/Snacks
- Collect bear cookie cutters or molds
- Cut bread with bear cookie cutters – spread w/ peanut butter or bear shaped French toast
- Make bear claws (w/ peanut butter balls & almond claws
- **Bears like honey (use as a dip)**
- blueberries

### Family Connections
- **Copies of story on loan**
- 2 sewing machines with volunteers to help make Corduroys on machine
- **Material scraps**
- Make video/DVD of children acting out story to show families at potluck supper
- **Need for pictures of real bears**

### Understanding Diversity
- **Different kinds of bears**
- Variety of bear storybooks (Pooh, Paddington, etc.)
- Money
- Buttons (size, shape, colors, # of holes)
- People in story (watchman, salesperson, mother, daughter)
- Differences and similarities of the toys
- **Bear habitats**
- **Real/pretend bears**

### Music/Movement
- Find bear songs
- Move, dance, etc., like bears
- **Move like rag dolls, cars/ trucks, rabbits, etc.**
- How you'd move if sad, happy, curious, mad, tired

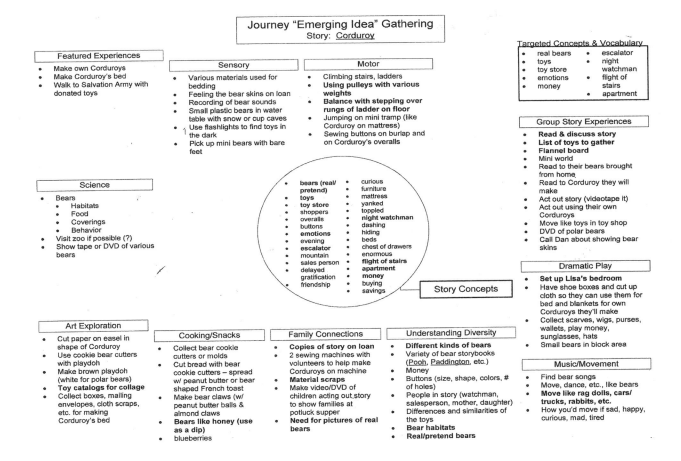

## STORYBOOK JOURNEY PLANNING SHEET©
### Sue McCord

Story:    Corduroy — Don Freeman
Dates:                                    Week I

### SCIENCE
Start a photo wall of real bears (polar, black, grizzly); add koala, panda, etc. next week.
Set up special box of real bear books from classroom books and public library

### MATH
Set out various play money (paper & coins) for children to explore.
Add cash register and money sorting box in anticipation of moving all of this to toy shop set up.

### ART EXPLORATION
Add brown, black & white paint to easel. Try variety of sticks as well as brushes.
Lay out toy catalogs to start class collage on their favorite toys (in prep for toy store set up)

### COOKING/SNACKS
M-grapes, orange slices, water
T-toast, peanut butter (tongue depressors for spreading), strawberries, apple juice
W-gummy bears, apple slices, milk
Th-banana circles, honey dip, blueberry juice
F-veggies, yogurt dip, water

### SENSORY
· Put out various materials that they can feel & sew (felt, burlap, fur, corduroy, fuzzy...) & buttons
· Search for recording of real bear sounds

### MOTOR (INDOOR/OUTDOOR)
· Set up pulleys to move things up & down like escalator
· Lay ladder down on classroom floor for stepping over rungs as they enter the room

**CONCEPTS**          Week One

real bears
pretend bears
toy store
money
*escalator
*night watchman
*flight of stairs
apartment
emotions (of Lisa & Corduroy)

*vocabulary to use/explain

STORY: Corduroy

### FAMILY CONNECTIONS
Send copy of story home to families.
Include in newsletter, we need:
-toy catalogs, buttons
-pix of real bears
-old toys children can part with for toy shop collection

### UNDERSTANDING DIVERSITY
Differences & similarities between real & pretend bears
Different kinds of bears – what do they eat, habitats, body features, etc.
Different places that humans live in – apartments, condos, trailers, houses, etc.
Emotions felt by Lisa & Corduroy

### GROUP STORY EXPERIENCE
· Read Corduroy.
· Look through book & talk about escalator, watchman, flight of stairs
· Discuss & list toys we want to gather for the classroom toy shop
· Flannel board telling of Corduroy

### DRAMATIC PLAY/ ENVIRONMENTAL SET-UP
Begin to gather what we need for toy shop w/ the children – shelves, check-out, $, toys, bags, etc.
Store them in toy chest until we're set up to start ( Remember purses & wallets for money !)

### SMALL GROUP EXPERIENCE
· Read Corduroy in small groups & "discuss" (maybe this could be an open choice option all week )
· Tap senior citizens, parents, volunteers to read w/ small groups

### MUSIC/MOVEMENT
· Teddy Bear, Teddy Bear
· The Bear Went over the Mountain
· Move like bears to drum beat
· Pretend to be different toys: rag doll, bear, car, jack-in-the-box

## STORYBOOK JOURNEY PLANNING SHEET©

Sue McCord

Story: Corduroy – Don Freeman

Dates:

Week II

### SCIENCE
· Add koala & panda bear to photo wall (discuss @ morning group time – then hang them)
· Show bear skins that Dan lent us of grizzly & polar bear

### MATH
· Sort & categorize buttons by size, # of holes, colors, etc.
· Explain money exchange for toy items in Toy Shop & "shop" with children to see if it's working

### ART EXPLORATION
Cut paper on one easel in shape of Corduroy
Playdoh w/ bear cutters
Put out white, brown & black paints to use w/ other colors

### COOKING/SNACKS
M-chicken noodle soup , water
T-thaw blueberries, mix w/ banana circles (eat w/ toothpicks), apple juice
W-carrot sticks, cheese squares, grape juice
Th-bear claws, water or apple juice
F-French toast bears, applesauce, milk

### SENSORY
· Look & feel the skins on loan
· Put blue food coloring in water table & add rocks, small pine boughs & miniature bears

### MOTOR (INDOOR/OUTDOOR)
Mini tramp for "jumping on the mattress"
Hide small bears in shaving cream – use tongs to "catch" them
Sewing Corduroy & stuffing him

### TARGETED CONCEPTS
· overalls
· hiding
· friendship
· buying toys
· saving
· mattress
· toppled
· play $

Extend from last week :
· Money
· Toys
· store

Corduroy

### FAMILY CONNECTIONS
· Need for 2 parents w/ sewing machines to help children make bears
· Plan for potluck dinner w/ families next week
· Send copy of new words we're exploring from story . Encourage their casual use at home

### UNDERSTANDING DIVERSITY
· Variety of toys in toy shop
· Different coins (penny , nickel , dime , quarter) for exploration and comparison
· Coins from different countries (put out magnifier glasses so children can explore designs on coins)

### GROUP STORY EXPERIENCE
· Tell story w/ mini world
· Act out story w/ simple props
· Video tape for children to see this week w/ group
· Tell story w/ their own Corduroy

### DRAMATIC PLAY/ ENVIRONMENTAL SET-UP
Continue w/ toy shop. Change toys that are for sale
Create Lisa's bedroom for dramatic replay extension.

### SMALL GROUP EXPERIENCE
Set up sewing machines w/2 volunteer parents for children to sew up their Corduroys & stuff them. (Store them on shelf between each step)

### MUSIC/MOVEMENT
· Move as if sad, happy , mad, tired (emotions of Lisa & Corduroy)
· Listen to recording of "When you go out in the Woods Today..."
· Sing songs from last week

## The Individual Planning Sheet

The Individual Planning Sheet was created to encourage communication among all persons working with children who have particular needs. Its use is intended for families, teachers, speech-language pathologists, occupational therapists, and other professional staff members. For example, occupational therapists and speech-language therapists can offer excellent suggestions in terms of physical challenges in the classroom and at home or unique ways to extend and encourage language and speech during children's play with the story.

CHILD'S NAME _____     DATE _____

**CURRICULUM AREAS**

-Motor                -Literature
-Sensory              -Dramatic Plan
-Music / Movement     -Projects
-Science              -Games
-Math
-Art
-Blocks
-Manips
-Food /snacks
-Literacy
-Outside

THE STORYBOOK JOURNEY
INDIVIDUAL PLANNING SHEET

STORY : _____
_____

**SPEECH /LANGUAGE FOCUS :**

**OCCUPATIONAL THERAPY FOCUS :**

**ROOM SET -UP**

**MATERIALS**

**SUGGESTIONS FOR HOME**

**SUGGESTIONS FOR CLASSROOM**

| GOALS | NOTES ON THIS SESSION | THOUGHTS FOR NEXT SESSION |
|-------|----------------------|---------------------------|
|       |                      |                           |

Storybook Journey © Sue McCord

Signed: _____     Date : _____

## The Storybook Journey

CHILD'S NAME _____ Ben _____ DATE: 2/08/06

| CURRICULUM AREAS | |
|---|---|
| -Motor | -Literature |
| -Sensory | -Dramatic Plan |
| -Music/Movement | -Projects |
| -Science | -Games |
| -Math | |
| -Art | |
| -Blocks | |
| -Manips | |
| -Food/snacks | |
| -Literacy | |
| -Outside | |

### THE STORYBOOK JOURNEY
### INDIVIDUAL PLANNING SHEET

STORY: _____ Corduroy _____

**SPEECH/LANGUAGE FOCUS:**

**OCCUPATIONAL THERAPY FOCUS:**

- Balance!

**ROOM SET-UP**

I have a mini tramp you can set up in classroom next week!

**SUGGESTIONS FOR HOME**

- If possible, find escalator for Ben to try (?)
- Go up and down stairs whenever possible!

**SUGGESTIONS FOR CLASSROOM**

- Keep ladder on floor for another week. Great balance for all the kids!

**MATERIALS**

| GOALS | NOTES ON THIS SESSION | THOUGHTS FOR NEXT SESSION |
|---|---|---|
| • Continue to work on balance<br>• Alternating feet on stairs | • Read Corduroy together and went up and down stairs throughout the building<br>• Ben's gaining strength and confidence! | Bring in balance beam -- use broadest side of beam. |

Storybook Journey © Sue McCord

Signed: _____ Barbara B. (O.T.) _____ Date: _____ 2/8/06 _____

Copy to: Family __X__
Teacher __X__

### Highlights of the Final Two Weeks of Corduroy

When it came time to sew up Corduroy on the sewing machine, a mother left the side door of the machine open so the children could see the inner workings. One boy was absolutely fascinated and spent most of the morning watching the mechanics at work. He wanted to sew even after making Corduroy and had the great idea of making a sleeping bag for his bear. From his idea, we suggested collecting things that could become beds for Corduroy if anyone else wanted to make him a bed. The project mushroomed into beds made out of all kinds of boxes, envelopes, and stapled paper. Blankets, pillows, and sleeping bags were made from scrap materials.

We discovered that beds are particularly interesting to young children, as they all have or share one. The teachers, children, and families started collecting pictures of every kind of bed or "sleeping place" we could find. They included a crib, bunk bed, cradle, basket, futon, water bed, hide-a-bed, Murphy bed, air mattress, sleeping bag, couch, hammock, twin/queen/king size, etc. It then moved on to doll beds, dog beds, cat beds, and other places animals sleep. Some families had photos of beds in places around the world! All of the bed pictures were glued onto file cards and covered in clear contact paper so the children could play with them: sorting, discussing, sharing ideas, relating similarities and differences.

A kindergarten teacher with her students undertook an extensive exploration of beds on a Journey with Corduroy. The children's discussion of Lisa and Corduroy's beds evolved into a long discussion of their own beds. The children drew detailed pictures of their bedrooms at home. The teachers and their families collected shoeboxes so the children could all have one to represent their bedroom space. Some made replicas of their rooms while others made their "dream bedrooms." Many different trash-to-treasure materials were gathered so that the children could represent things that were meaningful to them. (One child even had a wastebasket he made out of a blue detergent bottle top. (He was definitely a man of detail!)

It became quite an intriguing Journey project. Their original drawings of their rooms and each "bedroom in a box" were displayed in the hallway. It was a focal point of lively conversation among the children and families as they arrived for school and as they left after school. A small photo album was made of the total Journey adventure that families could check out overnight. This album was especially meaningful to families whose children rode the bus or who came to school in a carpool.

Photos of the Journey with Corduroy

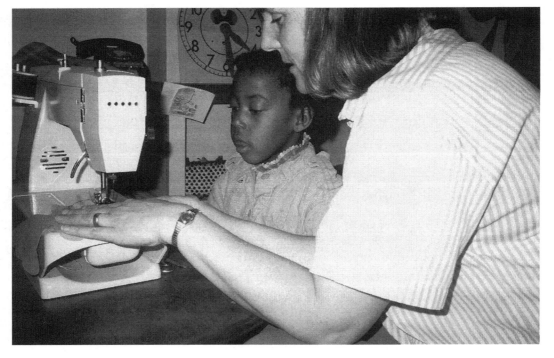

Sewing up Corduroy

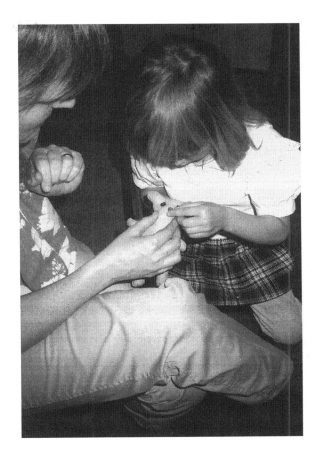

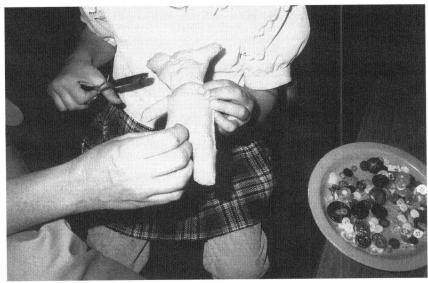

Hand sewing the features on Corduroy

Picking up bears with feet at clean-up time

Corduroy is the actor for story time.

Making bear claw cookies for snack

# REFERENCES AND RELATED READING:

Bodrova, Elena and Leong, Deborah (1996). *Tools of the Mind: The Vygotskian Approach to Early Childhood Education*. Englewood Cliffs, NJ: Prentice Hall.

Copple, C. and Bredekamp, S. (Eds.) (2009). *Developmentally Appropriate Practice in Early Childhood Programs Serving Children from Birth through Age 8*. Rev. Ed. Washington, DC: National Association for the Education of Young Children.

Derman-Sparks (1989). *Anti-bias Curriculum: Tools for Empowering Young Children*. Washington, DC: National Association for the Education of Young Children.

Epstein, Ann S. (2007). *The Intentional Teacher: Choosing the Best Strategies for Young Children's Learning*. Washington, DC: National Association for the Education of Young Children.

Epstein, A. S. (2009). *Me, You, Us: Social-Emotional Learning in Preschool*. Ypsilanti, MI: HighScope Press.

Hohmann, M. and Weikart, D. P. (1995). *Educating Young Children*. Ypsilanti, MI: HighScope Press.

Maxwell, K.L., Ritchie, S., Bredekamp, S. (2009*). Issues in Pre-K – 3rd Education: Using Developmental Science to Transform Children's Early School Experiences* (#4). Chapel Hill: University of North Carolina, Frank Porter Graham Child Development Institute, First School (available online at www.allianceforchidlren.org).

Miller, E. and Almon, J. (2009). *Crisis in the Kindergarten: Why Children need to Play in School*. College Park, MD: Alliance for Children. www.allianceforchildren.org in PDF format for downloading or P.O. Box 444, College Park, MD 20741.

Reynolds, G. and Jones, E. (1997). *Master Players: Learning from Children at Play*. New York, NY: Teachers College Press.

Wilson, David McKay (May/June 2009). Developmentally Appropriate Practice in the Age of Testing: Cambridge, MA: *Harvard Education Letter*, p. 2.

# *Chapter Four*

## Creating the Environment:
### Moving from Observation to Invitation

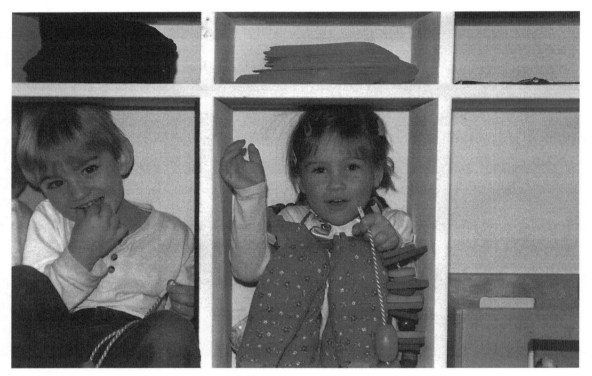

Spaces that become their places.

# Creating the Environment:

## MOVING FROM OBSERVATION TO INVITATION

"Young children strive to understand the world in which they live. They try to understand the visual images and concrete objects in their environment. Through the unique and concrete experiences that children have as they interact with their environment, they learn how the world works. The environment in which this learning takes place can enrich and expand the quality of children's experiences. Therefore, children, teachers, and parents must work together and use their resources in the most effective way." –Isbell and Exelby (2001)

### Part One
Spaces That Become Their Places

Creating an environment for young children is a way of cultivating what we value for children and the learning we want to foster in our settings. Sound environments reflect the development of physical spaces for learning through play. They also depend upon the emotional and social climate in which children and adults learn and live together. These components are inseparable and vital if we believe that children learn best when they are emotionally comfortable, actively engaged with their surroundings, and beginning to feel socially connected. It is important that this space invites and allows children to function safely and with the freedom and choice to

**Investigate**

**Discover**

**Experience**

**Transform**

**Risk**

**Experiment**

**Succeed**

**Fail without fear**

and become as intensely involved with what is meaningful and engaging to them as time and schedules allow.

The organization of this space for young children functions best when it makes sense to all who live there. If it is carefully developed, the environment can actually be viewed as a special prop for independent and shared learning. It can support and strengthen the activities that take place there. It can be arranged and adapted for children with varying abilities. Architecturally and as an accommodation for learning, the environment can offer pathways to all who live there for a novel way to understand and take on their world.

### Spaces from a Child's-eye View

Let's begin by entering our environment through a child's eyes – not only how it looks to the child, but also how it might feel. It helps to start by getting down on our knees, since that is the approximate viewpoint of a young child, and will give us quite a different perspective. By placing ourselves at the child's eye level, we quickly become aware that the children who navigate this space are really nose-to-nose with the backs of chairs, table legs, clutter on shelves, the bottoms of pictures, and adult knees. If we return now to our usual stance as adults, we scan over most of this and our eyes tend to focus on the surrounding walls and tabletops. Quite a different view, isn't it? We must constantly remember the setup needs to make sense to the children. How will they see it, experience it, and use it?

L.M. Morrow (2008) has stated that it is important to recognize that the physical environment has a substantial effect on children's learning and development. In the busy pace of our lives with young children it is sometimes hard to stop long enough to observe and reflect on what is really happening in our space. Take a moment. Look at the subtle or not-so-subtle messages the environment might be conveying to the children and their families as they enter this setting each day. Creating an atmosphere that matches our philosophy of child development means attending not only to the physical elements and configuration of space, but also to the psychological tone of warmth and caring that we wish to express. Thelma Harms (1979) has said that the way people treat children is as real a part of the environment as the materials, shelves, or space provided for block building. The adults' tone of voice, walk, facial expression, and stance all have an impact.

Children are exposed to a world of sensory overload everywhere they go today, and many children have trouble coping with this bombardment. For children to function and learn at their own level of comfort, we adults in their lives must consciously observe and monitor the use of the space, the atmosphere, and the tone in the room, along with the feelings of the children and adults themselves.

The monitoring might include a diagnostic scanning of everything that could contribute to an optimal environment of rich learning and emotional and physical comfort. We would call this scanning using our common "senses": what do we see, hear, smell, and feel in the environment and what effect might these sensory experiences be having on those who spend their day there? The physical and psychological atmosphere in an environment is basically affected by all that is happening in that space: human relationships, size of the room, number of children and adults, safety and appropriateness of the equipment, ventilation, heat, lighting, noise level, colors, surfaces, what and how things are hanging on the walls, organization, cleanliness, accessibility of materials, defined areas, pathways, and the variety of spatial levels. Each of these variables can enhance or detract from the overall atmosphere. Regulating temperatures and ventilation is imperative to a healthy body and, for almost all children; the need for private spaces and soft pillows is imperative for a healthy soul. Children react to their environment with every part of their being, and they deserve to have us pay careful attention to providing the most appropriate surroundings for their continuous growth. Humans and the Storybook Journey thrive in such an environment.

**Defining Spaces Inside**

Children's own needs and interests are supported or devalued by what a given setting provides. How spaces are arranged communicates expectations about how they are to be used. Adult modeling can help set expectations of how an area might be experienced. For example: reading or telling stories together in the quiet spaces or stretching out on the floor to observe the baby mice or fish; setting up the water table and paints in the "wet" area (which is preferably close to a source of running water); cooking and using Play-Doh or clay in areas that are easiest to clean up; and being noisy and active in the larger spaces that allow for freedom of movement.

Victor Lowenfeld had a wonderful way of saying how important provision for noise is in an environment for young children: "Noise is necessary, movement is necessary, and to be healthy they must be allowed to be exactly what they are – shapeless explosions of an over-plus of energy." Noise is a necessary part of young children's lives and a very important element to consider in developing spaces for young children. The wise thing to remember is to set up the noisy sections in the more active parts of the room (blocks, woodworking, and gross motor equipment and activities). Equally important is the creation of quiet spaces. Enclosed areas for individual or small-group story replays with flannel or magnetic boards, puppets, miniature worlds, listening tapes, books, and the like are very satisfying. They are also conducive to a concentrated pursuit of storytelling or imaginative daydreaming. Comfortable places to curl up, stretch out, or sink into befit such a quiet reflective space. One classroom I visited used only household lamps and natural light throughout the room. The effect was a cozy, soft, homelike setting. It was especially enticing in the book nook. Many children need to pull out from the pace, noise, and activity of an enthusiastic crowd. They need idle time for private thoughts and wondering. Pillows around a fish tank or ant village can often encourage or legitimize their efforts to calm themselves or just retreat for a while.

Many teachers and directors have found the following Environmental Scan Sheet an organized, quick, and useful way to look at their environment with their staff. They observe and list what they see on one side of the sheet first, and then go to the other side to record ideas for changes or extensions.

Some preschool settings have had teachers go into each other's rooms and review the environment with the Scan Sheet. The teachers then exchange ideas and support each other in the changes they'd like to make. (Other teachers have had a parent or the director come in to observe and fill out the sheet.) An explanation of the Environmental Scan Sheet and a blank form are included if you think this might be helpful to you.

# Environmental Scan Sheet:

An organized and useful way for staff to analyze the setup, use,
and care of the environment.

Setting up the environment as an invitation to come play with the story

## Environmental Scan Sheet

| A brief explanation of the Scan Sheet Categories: |
|---|
| **Noisy/Quiet:** |
| It's important to keep these areas as separate as possible. Loud sounds can be overwhelming for some children and they need an escape. Sound bounces off of hard surfaces, while soft acoustical materials will absorb sound (carpeting, rugs, curtains, acoustical tiles or panels). |
| **Light/Dark:** |
| Balance the direct, indirect, and natural lighting in your classroom spaces. For a cozy effect use incandescent area lamps, soft color on the walls, and warm white florescent tubes for ceiling fixtures. (The Soft White Long Life GE 60 watt bulbs give good light without glare!) |
| **Wet/Dry Area:** |
| Messy areas for cooking, paint, playdoh, clay, water tables, eating and the like are best situated close to a source of water and an easy surface to clean. Dry areas such as carpeting, rugs, wood and the like work well for floor play and group time. |
| **High/Low Levels:** |
| Create various levels with platforms, mattresses, claw-footed bathtub, lofts, large wooden blocks, over-turned bookcase, climbing equipment, various sizes of furniture... |
| **Open/Enclosed/ Space Definition:** |
| A variety of equipment can form enclosed or defined spaces: book cases set at right angles, fabric/curtain enclosures, rugs, couches, large boxes, small trunks or benches, tents, lattices, cubbies... |
| **High Mobility/Low Mobility:** |
| What is the traffic pattern in the classroom? How are the spaces defined for the quiet areas and separated from the very active, noisy areas? Observe the children's movement between their chosen activities – is the environment set up so that there is the least amount of disturbance between the high and low activity areas? |
| **Hard/Soft Textures:** |
| Sensory variations such as wall textures and colors, rugs, carpeting, linoleum, wood, pillows, curtains, cushions, natural materials, plants, bean bag chairs, suspended fabrics for enclosures and to lower ceilings, wall hangings, tents... |
| **Flexible/Fixed:** |
| Some classroom fixtures may be unmovable: i.e., sinks, lofts, counters, and the like. The more flexible the equipment, the more you and the children can rearrange the room for variety and utilitarian purposes. |
| **Stark/Cluttered:** |
| There is nothing more unnerving to most people than clutter. It can turn a potentially beautiful space into a totally disorganized mess! It can also be extremely distracting and disorienting for young children and most adults. The opposite of this is a stark environment that doesn't inspire children to become engaged. Observe the children's behavior and choose one area at a time to revamp. |
| **Together/Private Spaces:** |
| What spaces in the room would you define as places for groups to be together and what spaces can be private getaways? How are the spaces defined and are they adequate for the numbers, size, and activity level of the children in the setting? |

### Other Aspects of Your Classroom Environment to Explore:

| Authentic Cultural Representation in Materials and Environment |
|---|
| Racial, ethnic, modern life styles, home language, family situations, and varying abilities represented through various materials, i.e., books, music, artwork, dress-up, foods, puzzles, dolls, action figures, food containers, and the like. Visit and talk with families to gain a true understanding of what they would like to have represented. |
| **Aesthetics of Entire Room** |
| Children deserve a beautiful environment with color, warmth and different things to feel, see, and hear. Nature provides "seasonal gifts" all year. Pumpkins, gourds, flowers, seeds, rocks, shells, pods, birds, eggs, etc. We can also carefully display the children's artwork and photos in aesthetic ways. There are also beautiful fabrics, weavings, music, and so much more to grace our rooms. |
| **Use of Walls and Ceiling** |
| Enter your room and look at the walls and ceilings. What do you notice about the message they convey? The aesthetics? The colors? Is the children's artwork artistically displayed? What are the visual images and textures? Perhaps the most important things to try to avoid are cluttered walls and falling apart displays that have been hanging around for too long. To have the children's work caringly displayed values the uniqueness of each child's work and respects in a very real sense what is taking place in the classroom. |
| **Storage in Classroom (reachable recycled "trash to treasure")** |
| It is so important to have collections of usable materials on hand for children to use for their explorations and projects. How are the materials organized? Are they readily accessible to the children and are they rotated and replenished often? Does the storage of all materials make sense to the children? |
| **Storage Outside Classroom** |
| Perhaps the greatest treat for all teachers would be a HUGE storeroom! Since that is not usually possible, a small storeroom with shelving, hooks, plastic (see through) storage boxes, and an organizing principle that speaks to everyone using the room is imperative. Finding a parent who loves to organize and wants to help is what every storeroom needs! |
| **Living Things (plants, animals)** |
| Plants not only add warmth and beauty to a room, but they also provide a valuable experience for taking care of something living. Where do you put them? How do you keep them healthy? Animals are fascinating to young children and can provide meaningful experiences for them. They require care and supervision, and offer endless opportunities for learning through observation of their behaviors, attention to their needs, and a close encounter with their life cycles. They can also be very comforting to children who need to calm down or may be struggling with various issues. |
| **Children's Personal Storage** |
| Children need a place to put their personal things... a bin with their name, a cubby with their photo, a shoebox with their stickers or whatever you can manage in your classroom. It's important that all the children understand and respect that everyone has a place that belongs only to them. |
| **Family Space (hall, bulletin board, spare room...)** |
| If we want families to be a vital part of the classroom team, we need to be able to keep them informed about the class in action, the activities in the community, the experiences we want them to be a part of, the support systems that are available for them, as well as any concerns they want to address. How do we share information and make families truly feel welcome in our school? How do we keep "their space" alive and stocked with relevant and current information? |

## Environmental Scan Sheet

| Observe what exists now and take note: | Possible ideas for change and/or extensions |
|---|---|
| Noisy/Quiet: | |
| Light/Dark Areas: | |
| Wet/Dry Areas: | |
| High/Low Levels: | |
| Open/Enclosed/Space Definition: | |
| High Mobility/Low Mobility: | |
| Hard/Soft Textures: | |
| Flexible/Fixed Equipment/Furniture: | |
| Stark/Cluttered Areas: | |
| Together/Private Spaces: | |

## Other Aspects of Your Classroom Environment to Explore:

| | |
|---|---|
| Authentic Cultural Representation in Materials and Environment | |
| Aesthetics of Entire Room | |
| Use of Walls and Ceiling | |
| Storage in Classroom (reachable recycled "trash to treasure") | |
| Storage Outside Classroom | |
| Living Things (plants, animals) | |
| Children's Personal Storage | |
| Family Space (hall, bulletin board, spare room…) | |

**Children's Input in Defining Spaces**

Large blocks set up by "the boys" for their spontaneous band

One teacher of four- and five-year-olds in a child-care center became quite concerned about the use of space and materials in his classroom. He tried a dramatic remedy. He removed everything from the room and covered it with sheets out in the hall. When the children arrived the next day, the teacher greeted them in a totally empty room. You can imagine the children's surprise. After the initial shock and questions, the teacher asked the children to think about what they wanted to have back in the room. Books topped the list for the first order! (We were naturally thrilled to hear about that.) Blocks, a few chairs, and tables were brought back into the room as the children began to think about what they needed to create their environment. What was critical is that the children played a pivotal role in decision making about their space. They had to think about and discuss each new suggestion, and their requests were respected and implemented. There was focused attention on equipment, materials, spatial arrangement, and what was important for all who "lived" in this room. A renewed sense of ownership in the classroom, a commitment to a certain order, and a great opportunity to throw out junk or store unused materials were the gifts that resulted from this activity.

Not everyone would want to stage such an event or take such a risk, but this task has some elements that you might want to ponder. Children tell us, by their behavior in or avoidance of a certain area in the room, which spaces could benefit from analysis by the team and/or discussion with the children. When spaces are crowded, misused, or inspire children to begin to use each other as equipment, we need to look carefully at the children's needs, the arrangement of the physical space, and the equipment. Start with one area in your room that is a problem for whatever reason. Look to your parents, team, director, or supervisor as a resource. Perhaps one of them could observe the area and note what is going on or not going on in that space. Be certain to have the children discuss this with you also. Then you can begin to understand what changes you need to make. We have found that many times just switching the placement of centers—trading the dramatic play area with the book nook, for example—opens up a whole new interest. Of course, in the move you clean up, reorganize, add a few novel touches, and thereby renew interest. It's like having a new coat of paint in your kitchen!

One year, when we were doing the story of Molly Moves Out, a few of the children thought it would be fun to "act it out" and move all the household paraphernalia from the dramatic play area. They lined up the wooden trucks and trailers and worked so hard to lift the play stove, refrigerator, sink, and cupboard up onto the "moving vans." The morning was a flurry of endless movement and, I might add, chaos. For the engaged group of children, it was truly a case of relishing the process with no idea of any end product or logical plan of furniture arrangement. They had such fun balancing the equipment and problem solving how to keep it on the trailers while they were moving, then how to get it off when they stopped. The adults, however, had to finally call a meeting of all "van drivers" to help them develop a plan, as the equipment was being delivered to all different parts of the room and was distressing the would-be homemakers. It was fascinating to watch the children gain a sense of the environmental layout. They had gotten so caught up in the excitement of the moving process that they lost track of where they were moving or why. During our discussion, we realized that they used the space well that we had created and knew what happened where. However, when they started changing it, they really didn't have a sense of putting all the household stuff back as a unified package. Though it was not their intention, the results of the move gave the movers a much better sense of how and why each activity center was set up. The learning that took place for all of us was well worth the temporary upheaval.

**Spaces That Become Their Places**

All of us like to know we have a place to put things that are special to us—a place we trust to be used only by us and to hold things safely until we go home again. Children need those places too, and they learn quickly to respect not only theirs, but others: the bin with their name, the cubby with their photo, the shoe box with their sticker. As adults, we know that ownership in the room goes far beyond cubbies and bins. The exciting part is when children demonstrate that they know the room is really theirs. Boxes become hideouts and bedspreads are transformed into tent sides, creating marvelous private or special spaces. In England, many of the schools have walls that are alive with aesthetic displays of the children's artwork and a section of the room that is set up like a museum for looking at the clay or construction work of the children who live there. This setup values the uniqueness of each child's work and gives a very real sense of what is taking place in the classroom. Reggio Emelia programs devote a significant space or an entire room called an atelier for children to create and transform an array of materials into works of art. These projects are usually aesthetically displayed in the classroom or in a prominent space in the school.

The environment also provides a valuable backdrop for the interactive life of the players on this journey. Flexible space is necessary to accommodate the frequently shifting ideas at this young age. Planning for areas where children can re-create spaces for their own story reenactments is important. Furniture that can function in many ways is also an asset as it provides support for children's developing ideas.

In most programs across the country, funding limitations have necessitated and encouraged the most creative use of all available materials and equipment. An emptied shelf placed on the floor, so that the back is now the top becomes a delightful mountain peak from which to survey the world or a platform at just the right level for setting up small props for storytelling.

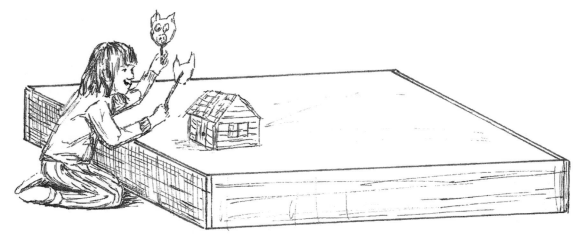

Tables can hold up sheets for impromptu houses for the three pigs or can be turned on their sides for puppet stages.

A doorjamb or two legs of an inverted table are ideal places to stretch a sheet and use that space as a puppet stage. Details can be painted or crayoned on the sheet for houses, barns, bridges, or whatever.

If adults encourage and model imaginative use of space and materials for spontaneous play, children will be more likely to do the same. One teacher in a child-care center threw a yellow bedspread over a dome climber, crawled underneath "the haystack," and started saying: "Little Boy Blue come blow your horn..." She had many little boy (and girl) blues who followed her in and later made haystacks of their own under chairs, tables, and then outside under the bushes. Children enjoy adapting spaces to their imaginative whims when the atmosphere promotes trust and empowers them to feel comfortable in their doing so.

## Spaces with Novelty and Variations

How often we hear child-care providers and educators lament that they wish they could build a loft or a pit into their environments. It's that longing for a change of levels, for some novel twist to keep the room interesting and challenging. Finances, shared spaces, rooflines, and other issues often make such variations in a room difficult. There are other ways to create novelty in a setting, however, by rearranging existing areas or developing new props for enhancing the play schema of the group. For example, we've all set up a play doctor's office with stethoscope, bandages, and the like. Did we also include a waiting room with magazines, chairs, and toys and a receptionist area with phone, appointment book, pens, and forms on a clipboard?

Doctor's office reception area

With most parents in the work force, a well-equipped office setup is likewise a real drawing card. The tools for writing, drawing, using calculators, adding machines, and the like invite endless opportunities for meaningful, manipulative literacy explorations. S.B Neumanand K. Roskos (1997), believe that children learning about literacy is integrally tied to practical action, resulting from the need to control, manipulate, and function in their environment. To set up an office, try taking two big refrigerator boxes and open them up halfway to form a secluded space. Cinder blocks and a wooden plank can be set up inside to form the desk. Two spackling cans can be spray-painted to become "office" chairs. Pencils, rulers, tape, scissors, markers, paper, stickies, telephone, an old adding machine, typewriter, or computer and other goods can be rotated for the duration of this project. In this way, the children can try the "tools of the trade."

Play "office space" made from cardboard refrigerator box,
2 cylinder blocks and a board "chairs" are empty plaster baskets

Changing the actual location of this little nook often rekindles the interest of some children or catches the attention of others who are just becoming engaged with the writing process. Books are distributed throughout the room for copying words if the children are interested, and various extensions – envelopes, sticky notes, stickers/stamps, small pads, and mailboxes – add a sense of purpose to beginning attempts at writing. So many stories refer to writing letters. A nook set up in this fashion encourages a very natural extension of their listening experience and offers other literacy adventures.

Observe how children rearrange their play spaces. They often create unique change that can be extended by providing related materials for them to use.

**Spaces Prepared for Story Replay**

When a carefully prepared environment is set up for a dramatic replay of a particular story, it supports the children's role-play. This area can be a revamping of the regular dramatic play area or a small space anywhere else in the classroom. Though the area may have specific props to invite the acting out of a particular story…children may create totally different scenarios with the provided props. This is where our observations are so important! We can "listen in" for clues as to where the children are taking the play and what we might provide for extensions.

What follows is an example of a setup that was created in a semicircle at one end of the classroom for <u>Goodnight Moon</u>.

Our giant bear was a substitute for rabbit, but not for long! He was replaced by a child wearing long ears and a cottontail that she found in a box of dramatic play props. In this case the teacher sat close by and read the story as the little girl rabbit rocked in the chair and got up at various points to hang the mittens, check the bowl of mush, and then, quietly whisper "hush." The setting was very simple at first. Other props were added as the children requested them. The teacher stepped out once the children seemed comfortable developing their own forms of replay.

A few weeks later, the dramatic play area was transformed into the house of the three bears. A long piece of cardboard from a washing machine box covered the back of the play refrigerator and sink. A space of one and a half feet was left between the sink and fridge and a door was cut out of that piece. We made a hinge with duct tape. It brought great activity to the area. The door was the big attraction. For the toddlers it was constant openings and closings, for the three- and four-year-olds it was very purposeful, and for the slightly older children it became a kind of saloon door to burst through on their way into the latest drama taking place in that space. Through extended play with a story, children begin to explore the environment and materials in new ways and have the freedom to rearrange them to fit their interests.

Retelling the story with houses the children have built

**Spaces That Include All Children**

Environments can set the stage in various ways for active learning, social contact, dreaming, thinking, and individual retreating from the tempo, volume, and complexity of the larger setting. In developing environments for the inclusion of a diverse population, where storybooks and extended literacy experiences are an important focus we may want to consider a number of issues, including the developmental range, varying abilities, and physical challenges of the children. We also want to focus on fostering positive interactions among peers.

In every group, the way each child perceives and relates to the world will vary. In an inclusive setting, these variations tend to be more dramatic, and the creation of an environment to meet diverse needs – especially if space is limited – takes careful thought and planning. A focus on the representation of story environments and the re-presenting of stories creates many options for children to explore in play. Our observations of their behavior should tell us whether the environment and the materials are engaging their interests, have personal meaning for them, and are accessible if they have physical challenges. Morrow (2008) has stated that with the support of appropriate materials and a well-designed classroom environment, instruction will flourish in preschool classrooms. Make the environment as important as the curriculum, and the two support each other.

The child who needs predictable, realistic arrangements to reenact a story might benefit from a small house set up in the dramatic play area, a clear path through the woods from home to Grandma's house, and a basket of goodies for Red Riding Hood to take to Grandmother. For other children, a pillow can serve as the bed, and they imagine the basket. While some children see everything in the room as a stimulus for a possible prop, others are more comfortable having the perceptual space carefully and realistically prearranged. One setting can accommodate both types of behavior, with the children free to move between their own setups and props and those the adults provide. The optimal goal is to nudge children toward a more symbolic representation of the story props – but only when they are ready to explore that next possibility.

Maintaining a balance between these two approaches is essential. Children who are developing and absorbing experiences in their own unique ways need to be able to go back and forth between the realistic environmental setups and those that are more abstract. They may do this by joining in, watching, or practicing in the security of the more private places they create at school. For some, the practice grounds are at home. It is helpful when families share what parts of a story their children are talking about or acting out in their home setting. Similarly, what teachers observe in school is helpful to evaluating the child's overall experiences and understanding of the story. Both parties can communicate with each other through exchanging brief notes, phone calls, and/or conferences.

**Spaces That Foster Interaction with Peers**

We all know that desks lined up in a row invite very different behavior from chairs arranged around small tables or pillows tucked in a corner. Encouraging children to be in touch with each other takes careful thought, not only in developing the environmental setups, but also in establishing the interpersonal atmosphere. Participation in reenacting a story encourages active interchange. Most stories have more than one character and thus entice various children to take on the various parts. A special enclosed area in the room for replay – puppet characters from a particular story or a miniature world setup, for example – creates a quiet, cozy atmosphere that can encourage the more timid children. Some children will be drawn by the appeal of the props and thus be in contact with other children. Some will be drawn to a particular child, small group, or the adult who has plopped himself or herself in the area. Paying close attention to the gathering and evolving use of the props, the presence of an observant/understanding adult, and the careful preparation of the space will invite children to come play out a story together. The size of the space is important too, as smaller spaces will dictate smaller numbers. The smaller the numbers, the more children will be encouraged to interact with each other. Watching and observing is an important stage of learning for many children, especially children with special challenges. Watching is also a preliminary phase of peer contact and interaction.

For days, Billy would choose to drive his toy truck and park it by the small enclosed area where children would retell stories, either with the flannel board or the miniature world props. He'd lean over the low shelf and watch without a word. When the storytelling was over, he'd drive off. We never saw him participate in the process of retelling a story at school. One night, while nodding off to sleep, his parents heard him say: "Who on bridge?" "No!" "Eat up..." Billy had taken in so much and was practicing in the safety of his own room. With time, perhaps he would try a reenactment with his peers. Watching and practicing alone was for Billy an essential prerequisite to peer play and part of his own unique style of mastery.

"Young children belong to more than one community, with their initial encounters generally being with their immediate and extended families and perhaps with nearby playmates. The early childhood program is usually their first community beyond those mediated by their parents. But while preschools want to be part of the community, joining it is a learning experience for them..." (Epstein, 2009).

**Space That Provides Access for Children with Physical Challenges**

Building accessibility is essential for including all children. It is amazing how ramps get built once an organization decides to make the commitment. Parents, community agencies, and volunteer groups seem to come out of the woodwork if someone makes this a priority. Once the wheelchairs and any needed special apparatus are in the room, it is important to study ways to arrange the space to accommodate the special equipment. More important, however, is finding creative ways to keep the equipment from separating the children from each other. If the group is on the floor and Joey is in a wheelchair, the levels further isolate Joey from the magic quality of being close to others at group time or at play. We can view this as a problem or as a beautiful challenge. A brainstorming session involving parents, teachers, support staff (occupational therapists, speech pathologists, psychologists), and children can be an exciting way to tackle it. Unique ways to position children and ingenious plans for adapting equipment can materialize from just such a session. Yes, it takes time and work, but the results are well worth the investment of energy. In fact, all children deserve this kind of attention to their basic needs.

**Part Two**

<u>Creating the Environment</u>:

Exploring the Play–Development Link

Part Two will look at the core areas of development and their link to play. This will set the stage for Part Three.

**Part Three**

<u>Creating the Environment</u>:

Bridging Development and Play through Story Reenactment

Part Three will demonstrate through <u>The Three Billy Goats Gruff</u> how the story provides the bridge joining play, development, and the creation of the environment

**Part Two**

<u>Creating the Environment</u>:

Exploring the Play–Development Link

Creating an environment that enriches and supports a child's core areas of development through play is of prime importance. Play is what young children want to do! If we've endowed them with the courage to risk and have not squelched their sense of wonder, they'll find a way! They want to, they're curious, their pursuit is self-initiated, and it is an enjoyable thing to do. Play is also often more complex than we realize. This is especially evident when we observe how difficult it is for some children to join others in play. They may have physical or emotional challenges, or issues with processing information or getting the gist of what is going on in the fast-paced transitions of creative play. Some children just may have difficulty relating to others and are shyly reluctant to join a group or communicate their desire to play.

Let us take the word P – L – A – Y and assign a corresponding core area of development to each letter. From there we will go into a deeper exploration.

**P** (physical)     = Physical

**L** (cognitive)   = Learning, Language, Literacy

**A** (emotional) = Affective

**Y** (social)       = Yourself in Relationships with Others

# Physical Development

Children in the early years are active little beings and participants in life. Their play is a continuous exploration using their bodies and senses to hear, see, touch, feel, taste, and smell. Their bodies carry emotional messages and communicate their feelings in an unspoken language. They want to master challenges and control their developing muscles through repetitive, intense physical play and practice. Play becomes the vehicle to integrate all the senses and provides an opportunity to begin organizing that sensory input for later use. A child moving through space and planning how to get off, on, around, and through various pieces of equipment, maintaining balance, and feeling safe reveals the complexity and interrelated aspects of the senses. Play and story reenactments provide excellent settings for physical and sensory activities and a means for the observant adult to heed the warning signs of a child having trouble with this critical aspect of development.

The occupational therapist on our team has really caught the spirit of the Storybook Journey and brought much more depth to our understanding of physical development. She has transformed ropes into beanstalks and regular climbers into triple-decker bunk beds for the three bears. Introducing the three layers of beds not only inspired delightful reenactments of the story, but it also gave us a great opportunity to watch the children climb, motor plan, and cope with the world from new perspectives. One little girl got under the lower bunk just fine, but when it came time to get out she was totally disoriented and seemed to freeze. One never knows in such a case if the emotional gate is closing any problem-solving skills at a time like this or if she perhaps just didn't have the repertoire of movement to experiment with getting herself out of this space. It wasn't until she started to cry that we realized she really saw herself as permanently lodged in that position. We talked her through moving her body in different positions, head down, crouching, and so forth, and she finally freed herself. When we shared this vignette with her mother at the end of the day, she said that was a frequent occurrence at home. Lori would crawl under the coffee table in their living room, turnaround, sit on her bottom, peer out at the world, and then would panic, having no idea how to get out. This shared information was extremely valuable in our pursuit of ways to provide experiences for Lori both at school and at home that would enhance her ability to problem solve around her special issues.

## Language and Learning (Cognitive Development)

"To play requires great flexibility in thinking, an ability to shift context and to add new ideas. These skills, which will be useful across an entire life cycle, do not come without practice." Elizabeth Prescott

Play allows children an innate and unquenchable drive to understand the world and to gain freedom and competence in it. Children want to be engaged participants in their own learning. The span of time we are touching on is Piaget's preoperational period of approximately two to seven years of age. This is a pre-logical stage of thinking in which children are egocentric, perception-bound, and intuitive. Their learning is a random doing, undoing, and redoing of their world through play. The power of language is intense and the desire to communicate, vital.

Teachers observing the complex thinking that takes place when children are playing and problem solving can gain valuable information about the cognitive workings and language of each child. Play is indeed the having and sharing of wonderful ideas! It is the practice grounds for communication. While observing in a child-care center one day, my attention was drawn to the dramatic play corner, where a group of children were busily involved in a "domestic dispute.

| Laticha: | "Can I play in your house with you?" |
| The Group: | "No!" |
| Laticha: | "I could be the sister." |
| Javad: | "No, we gotta sister." |
| Laticha: | "I could be the dog." |
| The Group: | "We gotta dog." |

Laticha wandered away and slumped in a chair a few feet away. "The group" watched and then went on playing. Javad kept looking over at Laticha – he appeared to be struggling with group dynamics and compassion for his friend, Laticha. Finally, Javad yelled out: "You could be the next door neighbor." Laticha leaped out of her chair, yelled back "okay," and immediately started to build an extension to the structure the group had built. The first thing she moved into her house was a phone. Communication occurs to the extent that one's thoughts and feelings are understood by another. This brief vignette, encompassing so much, reveals the inclusive and integrative value of play. There was compassion, having and exchanging ideas, problem solving, risk taking, rejection, verbal communication, body language, and a resolution that satisfied everyone's needs for the moment. Playing out the various themes in the course of the journey process also provides a unique practice ground for the children to develop a better understanding of each other, and of the world around them. "The greater the child's repertoire of action and thoughts, the more materials he has for trying to put things together in his head" (Elkind, 1987).

## Affective (Emotional Development)

Emotional development and the critical role of self-esteem in children's struggles to grow as whole persons is perhaps the most vital aspect of development. Young children are moving through the first three stages of Erikson's eight stages of human growth (trust, autonomy, and initiative). They are gaining a sense of self and discovering whether their worth is confirmed or denied through human relationships and their surrounding environment.

The Alliance for Childhood, a nonprofit research and advocacy group, reports that the push for academics in many early childhood settings is crushing what many researchers in early childhood development see as the most vital indicator of future success – play in the early years of school (Orenstein, 2009).

A surge of developmental research on the emotional life of children reveals the intimate interplay between affective and cognitive aspects of a child's life. According to Dr. T. Berry Brazelton (1984), a Harvard University researcher and popular author on child development, "It's about time we started looking at emotions more carefully! Everything we know about a child shows that healthy emotional development is the key to other kinds of growth."

In <u>Crisis in the Kindergarten</u>, a report also released by the Alliance for Children, co-author Edward Miller says, "Play – especially the let's-pretend, dramatic sort – is how kids develop higher-level thinking, hone their language and social skills, and cultivate empathy" (Miller, 2009).

Stanley Greenspan and his wife, Nancy Thorndike Greenspan, have written an excellent book, <u>First Feelings</u>. One of the great contributions of this book is the clear development of the theory that intellectual and emotional development are inseparable. Many examples of this theory will be woven throughout this Journey.

Sociodramatic play can provide a very valuable role in emotional release and understanding. Take for example the following observation of Betsy as she uses play to express her thoughts and feelings. Play is a way to test reality but keeps it safely masked in fantasy.

> Betsy yelled: "I can too scream because I am the mother screaming for you to stop screaming!" How wonderful for this four-year-old to explain to "her doll child" (and vicariously to the teacher) that she was "safely" screaming at her child in play to try on that role of control, power, and mother figure in her sociodramatic enactment of something she has either personally experienced or observed. Play is powerful. Becoming the "Bad Guy" – the wolf, troll, doctor or, in this case, the yelling mother – is vital to emotional development. Through the magic and escape of replay, young children begin to learn to manage their feelings and affective responses. To feel in control in a rather scary world – even if only momentarily – is a catharsis. The child's role-playing can provide us with a small window into her perception of the world; however, we do not always readily understand what we see and hear in play. "One might characterize emotional development as the application of mental processes to the world of feelings, interpersonal relationships, and inanimate objects to which the child is attached." (Greenspan, 1985)

The story can play such a valuable role in this emotional catharsis. It can often provide the structure or safe framework within which the child can gain an awareness of or perhaps even begin to work through unsettling feelings.

Jessie's reaction to the reading and acting out of *Little Red Riding Hood* is equally powerful. Jessie's mother died during Jessie's infancy and she had always called the grandmother who raised her "Mommy." In our reenactment of the story, every time Little Red Riding Hood took the basket of goodies from "Mommy" to give to "Grandma," Jessie left the group and paced anxiously in another section of the room or looked outside through the glass door with her back to the group. Perhaps the awareness on Jessie's part that Mommy was separate from Grandma in this story was unsettling. Her withdrawal from the flurry of activity might have been a significant step in her attempt to cognitively assimilate this emotional information on a very personal level. Our observations also gave us information we could share with Jessie's grandparents and father about the struggle this little girl was experiencing. To help Jessie work through the process of understanding what had really happened in her young life, it was critical for her family and the staff to find a way to bridge the gap with her. In this case, something very special happened! Both Jessie's maternal and paternal grandparents brought out pictures of Jessie's mother, including a treasured picture of Jessie being held by her mother. Together we made a book about Jessie's entrance into life, the death of her mother, her family now, and her days at school. This homemade book was a real catharsis for all of us, but its greatest gift was helping the grandparents realize that Jessie needed this information to begin to work through some of her deepest feelings. Like so many of us, her grandparents were trying to protect Jessie from the very thing she needed to know most: the truth. Little Red Riding Hood played a significant role for all of us!

Jessie had "created an inner world around the story, extracted its essence and applied it to a different situation." (Pearce, 1992)

## Your Self in Relationships with Others (Social Development)

Emotional and social development are often discussed together because they are uniquely connected. In this chapter, we're looking at the areas separately, but the core areas for all development are deeply interwoven. Play provides unequaled opportunities for development, as it is the fertile soil in which the social aspects of development can grow. I like to call the child's very early attempts at this process *social bumping*. Take, for example, the children who topple off their cardboard block wall, pretending to be Humpty Dumpty. They are naturally landing in close proximity of each other and are thus in playful physical contact. For very young, developmentally challenged, or shy children, this may spark one of their first social interactions away from home at a very primitive level.

It reminds one of puppies wagging their tails and circling each other. Igor Gamow (1987) shares another example:

> One characteristic of penguins is that large groups of them mill around the edge of the water off some very icy platform and while they are milling they are also actively bumping into one another until finally one gets bumped into the water. The moment one of the penguins gets bumped in, all the rest stop milling and bumping and observe the penguin which is now "in the drink," and if that penguin is not eaten by a leopard seal they all jump in.

Although Igor makes a different point in his article, I'd like to use his penguin pushing and puppy tail wagging as examples that can likewise relate to children's social probing. Children use this shared bumping and circling behavior as a way to check out a possible friendly encounter. Depending on whether the encounter is enjoyable and accepted, they will either repeat the activity or move on and watch. This preverbal social bumping is a beginning point of social interaction and communication and progresses into the very complex process of human relations. Katz (1987) notes:

> Although definitions of social competence vary on some of the details, they generally include the capacity to initiate, develop, and maintain satisfying relationships with others, especially peers. Social competence does not require a child to be a social butterfly. It is not a source of concern if a child chooses to work or play alone, as long as he or she is capable of interacting productively and successfully with another when desired or when appropriate.

Dylan, whom we met in the introduction to this book, was a young boy who, for the first three months of school, was unable to become involved with others beyond fleeting eye contact. For weeks he physically and emotionally isolated himself from his peers and the adults in his center. His behavior was a red flag. He was not only unable to initiate interactions, but on a far deeper level, he showed no desire to be a part of anything taking place around him. He was a social isolate in every sense of the word. It was only through the talented support of the patient, watchful, understanding staff in combination with Dylan's growing trust in his world and self that he was able to reach out, first to the consistent adults in his life and finally to the children. Peter Pan became the vehicle for this transformation, providing Dylan with the means to experience the world through the safety of walking in someone else's shoes. The story of *Peter Pan* became the vicarious tester of the social process . . . the substance for acting out feelings through a storybook character . . . the vehicle for moving toward others. As Dylan began to gain a sense of himself and an awareness of and interest in his peers, he slowly accepted others into his story-related play. Though they "flew" with him as Peter Pan in a very associative stage of socialization in the beginning, they later invited him into their play as a cooperative member of other story reenactments. He grew into a child who could comfortably balance his quiet times alone with his newly developed social competence in maintaining satisfying reciprocal relationships in play.

The use of stories as the core of our program plays a very significant role in the social development and communicative competence of young children. Socially, the story provides children with a central focus and common knowledge of a scenario to play out with predictable characters and sequenced situations. The story line is a scaffold providing each child with a vehicle for becoming an active, playful participant at a variety of cognitive, linguistic, social, and emotional levels. Feedback from peers serves as a social reinforcement. In the context of the story, children can be encouraged to communicate. Since everyone in the group is familiar with the story, the more-verbal children can carry the essence of the plot. The less-verbal children can fill in or chant "trip trap, trip trap" as they master the words through joyful repetition, practice, and peer acceptance.

Three "Billy Goats" crossing the bridge

The children's sense of being a part of the interaction enhances their learning and helps them to identify more closely with their peers. When Papa Bear is one of the less-verbal children, he can go through the motions while being encouraged by a more-verbal Mama: "Come on, Papa, we're going upstairs." Papa hears the language, follows the other bears, and becomes part of the social context.

"There is something special about social pretend play for preschoolers. When they engage in mature sociodramatic play (pretend play that involves communication with other children), children's interactions last longer than they do in other situations, children show high levels of involvement, large numbers of children are drawn in, and children are more cooperative – all of which have important benefits for children's cognitive (social), and other types of development" (Creasey, Jarvis & Berk, 1998).

Through our keen observation of children's play and our meaningful partnerships with parents, we begin to see how each child is progressing from egocentrism to a sense of self in relationships with others. Cooperation, collaboration, negotiation, and the intense and passionate pursuit of friendships are an ongoing process.

Play is children's most useful tool for preparing themselves for the future and its tasks. Flexible and imaginative thinking, communication, transformations, combinations, fantasies, engaged learning, emotional stresses and delights, human relationships, compassion, movement, and creative pursuits all occur in play. Children advance into new stages of mastery through play, practice, and the pursuit of their own interests.

Looking to the book for clues as to what comes next in her
story replay of The Gingerbread Boy

**Part Three**

<u>Creating the Environment</u>:

Bridging development and play through story reenactment

A variety of experiences with a story gives children a sense of mastery without drill. These experiences create the capacity for a deeper knowledge base of the story and the children's satisfying personal engagement through hands-on participation. The creation of the environments and the making or gathering of the materials the children may need are a valuable part of the process. While on a Journey with a story, extensions are used to involve children in play with all aspects of the curriculum, environment (inside and outside), choice of materials, and peer relationships. Extensions nudge children to experience and experiment in all areas of their development: physical, cognitive, communicative, emotional, and social.

Using the paradigm of P – L – A – Y from part two, and the story of <u>The Three Billy Goats Gruff</u>, we'll explore engaging play, the use of both the indoor and outdoor environment, and how one story can involve all areas of development.

<u>Story review</u>: <u>The Three Billy Goats Gruff</u>

This story is a favorite among the classics. It's a tale about the adventures of three billy goats of progressive sizes who have only brown grass left to eat in their field. There is a lovely meadow available…but they have to cross a bridge…and a mean troll lives under the bridge! Each billy goat has to face the troll before triumphantly reaching the delicious meadow on the other side.

**<u>P – L – A – Y and the Three Billy Goats Gruff</u>:**

Exploring the use of the environment and story concepts and content to enhance the core areas of development through children's play

**P = physical play with the three "billies"**

Create a variety of bridges to cross so all children can be challenged and/or find a bridge they feel secure enough to try.

- ➢ a low table
- ➢ 2 saw horses or large wooden blocks with a wide board on top
- ➢ foam rubber packing blocks to use as stepping stones

> ➤ 2 parallel pieces of tape so a child in a wheelchair or on a scooter board can go "over" a bridge
> ➤ a partially filled water bed mattress where everyone falls and giggles
> ➤ climbing equipment used in different configurations
> ➤ mini tramp
> ➤ balance beam
> ➤ a real bridge is great fun if you have one nearby

Experiment with materials you have available and use one challenging bridge and one easy alternative so everyone can participate in the story replay if they choose. Use existing climbers and slides outside for impromptu bridges or hay bales with a plank across the top.

Having the children help set up the environment with the various bridges during the Journey will give them opportunities to lift, lug, drag, push, and haul the equipment. (This is an excellent time for teachers to observe each child's motor planning and muscle strength.)

**For small muscle involvement**

> ➤ at snack time have children pierce three "grape" billy goats with a toothpick after they cross a large pretzel stick bridge that rests on two squares of cheese. The troll is a fat piece of cut carrot.
> ➤ offer wood scraps, various-sized paper tubes, all sizes of jar lids, corks, and other materials for children to create their own miniature worlds for three billy replays.

**Outside**

In the book <u>Parabola</u>, Richard Lewis talks about children's "whyness" and "how comeness" of every ant, pebble, shadow, and stone…exploring the meaning, touching, experiencing, and building that special relationship between themselves and the things in the natural world. When you go outside with your children now, try to find a wonderful place that might have any or all of the following: stones, pebbles, rocks, pine needles, leaves, horse chestnuts, acorns, pinecones, twigs, puddles, brooks, bushes, bark and the other marvelous natural resources that the children can discover. Tell the <u>Three Billy Goats Gruff</u> using nature to supply your props, for example…three different-sized rocks for the goats and an ugly pinecone for the mean troll. Let's move away from store-bought materials and instill the simple pleasures of creating and imagining. These natural props are also readily available when children want to play out these stories at home.

## L = language and learning (cognitive development) with "The Three Billies"

### Sequencing

> ➢ observe children replaying the story in different modalities to see if they have mastered the sequence of events. Use:
>   - flannel boards
>   - puppets
>   - mini worlds
>   - dramatic play
>   - art work

### Substitution

> ➢ observe the children's use of abstract things to represent goats and troll such as:
>   - unit blocks
>   - scrap items from trash-to-treasure bins: corks, jar lids, buttons, paper tubes…
>   - nature collections: rocks, shells, bark…

### Creation

> ➢ encourage the children to make up their own versions of the story: instead of Billy Goats… what could it be? Where do they live? What or who are they afraid of?

### Vocabulary

> ➢ what do these words mean and what other words are there for: gruff, meadow, mean, sizes (i.e., big, bigger, biggest, small, medium, large, etc.), and troll?

**Concepts**

The Three Billy Goats' seriated sizes and "threeness":

➤ try seriating all kinds of materials: buttons, shoes, mittens, the children, blocks, cups, and natural resources...

➤ play with the concept of three for snack (three crackers or three raisins...), three of each item in water table, go up three steps and sit, then three more and kneel; only three colors of paint...

➤ put out other stories with three of the same characters: Three Bears, Three Pigs...

➤ also exploring concepts of fear (i.e., troll and other scary things)

➤ explore types of goats and their products

➤ do a study of bridges

**Open-ended questions to probe children's thinking**

➤ what could the troll have done if he really wanted to catch the billy goats?

➤ could the billy goats have gotten to the other side of the stream any other way? (e.g., by borrowing a boat? By sending the biggest goat over the bridge first to get rid of the troll?)

➤ why do you think the troll was so angry?

**Understanding other versions of the story**

Children need to understand the original version of a story before catching the twists and humor of a "knockoff." Play around with making up a silly version where you change a few things at a time. For example, have the story of the three trolls and a billy goat is under the bridge or the biggest billy calls his father or mother on a cell phone for advice. Published versions to try:

The Troll – Bridge Troll – Patricia R. Wolff

Three Cool Kids – Rebecca Emberley

The Three Silly Billies – Margie Palatini

**A = affective (emotional development)**

Bringing their attention to the emotions or potential emotions in a story is a positive way for children to begin to identify their own feelings. Now and then, ask the children…have you ever felt this way or have you ever had this feeling?

**Talk about**

> ➤   the angry feelings of the troll
> ➤   the fear or courage each billy goat may be experiencing (relate to fears the children might want to talk about)
> ➤   the fierce or protective feelings of the biggest billy goat gruff
> ➤   the relief each goat must have felt when he or she reached the meadow safely
> ➤   the panic the troll may have felt when he lost control of "his" bridge
> ➤   do you think the billy goats' mother and father worried about them?

**Look at illustrations for**

> ➤   the billy goats' expressions before and after crossing the bridge
> ➤   study the troll's face for clues to how he's feeling

**List and listen**

> ➤   have the children help you list how the goats and the troll may have felt in this story:

| | |
|---|---|
| *mad | *afraid |
| *sad | *mean |
| *angry | *cowardly |
| *fearful | *happy |
| *annoyed | *safe |
| *scared | *sorry (for troll) |

**Act out**

> ➤ talk about pretending to be each of the billy goats or the troll and act out how they may have felt, for example:
>   - the littlest goat – he was so frightened..how would you walk or look if you were that littlest goat?
>   - the troll – how would you jump up from under the bridge if you really wanted to look mean and angry?
>   This is a meaningful way for children to "practice" a variety of emotions in a context they can control. It is also important for children to learn to read the expressions of others. This is a skill that is an important part of social interactions and relationships.

**Y = yourself in relationship with others (social development)**

The ability to develop friendships is such a vital part of being human. Stories can provide the common thread to foster communication and meaningful interaction. Reenacting a known story can provide a marvelous practice ground for children to begin developing relationships with their peers.

**Address**

> ➤ at group time or at snack it might be interesting to pose the question of how the billy goats and the troll could become friends
> ➤ how could they have worked out the bridge crossing in a more friendly way?

**Role-play**

> ➤ working in small groups, try acting out the above questions with the children. Through the characters, they can experience some of their own struggles with negotiating relationships.
> ➤ using the materials for story replay, invite children to negotiate role assignments themselves. Try having four children with puppets, mini worlds, or a flannel board taking

on the four characters in the story at group time (with the teacher as mentor). Have the other children observe the process. This takes time and practice, but is so valuable in helping children join in social exchange. Having families replay the story together at home is a very reassuring way for children to gain confidence to try acting it out at school.

**Encourage**

➢ Try teamwork in setups and cleanups for all the story activities in the classroom. A great example of this was when we brought a real goat named Norman into our classroom the last day of our Journey with The Three Billy Goats Gruff. We had Norman out on the playground, but he kept coming up to the back door and butting it with vigor. We decided he really wanted to be inside, so we let him come in. This was a splendid adventure! He walked all around the room, seemed curious about everything, and loved nuzzling the children. The greatest excitement was that Norman did not use the bathroom...of course. The children were fascinated by his tiny, round "deposits." Everybody wanted to help clean them up. So...we had teams of two – one with broom and one with dustpan follow Norman. Luckily, he delivered enough during the morning so every team had a turn. We talked often about the great effort of the class on this task and their ability to cooperate as teams! Unfortunately, not all cleanups are as fascinating!

**Working together**

Other opportunities to have children involved in common experiences that bring them together might be:
➢ moving equipment and furniture around for story props
➢ setting up environments that encourage children to interact, for example:

- cozy nooks that will hold only three or four children
- a swing, seesaw, or other equipment that requires two children in order to function
- setting up one long piece of paper on a table with only two chairs and one box of magic markers

- hanging two pieces of paper on one easel
- providing a small table with a game board and only two chairs

The classroom can become a locus of learning, sharing, and building relationships around story replays! The story of <u>Three Billy Goats Gruff</u> and so many others have provided the classroom with gateways to friendship. You'll surely enjoy your own adventures if you're willing to observe the children for your directions.

**Spaces outside for story replay**

Extending beyond these indoor spaces – to explore meadows, ponds, rocks, and ditches to ride on escalators as a corduroy bear or to sit on walls all over town as Humpty Dumpty – is also part of the environment. The outside world offers children the feel, sights, and smells of the world at different times of day and in different weather and seasons. Children know how to explore every inch. Greenman (1988) wrote:

> The outdoors has weather and life, the vastness of the sky, the universe in the petals of a flower. But many programs, following the model of schools, have seen the very qualities that make the outdoors different as obstacles or annoying side effects. The openness is tightly constricted; weather provides a reason to stay in, and landscape and life are things to be eliminated. A playground, considered the primary, if not the only outdoor setting, performs the same function as a squirrel cage or a prison exercise yard—it is a place for emotional and physical release and a bit of free social interchange.

Greenman has gathered the most comprehensive information on what children want to do outside. He suggests many alternatives to the standard playground. His chapter on outdoor learning is an excellent resource and well worth exploring.

The natural materials and spaces of the outside world provide unique opportunities for storytelling. When my children were little, they would gather dried grass, twigs, and assorted bricks to complete bush and tree root enclosures representing the houses of the three pigs or the witch's house for Hansel and Gretel. They used leaves to build nests, acorn tops became fairy cups, and pebbles from the nearby brook were the gold coins for the giant to count. At the beach, the sand and the shells provided endless extensions to their imaginative play. At one point in their lives, they would dig huge sand pits to hunker down in, feeling warm and safe to spin their dreamy tales in these private enclosures.

Going to a wooded area or a place with high bushes or a few trees adds a new dimension to telling <u>Little Red Riding Hood</u> or <u>The Three Bears</u>. One class went outside to the playground after reading "The Three Bears," and the children spontaneously started to play out the story. The bowls were differently sized pails, the sand was the porridge, the sandbox ledge served as the table, and the children created anything else they needed out of whatever they could find. When it came to beds, Fred just took a stick and made three differently sized circles on the ground and told everyone which bear would sleep in which "bed." No one questioned that those circles were indeed the beds.

As teachers, we want the inside and outside environments for young children to offer an invitation to enter into a safe and welcoming place away from home...

A place where children know the environment is theirs and they can turn old
sheets into capes and jar lids into taps for their shoes...

A place that encourages and supports their physical pursuits...

A place to experience the joy of building friendships with their peers...

A place that embraces play as a child's journey with learning...

A place that respects the uniqueness of each child!

## REFERENCES AND RELATED READING:

Bergen, D. (1987). *Play as a Medium for Learning and Development: a Handbook of Theory and Practice*. Portsmouth, NH: Heineman.

Carion, R. (1956). *The Sense of Wonder*. New York, NY: Harper & Row.

Casey, T. (2007). *Environments for Outdoor Play: A Practical Guide to Making Space for Children*. Thousand Oaks, CA: Corwin Press.

Copple, C. and Bredekamp, S. (Eds.) (2009). *Developmentally Appropriate Practice in early Childhood Programs Serving Children from Birth through Age 8*. Rev. Ed. Washington, DC: National Association for the Education of Young Children.

Creasey, G., Jarvis, P. & Berk, L. (1998). Play and Social Competence In Saracho, O. and Spodek, B. (Eds.) *Multiple Perspectives on Play in Early Childhood Education*. (p 116-143) New York, NY: Suny Press.

Debruin-Parecki, A. (2008). Effective Early Literacy Practice. In L.M. Morrow (Ed.) *Creating a Literacy Rich Preschool Classroom Environment to Enhance Literacy Instruction*. (p. 2) (p. 12) Baltimore, MD: Paul H. Brookes ).

Dooling, D. M. (Ed.) (1979). *Parabola: Storytelling and Education* Volume IV, Number 4, November 1979. Brooklyn, NY: Parabola.

Edwards, C. P.; Gandine, L.; and Forman, G.E. (Eds.) (1993). *The Hundred Languages of Children: The Reggio Emilia Approach to Early Childhood Education*. Norwood, NJ: Ablex Publishing Corporation.

Epstein, A. S. (2009). *Me, You, Us: Social-Emotional Learning in Preschool. Ypsilanti, MI: HighScope Press*, p. 70.

Feldman, J. R. (1997). *Wonderful Rooms Where Children can Bloom!* Peterborough, NH: Crystal Springs Books.

Frost, J. L. (1992). Reflections on Research and Practice in Outdoor Play Environments. *Dimensions of Early Childhood*, 20(4), 10.

Gamow, I. (1987). The Scientist as a Story Teller. In M.A. Shea (Ed.). *On Teaching*. Boulder, CO: University of Colorado, p. 25.

Greenman, J. (1988). *Caring Spaces, Learning Places: Children's Environments that Work*. Washington, DC: Exchange Press.

Greenman, J. (1998). *Places for Childhoods: Making Quality Happen in The Real World*. Redmond, WA: Exchange Press, Inc.

Greenspan, S. and Greenspan, N. T. (1985). *First Feelings: Milestone in the Emotional Development of your Baby and Child*. New York, NY: Penguin Books, p. 85.

Harris, V. (1991). The Playground: An Outdoor Setting for Learning. In *Supporting Young Learners: Ideas for Preschool and Day care Providers*, Eds: N.A. Brickman and L.S. Taylor. Ypsilanti, MI: HighScope Press.

Isbell, R. and Exelby, B. (2001). *Early Learning Environments that Work*. Baltimore, MD: Gryphon House, Inc.

Jones, E. and Cooper, R. M. (2006). *Playing to Get Smart*. New York, NY: Teachers College Press.

Jones, E. and Reynolds, G. (1992). *The Play's the Thing: Teachers' Role in Children's Play*. New York, NY: Teachers College Press.

Katz, L. (1987). *Dispositions in Early Education: What Should Young Children be Doing?* Urbana-Champaign, IL: Bulletin 18.

Klugman, E. and Smilancky, S. (1990). *Children's Play and Learning: Perspectives and Policy Implications*. New York, NY: Teachers College Press.

Krilchensky, S.; Prescott, E. and Walling, L. (1977). *Planning Environments for Young Children's Physical Space* (2nd Ed.). Washington, DC: National Association for the Education of Young Children.

Louv, R. (2008). *Last Child in the Woods: Saving our Children from Nature-Deficit Disorder*. Chapel Hill, NC: Algonquin Books.

Neuman, S. B. and Roskos, K. (1997). Literacy Knowledge in Practice: Contexts of Participation for Young Writers and Readers. *Reading Research Quarterly*, 32 (1), p. 10.

Olds, A. R. (1979). Designing Developmentally Optimal Classrooms for Children with Special Needs. In Samuel J. Meisels (Ed.). *Special Education and Development: Perspectives on Young Children with Special Needs* (91-138). Baltimore, MD: University Park Press.

Orenstein, P. (2009). *Crisis in Kindergarten: Why Children Need to Play in School*. www.allianceforchildhood.org in PDF format.

Pearce, J. C. (1992). *Evolution's End: Claiming the Potential of our Intelligence*. New York, NY Pearce Harper Collins. p. 158.

Segal, M. and Adcock, D. (1981). *Just Pretending: Ways to Help Children Grow Through Imaginative Play*. Englewood Cliffs, NJ: Prentice Hall.

Vergeront, J. (1992). *Places and Spaces for Preschool and Primary* (Indoors). Washington, DC: National Association for the Education of Young Children.

# Chapter Five

## Props for the Journey:
## Explorations with Found Materials

Spontaneous props for the journey

# Props for the Journey:

## EXPLORATIONS WITH FOUND MATERIALS

"Using everyday materials clarifies the notion that concepts are not in the materials
but rather in the relationships the child makes between materials."
–Ann Hammerman

Materials can provide the tools for learning things that no one can teach. When open-ended materials such as water, sand, mud, clay, paper, blocks, and trash-to-treasure items are consistently available, children become engaged. They act upon them, organizing and changing them, exploring the possibilities and creating relationships among them. During this process, they begin to gain an understanding of the properties of the materials with which they're working, experience the effect their actions have on the materials, and enjoy a new sense of wonder about themselves and the world around them.

The atmosphere in the room must be one of valuing and encouraging the child's attempt to use what is available by testing, discovering, and integrating "junk" items into their ongoing play schema. Paper tubes can roll, unravel, and spin. They can form marble runways, car tunnels, silos, or binoculars. They can be lined up in sequence as the three bears or represent all the members of their family. "When materials are not limited by boundary or form, they remain forever tools which a person uses differently as he grows to perceive the world differently" (Cohen, 1972).

Children are spontaneous researchers spurred on by their natural curiosity and attempts to make sense of their immediate surroundings. One day while doing childlike "research," Matt discovered that by cutting three sides of a square space on a piece of paper he had created a "flipper." Held this way it became a garage door (see Figure 1). Held another way, it looked like a house door (see Figure 2). He went on to try it with cardboard, which worked better, and wood, which didn't work at all. Like Matt, other children want to push it, pull it, twist it, combine it, beat it, mix it, drag it, poke it, control it. They want to explore and manipulate real objects with their senses, their bodies, their minds, and their peers. They want to build on what they know, make decisions, and see results.

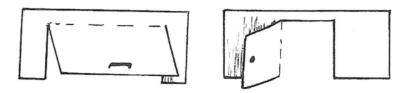

Fig. 1 A piece of paper becomes a garage. Fig. 2 held another way, a house door.

## I.  Honing Our Skills

To support a child's interests and investigations, adults face the continuous challenge to hone their skills of:

- Observing
- Experience-priming:
  - ➢ provision
  - ➢ organization
  - ➢ rotation
  - ➢ exploration
  - ➢ preparation and
- Tone setting
  - ➢ time
  - ➢ attitude and atmosphere
  - ➢ diversity
  - ➢ presentation
  - ➢ material gathering and storage
  - ➢ constructive responding

For each of these skills our goal is to encourage, enhance, and extend children's opportunities to use materials to support their emergent literacy development and comprehension. While early childhood programs use materials to integrate *all* development, this chapter will focus mainly on the use of materials as they relate to story reenactment.

**Observing**

Dorothy Cohen (1978) used to say that "children reveal themselves in special children's ways!" Observing them carefully gives us clues and information to see them as they are and as they see themselves. During our observations, it's important to be aware of what is significant to children. How often have "special" gifts wrapped in fancy paper been cast aside for what really has meaning: the *box* that contained the present! When we observe each child carefully as an individual and as part of a social context, we can begin to develop options and choices for individual children that will help them derive personal meaning from their experiences.

Brian was just such a child. After weeks of seeing him explore the preschool in his own way — touching things and pouring water for days, oblivious to the rest of the world — we set up a story replay with Brian in mind. We were doing the story of <u>Little Blue and Little Yellow</u> by Leo Lionni. We set up a Plexiglas easel by the glass door so that the light would come through and give Brian a large transparent surface where he could explore the marvels of paint. He was totally engaged in the process of mixing the colors on the easel and in the paint cups. The light shone through in an amazing way. Perhaps for the first time he really could bask in the joy of "seeing" vivid colors with the very limited sight he has had since birth. Perhaps this is just what David Elkind (1987) meant when he said, "Education of children must be in keeping with their unique modes of learning." Our observations reveal those unique modes and help us to choose materials that will enhance children's experiences and options.

Through our observations, we begin to learn when to nudge children gently from realistic materials to those that are more abstract. We can also see what challenges and what frustrates each child; who risks and who withdraws; who generates an abundance of ideas and who needs inspiration; who can approximate with confidence and who feels safer copying a peer or enticing an adult to make it for them. Our challenge is to move from observing the child to setting up an invitation to come play and create. We want to set up materials so that children can explore and use their imaginations to the fullest!

## Experience Priming

Careful attention to how we prepare or prime the environment both physically and psychologically is paramount to the journey. In our sincere attempt to teach, we can inadvertently rob children of their own discoveries. "We ignore what children have to learn and instead impose what we want to teach, thus putting young children at risk for no purpose" (Elkind, 1987). It is therefore extremely important to prepare the learning experiences that children can relate to and explore over time. An example of this might be what took place in one classroom that was journeying with Charlie Needs a Cloak by Tomie dePaola. This is a delightfully simple story that starts with Charlie needing a cloak. He goes through all the steps from shearing the sheep to weaving the cloth. (The illustrations really tell the story.) The teacher started the Journey with a weaver coming to the classroom to demonstrate all of the steps involved in preparing wool so that she can weave. She also brought two fellow weavers with smaller looms so the class could divide into small groups to experience weaving one at a time. This experience was a grand "priming" for the children to understand not only the materials, but also the process. So often we take a field trip or bring in a "demonstration" to end a story. We might want to vary that when appropriate and start with the field trip, demonstration, or visitor as a prime. The class went on to explore all kinds of weaving, dying with different herbs and veggies, and exploring many varieties of wool. The story carried a deeper meaning because they could attach the words of the story to their own experiences.

Inspiration from the master weaver

Creating our own loom from chicken wire

Admiring the results

The young children did a very free-flowing shared experience weaving old torn-up material into chicken wire that was enclosed in a circle. One child at a time could get "inside" and weave by herself. Others could join in from the outside feeding the material to the one in the inside.

We can also view priming as a preparation of the classroom for children's purposeful involvement in their pursuit of knowledge. Priming such an environment involves provision, organization, rotation, exploration, and a thoughtfully prepared setup of the materials.

- ***Provision***

  Open-ended, hands-on materials must be accessible to children at all times. Children think best with all of their senses and need to be able to see, touch, manipulate, and feel empowered to transform materials. Open-ended refers to materials that do not have a specific "correct" use and thus inspire the child's impact on them; sand, water, clay, paints, wire, and mud are examples. They are multipurpose materials that allow random experimentation and a means to extend children's imaginations.

- ***Organization***

  Organization of the materials must make sense to those using the space and should encourage independent choices and cleanup. The accessibility of such materials is paramount if children are to creatively pursue development of their own projects.

- ***Rotation***

  Rotation of materials from storage space to classroom is another way to kindle interest. If egg cartons, Popsicle sticks, bottle caps, yarn, string, and other materials have been out for a long time and space doesn't allow for additions – rotate! Put different things in your bins, baskets, or boxes. Just changing "stuff" can prime curiosity and creativity. (Many have found that plastic see-through shoeboxes with lids work well for storage and display. The commercial, divided cardboard shelves with nine spaces for holding shoeboxes are excellent for an orderly arrangement in both the classroom and the storage room. They organize and display the materials for easy viewing, accessibility, and rotation.

- ***Exploration***

  In-depth exploration of one material at group time is another way to prime the creative flow. For example, if a child has brought in a bag of spools to add to the class collection of materials, hold up one spool at group time to brainstorm its uses. Children will feed off each other's ideas for using it as a bubble blower, a bead for stringing, a ramp roller, a wheel for a small car, a base for a dollhouse table, and more. This group priming before adding the spools to the project area of the room generates interest and ideas for later use. Writing the children's suggestions as a list with quick illustrations to assist in "reading" what they have shared is a helpful literacy nudge in the recycled "trash-to-treasure" project area.

- ***Preparation***

   Preparation of thoughtful setups invites children to try, invent, discover, be challenged, and enjoy. It's a little like providing appetizers to unexpected guests. *It isn't as much an issue of what we have or how much we have as how we vary the invitation* to try some of the same old stuff. Even carrots can seem very appealing according to how we cut, display, and present them. This is akin to what Chittenden said that teachers should do to arouse curiosity: introduce the novel in the context of the familiar. We want to encourage that "Gee, I'd like to try this!" feeling. Putting crayons out in various ways to inspire their use is a fun example of this process. We've tried arranging them for individual use in upturned egg cartons and plastic adhesive bandage boxes, and lying flat on meat trays or in a small pumpkin shell for Halloween. Presentation of materials can also prime the social aspects of learning. Putting all of the crayons in one basket at the center of the table invites sharing, negotiation, and patience! It provides a marvelous opportunity to observe children's ability to navigate in the sometimes uncomfortable situation of having to wait for the color they want or deciding to grab the whole basket for themselves.

To stir up curiosity, we have also done things like put a story-related group of puppets in a closed box in the middle of the floor. Some just walk right around it, while others have to peek in the box to explore what is inside and begin to interact with the contents. Once we wore swim flippers on our feet to greet the children in the morning as a way of opening up discussion on the first week of the story, *Frog and Toad Together*. One classroom has a big stuffed bear that usually resides in the book nook. One day the staff put a yellow cowboy hat on his head and a scoop in his paw and moved him over to the water table that was filled with the kind of colored pebbles you would put in a fish tank. He was a drawing card for some very creative play. One teacher put a rope down the slide and pretended to be rescuing children from the "water." The children were Timothy Turtle, Captain Hook, or just themselves. The teacher and a group of children would stand at the top of the sliding platform and hold the rope, while the child on the other end would climb up the slide (the plank for Peter Pan and the lost boys), going hand-over-hand on the rope. It was a simple idea, but fun and great for building upper-body strength. Another teacher used colored scarves on the slide. The children would lay a scarf down on the slide and zip to the bottom on a slippery flash of color. This takes time and inspiration, but the results are well worth the effort. It can eliminate some of the ho hum of setup and adds an element of fun to rearranging a given space or re-presenting materials in a variety of unique ways.

## Tone Setting

It is important to create an atmosphere of acceptance in the context of challenges. There also needs to be time to experiment with many materials so that children see their options. *If* they feel supported and valued for their efforts, ideas, and unique ways of interpreting the world, they are far more willing to independently master the mechanics and problem-solving skills necessary for developing their story props with tape, scissors, paper, stapler, and brads. Frustration can build for some children as their mind's idea and the capabilities of their small hands don't always match. It is during such times that a patient, caring adult who can just slip in beside a child for a few minutes and "self-talk" the child through the problem is very helpful. As children work, teachers interact with them, prompting them to discuss their ideas with each other and with the teacher, to use a different strategy, to try out a new solution to a problem, to look for other materials, or to show them how to use a tool (Jones, 1993; Carter & Curtis, 1994).

The following examples will demonstrate how two observant, present teachers extended learning with different strategies and suggested solutions to each frustrating incident. In the first classroom, a four-year-old boy was so upset trying to hold his sock puppet with one hand while sewing the eyes on with his other hand, that he was about to throw the whole thing across the room. His teacher saw the struggle and told him: "I remember when I first made a sock puppet. I could never figure out how to put on the eyes with only one hand to work with…I think I remember now what helped me." The teacher went on to fill a recycled detergent bottle with sand and began talking her way through each step. She pulled a spare sock over the bottle (all the features for the puppet were already on the table) and fastened the button eyes on her sock with bread bag twist sealers using both hands. The child watched intently and then proceeded to experiment with a whole new set of options. The tone was one of here's an idea that might help – there is no right or wrong, just a different way to go about a task, and you can try this idea or invent your own way.

Another example reveals an astute teacher who was able to guide two children through a dilemma with a suggested strategy. Tom, Sojung, and their teacher were sitting at the Play-Doh table and Sojung had a pile of Play-Doh encircled with her arms, signifying this is <u>all</u> mine! Sojung was an engaging young child with Down syndrome from Korea who could speak neither Korean nor English, but clearly learned a variety of marvelous ways to communicate her message. Tom asked Sojung for some more Play-Doh because he had only a tiny piece. Sojung stared at him, crouched lower over the Play-Doh, and didn't budge. Tom then put his small piece of Play-Doh in his out-stretched hand saying: "Can you give me some of your Play-Doh? Sojung took it out of his hand and put it back in her pile. "Hey – she took my piece!" The teacher explained: "You know, Tom, I think when you put your hand out to someone with something in it, that means: "Here, this is for you." When you put an empty hand out it means: "May I please have some?"

Tom pondered that for a moment and put his empty hand palm up to Sojung. Sojung immediately pulled off a good-size chunk of Play-Doh and put it in Tom's hand. Tom was absolutely de-lighted and sang out: "It worked!" When Sojung saw his excitement, she responded by giving him one more little piece.

Materials certainly provide an excellent catalyst for all kinds of learning opportunities…not only for the children, but also for the intentional teacher.

- *Time*

    Time is also an important element of tone setting. Children become more deeply engaged and invested in their projects if they have the time to explore something of interest in considerable depth. Too often, a child's school day is so full of transition and interruptions that sustained time for one project is rare. This is tremendously det-rimental to developing a child's concentration and learning. Research has shown that since the arrival of television, children's attention spans are about as long as a segment between commercials! Our school schedules only exacerbate the situation. Time is also an element in regard to access to many materials. Some programs whip out a new ma-terial each day: clay one day, wood scraps one day, and sewing one day. The materials are then boxed up and put away for another time later in the month. Having the same materials out over an extended period invites children to master, invent, and expand on their ideas. When certain materials are available for long periods, children turn to them as needed resources for their projects. Sometimes just seeing the material will spark an idea for the needed airplane wing, puppet nose, or magic wand. It takes a keen awareness of what materials are being used and how they are being used to know when to introduce new items and combinations and when to put away others for a while.

- ***Attitude and Atmosphere***

  An attitude and atmosphere of acceptance are essential for children to feel comfortable in their attempts to try new ways, take risks, share their ideas, and develop flexible thinking. For example: the teacher is making plaster and gauze masks with the class. They are messy masks and need to cover the children's faces while being formed, dried, and hardened. A few of the children want masks, but are not comfortable with the medium or with having their faces covered. If the atmosphere in the room is one of acceptance, the teacher can offer alternative strategies for making masks: paper bags, paper plates, boxes, or other wonderful options

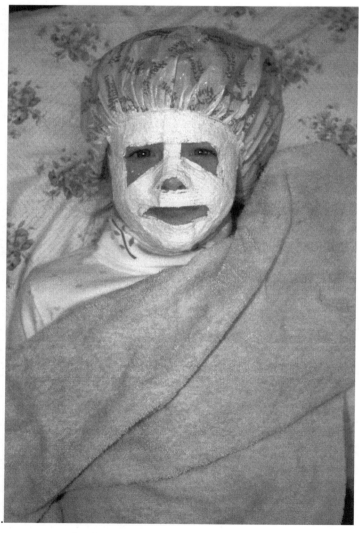

Plaster and gauze mask making

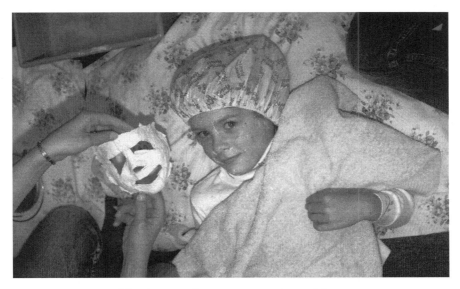

Plaster and gauze mask making

Alternative choices for masks

The finished "wild things"

As adults, we want to keep the spontaneous expression of children unencumbered by how we might think a mask "should" be made. Children will explore the materials and use them creatively when adults welcome their experimentation. Parents sometimes need help understanding children's attempts to represent their world. They need to be reassured that what children do is a process and that this process and willingness to try are what counts. A workshop or exhibit showing stages of art development as well as other available resources helps parents appreciate and understand all that is involved in a child's work.

- **Diversity**

  It is important to ensure that materials reflect the diversity of families in our schools and in our lives. Every child needs to feel welcome, comfortable, and accepted in the classroom. It is important to encourage children to bring things from their homes and for teachers to supply things that are familiar to them (labels in all languages and written symbols; pictures, magazines, and books of many cultures; empty food boxes for the dramatic play area that include different ethnic cuisines; dress-up clothes that represent what children's families really wear. It is equally important for all children to experience these differences and become comfortable and aware of their own feelings. Making crutches, walkers, leg braces, and hearing aids available in the room gives children a chance to discover and better understand what it is like to need such equipment to function in the world. These materials open up the possibilities for many avenues of playful exploration, explanations, and a deeper understanding of our similarities and differences.

- **Presentation**

  A certain spirit of delivery and investment of energy by adults conveys a subtle but powerful influence on the climate of a setting. One home child-care provider who is in touch with the simple joys children experience when adults join in their world, exudes just such a spirit. Her whole house is a stage and unbelievable things turn into costumes. A unique feature, though, is her fairy glue pot. This caregiver is undaunted by the meager funds available for materials. She has found, as we all have, that for young children, the joy in gluing is more in watching the dripping process than it is in adhering two substances. Glue, unfortunately, is expensive. This clever lady invented the individual fairy glue pot. It's a tiny container made from a strip of paper bag about three-fourths of an inch wide and three to four inches long. It is wound around a finger into a cylinder then glued to a small cardboard base. The child's name is written on one corner. The cylinder holds just enough glue to do whatever project the child is working on (refills are possible, of course). The magic of it is that the children never feel deprived by having such a small portion. Instead, they delight in the presentation and the charm of using their very own fairy glue pot.

**II.** <u>**Materials Gathering**</u>: A smorgasbord of delicious collectibles and their storage containers.

"For children to be in a group is a situation of great privilege, as if inside a great transformational laboratory." –Loris Malaguzzi

Yes! We want to gather and have readily available many natural and recycled materials to develop a "laboratory" in which children can experiment and devise their own works of creative ingenuity!

<u>**Materials Gathering:**</u>

Most schools have a limited budget for materials. This encourages an interesting mix of commercial and homemade materials. It is this author's belief that both are necessary, but I'd prefer to discuss the use of recycled materials, as I believe their value is often underestimated. They can be an excellent resource for both the adults and the children in the room. If the adult uses them to create learning devices, it's important to make them aesthetically pleasing and safe. An example might be to use colorful plastic bottle tops for game markers instead of the metal screw-off tops that can become rusty and sharp. One also needs to look at the expense involved in making something recycled aesthetically acceptable instead of buying something new. Covering a cardboard box with $15 worth of contact paper to create a play stove or sink might be penny-wise but pound-foolish. Perhaps investing in a commercial set in the beginning would be more appropriate and would save money in the long run. This is especially true for a popular item that will get much use.

Gathering collectible castoffs or trash-to-treasure items requires the help of parents and children in saving and transporting such treasures for the class. Communicating and demonstrating the importance of these items to the children's development and the curriculum helps families begin to balance this with the constant media hype about high-priced toys "guaranteed" to better educate children. By modeling the intrinsic value of everyday, open-ended materials as viable learning tools in school, we are also encouraging their use at home.

The availability, storage, selection, and choice of materials are critical considerations in managing any environment for young children. Children need to be able to see what is available, where it is stored, and what expectations there are for the care, use, and clean up of such materials. These materials are a highly valued source of creative extensions to stories. Differently sized boxes, scraps of wood, or toilet paper tubes can form a base for a variety of animals or people. Putting details on such as ears, eyes, and wild hair is completely up to the children and often inspired by the availability of the materials and the devices for attaching and transforming the materials.

The following is a list of trash-to-treasure items to collect, display, and store so that children can transform and combine them in their marvelously unique ways. Guided by what they learn from experience, children will build on their own repertoire of ideas and possibilities.

<u>Trash-to-Treasure Collectibles</u>: Think of colors, shapes, textures, and sizes.

*boxes

*bottle tops

*jar lids

*cardboard tubes (T.P. and
  paper towel)

*egg cartons

*foam rubber packaging

*sponges

*buttons

*baby food jars

*wood scraps

*cotton balls

*yarn

*string

*thread

*popsicle sticks

*tongue depressors

*toothpicks

*Venetian blind slats

*magazines

*catalogues

*paper plates

*ping pong balls

*shower curtains (to spread under messy projects)

*socks

*scrap paper

*wallpaper scraps

* wrapping paper

* water bottles

*see-through plastic containers

*spools

*ribbon

*clothespins

*corks

*felt scraps

*straws

*pipe cleaners

*thin wire

*old keys (check for lead!)

*dress-up

-hats

-shoes

-big boots

-nightgowns

-pajamas

*tennis balls                         -purses, wallets

*fabric scraps                        -dresses

*old jewelry                          -shirts

*sandpaper scraps                     -slips

*margarine cups                       -ties

*styrofoam trays                      -scarves

*cardboard scraps (e.g. back of
  lined paper or note pads)

## Nature Collectibles

pinecones                             shells

pods                                  rocks

beans                                 pebbles

feathers                              seeds

twigs                                 dried flowers

straw                                 leaves

acorns                                horse chestnuts

bark

## Supplies for attaching found objects

glue                                  strips of fabric

tape (scotch, masking)                yarn

staples                               shoe laces

hole punch                            paper clips

bag twisters                          binder clips

thin wire                             rubber bands

string                                brads

spiral coil                           needle & thread

clothes pins                          colored telephone wire

## Other Sources of Collectibles:

Sometimes older siblings, friends, relatives, janitors, and senior citizens have collections they no longer want. Solicit such things as: gumball machine trinkets, jack-in-the-box prizes, cards, miniature cars, dolls, dinosaurs, and the like. Take-aparts – old vacuums, windshield wiper motors, clocks, radios, typewriters, and fans – are wonderful sources of reusable materials.

Children have transformed these castoffs and collectibles into body parts for robots, musical instruments, beds for the three bears and Corduroy, bridges, pretend food, puppets, billy goats, facial features, dollhouse furniture, miniature worlds, and so much more. Children have the ability to endow their playthings with significant meaning and to use them in magical ways to tell a story. Watching their physical and cognitive skills evolve through the use of these open-ended materials justifies the collection and storage of all that "stuff." These recycled materials are truly more treasure than trash.

## Trash-to-Treasure Storage Containers:

*Shoe boxes:*

Clearly label boxes and place them on low shelves so the contents are easily seen and readily available. Putting the lid on the bottom reinforces the box and makes the lid readily available when you want to put it away.

*Plastic detergent, milk, and cider jugs/containers:*

Cut off tops of containers and thoroughly wash out the contents. Label with permanent markers. See-through plastic milk and cider jugs work particularly well. Another possibility is to cut a large opening on one side of the jug. The handle can then stay intact and allows the children to remove it from the shelf.

Many supermarkets now store their bulk candy in marvelous see-through plastic bins with removable "trap" doors in the front. They throw the bins out—but will save them for you if you make arrangements ahead of time. They stack and are fun to use!

*Copy paper boxes:*

Paper from commercial copying machines often comes packed in strong cardboard boxes with lids. Check local schools, churches, colleges, and business operations. Wood scraps, fabric, wallpaper, and the like can be neatly stored and labeled in these boxes.

*Wooden boxes:*

You can obtain wooden boxes free if you know someone at a liquor or import store that uses such boxes. Even if you need to buy them, the fee is small considering their durability and possible uses. I've found it hard to find shop owners who will "share" them, but I keep trying. They make excellent shelves or larger boxes for storing bulkier collections.

*Large paper bags:*

Two large paper bags (one inside the other) with their tops folded down create a quadruple-thickness storage space. These can be labeled colorfully and easily replaced when they wear out.

*Deep box lids:*

The best box lids to use for storage are those from copy machine paper boxes. They are rectangular and allow spreading of materials for easy visibility.

*Discarded drawers:*

Sometimes drawers outlive old desks, dressers or kitchen cabinets. Save them— they make excellent, sturdy storage bins.

Tool boxes, plastic ice trays, and egg cartons:

The well in these items make excellent storage units for buttons, beads, washers, and the like. Garage and farm sales often have old tool boxes. Wash out, dry thoroughly, and spray paint.

*Gallon milk cartons:*

Cut milk cartons in half lengthwise for small-item storage (clean them well!).

Other helpful small-item storage containers:

- small boxes that once held jewelry
- yogurt containers
- margarine tubs
- large cardboard ice cream containers from school cafeterias, ice cream stores, hospitals, and other places serving large quantities of food
- strawberry baskets

### III. **Props to Enhance Story Replay:**
A Gathering of Simple Ideas

Creating Story Props:

A significant part of the Journey is to live with each story for as long as the children are engaged and the extensions of the story are meaningful. Over the course of a Journey the story is read, told, and retold with a variety of interesting props. Most of the props discussed below can be made from the found materials that were discussed previously. The aim of this section is to encourage adults and children to be able to easily provide props so that story retelling, in a number of different modalities, can always be a vital part of the curriculum.

When teachers are creating props for the group retelling of the Journey story, it is a wise idea to make two sets of flannel board characters, puppets, mini worlds, and anything you wish to keep in good order. Most teachers keep one set for their use only and put the other set out in the classroom for children to play with on their own or with their peers. All of this takes time! Encourage families, friends, senior citizens, and any other talented individuals to help you create the second set or… both sets for that matter. ☺ Children will use the trash-to-treasure smorgasbord to create their own props if this is encouraged. Making their own personal mini world is a wonderful way to extend the story to their home settings for retelling with siblings, parents, or by themselves.

**Books as Props**

*Japanese Picture Story Cards*

The Japanese picture story cards are called kamishibai, which means "paper theater." A kamishibai man used to gather children in Japanese neighborhoods and tell stories using these cards. Kamishibai Man by Allen Say (2005) is a delightful new children's book that tells the story of a kamishibai's life. It is a lovely way to introduce these cards to the children after you've made a set.

The story illustrations are on the front of the card and the words appear on the back. This arrangement allows the reader to face the children and look right at them more easily than when holding a book off to one side. You can also hold up and rotate the cards around the circle so the children can see the pictures as you continue to read. To make a set of cards you need:

- plastic insert pages
- three rings
- oak tag cut slightly smaller than insert pages

- your own illustrations, magazine pictures, coloring book pictures, or an old or second copy of a paper book you can cut up to use the illustrations

Cut the oak tag, and arrange story characters or scenes for each "page" of the story on one side of each card with accompanying words on the back. When the glue is dry, slip the oak tag into the plastic insert pages, order them in sequence, and attach with rings.

When a book has gone out of print, we check it out of the library, copy the whole thing (enlarging the pictures), color in the illustrations, and make it into a story card set.

*Big Books*

When books become dog-eared or the bindings are no longer holding the pages together, pull the book apart and make a big book out of it. Cut off the frayed edges of the pictures and glue them onto oak tag. Write the story in larger print under the pictures to help those children interested in seeing the words as you read to them. Cover the pages with clear contact paper and use rings to bind the pages. The real advantage of a big book is the feeling of being "surrounded" by these large pages and having giant words to explore.

## Books for children's original stories

Use the cardboard backing from writing tablets and cover them with cloth, colored paper, wallpaper, wrapping paper, or plain white paper. These will form the front and back covers of a book. Place paper in between the covers and hold together with staples, rings, shoelaces, or yarn.

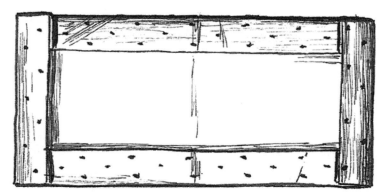 

Fold a clothing box flat (as the retailers do to store their boxes). Glue a piece of paper over the folded sides. Take about 10 sheets of paper and lay them down on top of the paper you've just glued. Sew right down the middle of the paper. Fold in half and you have an instant book with a box lid cover. Decorate the cover with any of the ideas mentioned above.

One teacher uses *old catalogues* for her classroom books. The children glue white paper over each page and the book is ready for use. It's sturdy, compact, and doesn't put all that colored ink into our environment!

Enclosing photos, old book pages, and the child's original work in Ziploc plastic bags makes a useful book configuration. Place each page in a bag, zip it closed, and place one or two rings close to the "zipper" to hold the book together. Large snap clips also work to keep the book together.

**Miniature World Props**

Miniature worlds are just what the words convey. They are small versions of the story props that children can use to retell a story alone, in small groups, or with the whole group. Children can create their own or use those created or gathered by the adults. It's wonderful to see how children assign new meaning to the materials available.

One day we told the story of Rumplestiltskin with action figures fashioned from puzzle piece figures and dressed-up <u>Star Wars</u> characters. Princess Leia made a wonderful miller's daughter and the children tolerated the transformation. The castle was built of blocks. The spinning wheel for the miniature figures was actually a disguised, broken toy motorcycle turned upside down and lodged between two blocks. The children were drawn to retelling this story by the appeal of the miniatures representing Rumplestiltskin.

*Miniature World Storage*

Shoeboxes work well with a label or symbol of the story on top and on the exposed side of the box. If you take a photo of the pieces that go in the box and tape or glue it to the inside lid, it helps children check to see if they have all of the pieces gathered for the next person who will use them.

Children often seem to be drawn to opposites – either very little or very big versions of the storybook characters. Because storage is a chronic problem, we have naturally concentrated more on miniatures, but there is great value in <u>*maxi world*</u> characters as well. For the giant in <u>Jack and the Beanstalk</u>, we borrowed some jeans and a shirt from our biggest dad in the class. The children stuffed the clothes for his body and a pillowcase for his head. They stuffed his legs into big boots from our dress-up box. Two children held him up and moved him around like a human-sized puppet. For one young boy in the room named John it was very comforting because he felt a sense of control over the giant. The giant didn't yell "fee fi fo fum" unless John made him say it and he didn't move until John and a peer made him move.

<u>Spontaneous</u> mini worlds can be plucked from nature or found materials. A rock can be a troll, wood scraps can become magical chariots that roll in on spools, and monkeys can be corks with bottle top hats. The possibilities are endless! If the children watch you make these improvised leaps of fun, they'll be inclined to do the same thing.

FRONT: Three Bears made of felt-covered plastic lotion bottles, LEFT BACK: large clips hold pig, wolf and photo of child with skeleton, RIGHT BACK: T.P. tubes hold up farmer and wife puppets.

<u>Small bottles</u> of shampoo, conditioner, body lotion, and other toiletries make fine bases for story characters. Empty the bottles, rinse, and dry. A glue gun works best to attach felt clothes and anything you want to use for features. These details enhance their realness and usher children into the replay.

<u>T.P. or paper towel tubes</u>. Toilet paper tubes can become characters for a mini world and can also hold up story characters for replay. Copy characters out of a storybook, cut a picture out of a magazine, have a teacher or a child draw the character or characters, and attach them to a T.P. tube with a stapler. They stand up well and are very easy to make. (When the pictures are floppy, glue them on thin cardboard or a manila folder before stapling them to the tube.)

<u>Clip characters</u>. There is a clip called a binder clip that is a perfect base for a stand-up-mini world character. You place a picture of the character you want to stand up in the pinch part of the

clip. The character can be drawn on a manila folder, index card, or thin cardboard. It can also be a picture from a coloring book, magazine, storybook, or catalog. Once the character is in the clip, take the "pinchers" off by squeezing them and wiggling them out of their holes. Once out, flip the clip over and the character will be ready to play his or her role.

Other sources for mini worlds.  There are more possibilities for mini worlds. Not all of them have to be homemade. There are commercial figures of story characters in many school catalogs, as well as garage sale items, family collections, and puzzle piece figures. They can be inserted in the bigger size binder clips if you want them to stand up.

**Puppet Props**

Puppets are mini magical creatures. They can portray personalities, different voices, actions, humor, and feelings. Puppets can capture children's attention, spark their imaginations, and modulate their moods. Slip a puppet on your hand when a child is having trouble with a peer or is struggling with separation. Start talking to the puppet with your back to the child. Have the puppet make reflective comments such as: "I feel sad when my mom leaves too, but she always comes back!"…pause…"…sometimes she even comes back early."…pause…and peek to see if there is any reaction. This can be one of those magical movements if the child is curious about who's talking and is ready to be distracted.

Anything can become a puppet if children and adults have been encouraged to use their ingenuity and unique ideas. Organized treasured trash will inspire creative features, limbs, and outfits. The puppets to follow can be used as a base for developing storybook characters or children's unique creations from their untethered imaginations.

Teachers…keep a puppet in your pocket! They are wonderful at saying something you really want children to hear.

| Basic puppet ideas |
| --- |

*Bag puppet:* Lunch-sized paper bags fit easily over a young child's hand and work well as a short-lived puppet.

*Sock puppet:* A child's sock is often more comfortable for the child to manage. However, it's fun to have a variety of sizes, since some children love the big floppy look of an adult-size sock. Telephone wire cut in small pieces works well for attaching things to serve as eyes and nose.

*Stick puppet:* A child's drawing, tracing, or magazine pictures can be glued or stapled to a stick to create a very simple puppet. An upturned egg carton with a slit in each "bump" can hold the characters in place until "their parts" come in the reenactment.

*Dangling puppet:* Instead of gluing the character to a stick, punch a hole in the top of the character and reinforce with notebook reinforcers or tape. Then thread yarn, string, or elastic through the hole, knot one end and tie the other end to the stick. Now the puppet moves as the child wiggles the cord.

*Detergent bottle puppet:* Any clean plastic bottle that will fit over a child's hand when the bottle's bottom is removed is fine for this puppet. If any of the edges are rough, just put masking or freezer tape around the newly cut edges. Have children really look at the shape of the bottles. Can they imagine animals, special people, robots, or machines?

*Cloth and ring puppets:* This is one of the simplest ideas and requires only a small sheet or handkerchief scrap and a plastic curtain ring. It is particularly good for young children because the plastic ring helps to keep the puppet secure on the child's finger. The sheet scrap (about four by four inches) is placed over any finger and then the ring slips over the material and the finger. The child can add features to the puppet or play with it as it is.

*Cup puppet:* A Styrofoam or paper cup is just the right size for a child's hand to fit inside. The cup is the base to which you can add other items for features and limbs. The cup can either be the whole puppet or just the head. A cloth scrap on the hand with the cup on top creates a head and body effect.

*Tube puppet:* A toilet paper tube cut to all lengths can fit over a child's fingers and form an instant base for a puppet. It can also be used as antlers, legs, arms, or skinny bodies for other character creations.

*Mitt puppet:* This is a more durable puppet made from an old scrap of sheeting, pillow case, or muslin. A paper pattern is made by tracing a child's hand to form a "thumbless" mitten shape. Transfer this to material, then cut and sew around three sides. If a child is intrigued with a pattern idea, the concept of ears, hands, paws, and different-shaped bodies can be explored.

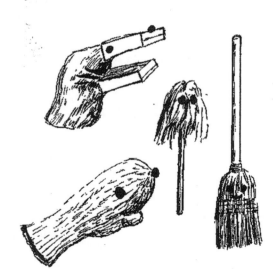

*Other puppet* base *possibilities:*
- rag dish mop
- dressed up broom (use handle to move puppet around)
- cereal boxes slipped over a hand
- sponge mitt (used to wash cars)
- mittens (the thumb can be the animal's ear or mouth)
- two gelatin boxes and a sock

## OTHER IDEAS FOR STORYTELLING PROPS

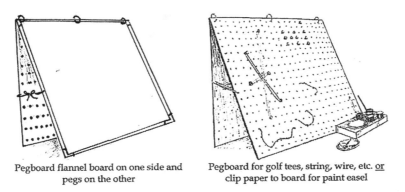

Pegboard flannel board on one side and pegs on the other

Pegboard for golf tees, string, wire, etc. <u>or</u> clip paper to board for paint easel

Pegboard 1: flannel board on one side and pegs on the other
Pegboard 2 : for golf tees, string, wire, etc., or clip paper to board for paint easel

### Pegboard Easel Storyboard

The pegboard easel storyboard, pegboard easel manipulation board, or paint easel is a very versatile piece of equipment for storytelling, for use as a small manipulative board, and as a paint easel. Pegboard comes in many different lengths and with a variety of hole sizes. (If you want to use one side as a pegboard with golf tees, be sure to bring a golf tee to the hardware store with you so that you can get the right size hole.) Depending on space, storage, and number of children who will use it at one time, the size of the board can vary greatly. I've used two pieces of pegboard measuring 22 by 24 inches with a differently sized hole on each side. Connect the boards together at the top with two shoelaces, leather strips, string, or the like. Ring binders also work very well. Tie the sides together at one edge to keep the boards from collapsing.

### *Pegboard Flannel Board*

Cut a piece of flannel about an inch larger all the way around than one panel of the pegboard. Hem the flannel. Cut four pieces of elastic and sew them across the back of each corner. These will then slip over each corner of the pegboard to form the removable flannel storyboard. Placing two of these easel storyboards on the floor provides a divider in a room with storyboards on one side and manipulatives on the other. You can also place them in the hallway for an announcement board or on a table for a different perspective.

### *Pegboard Paint Easel*

Cover the board with plastic or aluminum foil for easy clean up. Attach paper with two clothes-pins and spread newspaper or an old shower curtain underneath for protection. Use a sponge with holes cut in it to hold film canisters or small jars with paint and a margarine tub with water. Set it on a tray or box lid with brushes and a rag. This is an excellent surface for "painting a story." Leo Lionni's Little Blue and Little Yellow lends itself well to this type of easel.

### *Pegboard Manipulative Board*

Select your hole size according to what you want children to be able to manipulate through the holes. The possibilities are endless. You might provide the following objects:

- golf tees
- telephone wire
- thin wire
- shoelaces
- yarn (with or without needles – dipping one end of the yarn or string into colorless nail polish will stiffen so it acts very much like the end of a shoelace)
- plastic bag twists

Include: beads, buttons, spools, shells or rocks with holes, washers, scraps of colored paper, felt or vinyl, and a hole punch

One child cleverly filled the pegboard with golf tees, removed some randomly down the face of the board and rolled ping-pong balls and large marbles through the open spaces. It was a hit with everyone and opened up a whole new realm of ideas.

Another child took the class button collection over to the easel and with telephone wire retold the story of Frog and Toad and the lost button. He took a long piece of wire and as he told the story he poked the wire through a different hole, making a big loop to hold all of the various buttons that frog found for toad — one with two holes, another with four holes, thick ones, thin ones, different colors, and so on. As he spun the story, it was as if the wire were traveling on a path through the woods. One *never* knows what will evolve into an inspiring story "place."

## Other Felt/Flannel Storyboards

The flannel board offers a simple medium for children to retell a story either alone or with others. There are many ways this can be made:

### Cigar Box Stories

The lid of a cigar box provides a good place to glue a piece of flannel or felt. Felt is more expensive, but it does not fray and tends to hold a little more securely. The box itself can hold the characters for the story replay. This is also a good container for transporting while traveling. A book and flannel pieces of the story characters make this a fun birthday or going-away present for a child.

### Masonite

Cut two pieces of *Masonite* 12 by 9 inches, and fasten the pieces with two small two-inch hinges. Measure the flannel one inch larger all around the opened board so that it can be folded over on all sides and secured with wide mailing tape or masking tape.

### Box Easel

Take any size square cardboard box and cut off the top flaps. Cut 2 sides on the diagonal to form a base for a flannel board or a paint easel. Attach flannel with glue gun.

### Magnetic Boards

Anything that holds a magnet can become a storyboard: the refrigerator door or sides, file cabinet, radiator covers, hospital bed bars, and metal shelves. Portable versions can be cookie tins, baking sheets, and stove mats. These can lean up against a pegboard easel, wall, back of a chair, or sit on a child's lap.

Magnetic tape that has adhesive on the back can attach any character you may want to use on the metal surface. This tape is available in fabric, hardware, and novelty stores.

One family found that their child, Lauren, was very content to play on the floor using the refrigerator as her storyboard, especially when her mom or dad were in the kitchen. She would retell stories that her mom had made from an old coloring book. The storybook characters were cut out, colored, and backed with magnetic tape. Lauren would line up the characters on the floor and use them one at a time to tell the story. The refrigerator door was her backdrop.

### Story Characters or Props to Use on Boards

Felt pieces and Pellon material will adhere to a flannel or felt board on their own. Just cut out the shapes, characters, or props you desire. With Pellon, you can use magic markers for the details.

### Other Suggestions for Story Character Props

- photographs
- magazine pictures
- coloring books
- the children's own drawings
- two copies of the same book (old ones from garage sales, store closings, etc.)
- commercial flannel sets of stories

Cover each paper or tagboard character with clear contact paper to preserve it. Attach any of the following to the back of each piece so it will stay up on the storyboard:

- strips of coarse sandpaper
- small piece of Velcro
- small wad of tic tac (used to hold pictures up without marring walls)

### Make Your Own Slides for Storytelling

This experience is for children who are ready to become involved in a process that requires a series of steps and the ability to draw in a small space without feeling frustrated. (We did this with a group of five- and six-year-olds, and they loved it.) We practiced on pieces of paper that had boxes the same size as the slide dimensions, an inch by an inch and a half. It was a challenge to keep inside the squares when the children were used to drawing on much larger pieces of paper. Some really liked drawing tiny figures in one square, others drew "designs," and a few ventured to put together a series of illustrated slides to go with their story. As each child finished a slide or slide series, he or she would come over to the projector and see the slides "come alive" on the wall, and then tell the story to anyone who would listen.

You'll need:

- transparent slide paper (overhead projector sheets work)
- slide encasements
- special pens (overhead projector pens)

These are best purchased at a photo or office supply store, unless you are familiar with the slide creation process and can order materials from a catalog.

### *Flashlight and Cellophane Windows*

For telling a story where color is an integral part of the story line, it's interesting to tell the story with paints, markers, colored paper, or cellophane "windows." The lightweight cellophane can be wrapped around a cardboard tube (toilet paper, paper towel, or larger commercial cardboard spools) and secured with tape or rubber bands. Another idea is to cut holes in pieces of strong cardboard and over these holes tape heavy-duty cellophane (like the gels they use in stage lighting or the colored plastic theme paper folders. The gels cast a much stronger color.) A flashlight inserted into the tubes or placed behind the colored cellophane gels will cast that color on the white walls or ceiling. In retelling the stories of <u>The Great Blueness</u> or <u>Little Blue and Little Yellow</u>, this is a particularly meaningful extension. For <u>Little Blue and Little Yellow,</u> we tape two pieces of cardboard together to form a "hinge" with yellow cellophane on one side and blue on the other. When Yellow and Blue hug each other, we close the two pieces of cardboard together and the spot on the wall turns green. This process has a certain magic quality that intrigues children. They are interested in later experimentation on their own.

### *Child's Own Gestures as Props*

It is interesting to use a child's own gestures, posture, expressions, and large body movements as props. Peggy Hackney (1988) states: "…the first step in any creative process is the art of merging, identifying, and becoming one with that which is there to be known. Young children learn through identifying. They learn the nature of 'cat' through becoming one." Reenacting a troll, a giant, mean witches, or a fairy godmother requires that a child begin to identify with that character and try to move and act in such a way that it communicates how each of these characters might feel. It deepens the child's understanding by doing and physically makes internal thoughts and feelings external. It reveals the child's observational skills, attention to detail, experiences, and ability to integrate and act upon a wealth of information. Don't you think a child would enjoy being a "living prop" and seeing him or herself as a miniature world that's come to life?

### *Constructive Responding*

It might be helpful as we close this chapter to reflect upon how we respond and give feedback to young children's prop-building attempts. It is often a struggle for them as they endeavor to get their hands to cooperate with the ideas that dance through their minds. When your hole puncher is hard to work with one hand, glue seems to stick to everything except what you want to hold together, and fastening wheels to a car so they still move is frustrating if not impossible, it can drive a little fellow to throw it all on the floor and cry.

How children respond to each other and are responded to by adults that are significant to them is a powerful dynamic. It is an arduous task to balance one's response in such a way that it encourages children and stretches them in meaningful ways without slipping into global praise or stepping on their sensitive egos. Accepting their spontaneous attempts and encouraging new and harder possibilities is our challenge.

David Hawkins (1970) talks about the creative capacity for synthesis, for building a framework for assembling coherent episodes of experience. Prop building provides the chance to do this in many different modalities and to practice, invent, internalize, and master the process and the story. This chapter has suggested many ways to provide the capacity for this synthesis, and I believe it is important to share some thoughts on the feedback loop in this process. If we organize these thoughts in terms of the "I" words (*interaction, intervention, integration,* and *interference*), it will help us to keep them in mind as we work with children and our colleagues. The following discussion of these aspects of feedback explains guidelines that are comfortable for me. You may want to discuss them with your team or change them to work for you.

### *Interaction*

Communication occurs to the extent that others understand one's thoughts, actions, and feelings. Sometimes it does not involve spoken language. As adults, then, it's important in our interactions with children to be sensitive to what they are doing, to observe, and to quietly understand what is going on before moving into their world or agenda. We are joining children on their terms.

Rita Weiss, a former professor and administrator at the University of Colorado at Boulder, called this S.O.U.L.

S – approach the child <u>S</u>ilently

O – <u>O</u>bserve what is occurring

U – gain an <u>U</u>nderstanding of what the child is doing or attempting to do

L – <u>L</u>isten and <u>L</u>earn before interacting or intervening

### *Intervention*

An interaction becomes an intervention when another idea is interjected to extend the child's thoughts, actions, or prop-building process. It's a supportive nudge to open up other possibilities. Sometimes children become stuck and need opportunities to see other alternatives or choices. It might be different ways to build things, rearrange or reinforce form, change the endings of stories, or interact with others. The ability of adults to know *when* and *how* to intervene is the essence of sensitive teaching.

### *Integration*

Children gather information from many different sources. Our observation of their transformations of props and materials as well as their interactions/dramatizations with peers and adults will give us valuable clues as to how they are integrating the story information.

### *Interference*

We all know what happens here. The adult/child agenda becomes blurred and we intrude in ways that are not in the child's best interest. Our intentions are usually noble, but we lose track of who is creating.

## SETTING UP MATERIALS TO INVITE PLAYFUL EXPLORATION

Place the dress-up corner mirror on its side so children can explore
With a double image as they draw or paint.

See if you can find an old record player that still spins; add baby food jars,
water, food coloring and eye droppers, set to lowest speed.
Great for hand-eye coordination & color mixing.

**EXPERIMENT WITH A VARIETY OF THINGS IN THE WATER TABLE**

This table has half blown up balloons, red food coloring, and miniature bears. The bears were added by the children who tried to balance them on the balloons.

Water table liner is lowered onto box and chair to give children a different height to explore. The table is filled with new fish tank pebbles and plastic tubes, great for sound effects.

Using a "c" clamp turned upside down with wire for cutting the clay or balancing "blobs" gave a wonderful format for experimentation.

Have you ever tried painting on snow?

Set up a wide variety of blocks and a board to encourage some serious building.

The board and block set up seemed to inspire a very thoughtful arrangement of the various shapes and sizes of blocks.

In a workshop for teachers, they were assigned to use all the blocks and jar lids to build a safe village for the pig family. Jar lids are a fine addition to the block area!

Two pieces of paper on one easel to invite peer interaction.

John Holt expresses a similar philosophy when he states:

The adult's role is to provide the environment, to see that materials are accessible, and then to give children the opportunity to explore and think for themselves. In this process, the adult must learn *when* and *how* to intervene, for the intervention is crucial to the dialogue. In this process it is not so much the adult's knowledge of scientific principles that enables him to play his role skillfully, but his ability to establish the climate which everyone...adults and children...are encouraged to engage in the quest of wondering, relating, experimenting, discovering, and thus learning.

We all learn in our endeavors with small children. Their novel approach to life and materials can rekindle our own distracted curiosity.

## REFERENCES AND RELATED READING

Carter, M. and Curtis, D. (1994). *Training Teachers: A Harvest of Theory and Practice.* St. Paul, MN: Redleaf Press.

Cohen, D. (1972). *The Learning Child.* New York, NY: Pantheon.

Cohen, D. H. and Stern, V. (1978). *Observing and Recording the Behavior of Young Children.* New York, NY: Teachers College Press.

Copple, C. and Bredekamp, S. (Eds.). *Developmentally Appropriate Practice in Early Childhood Programs Serving Children from Birth through Age 8.* Rev. Ed. Washington, DC: National Association for the Education of Young Children.

Derman-Sparks, L. (1989). *Anti-bias Curriculum: Tools for Empowering Young Children.* Washington, DC: National Association for the Education of Young Children.

Edwards, C., Gandini, L. and Forman, G. (1998). *The Hundred Languages of Children: The Reggio Emilia Approach – Advanced Reflections.* Greenwich, CT: Ablex Publishing Corporation.

Elkind, D. (1986). Formal Education and Early Childhood Education: An essential difference. *Phi Delta Kappan Journal,* pp. 631-636.

Hackney, P. (1988, winter). Moving Wisdom. In *Context,* p. 18.

Hawkins, D. (1970). I, Thou, It. In *The ESS Reader.* Newton, MA: Elementary Science Study.

Hawkins, F. P. (1969). *The Logic of Action: Young Children at Work.* New York, NY: Pantheon Books.

Johnson, P. (1993). *Literacy through the Book Arts.* Portsmouth, NH: Heinemann.

Jones, E. (1986). *Teaching Adults: An Active Learning Approach.* Washington, DC: National Association for the Education of Young Children.

Topol, C. W. and Gandini, L. (1999). *Beautiful Stuff: Learning with Found Materials.* Worchester, MA: Davis Publications, Inc.

Say, A. (2005). *Kamishibai Man.* New York, NY: Houghton Mifflin Company.

Walker, L. (1995). *Block Building for Children.* Woodstock, NY: The Overlook Press.

Weiss, R. (1981) INREAL Intervention for Language Handicapped and Bilingual Children. *Journal of Early Intervention,* October 1981 vol. 4 no. 1 40-51

Wiseman, A. (1973). *Making Things: The Handbook of Creative Discovery.* Boston, MA: Little, Brown, and Company.

Wiseman, A. (1975). *Making Things: The Handbook of Creative Discovery* (Book 2). Boston, MA: Little, Brown, and Company.

# Chapter Six: Part *I*

# The Journey With Families:

### BUILDING THE HOME-SCHOOL PARTNERSHIP

➤ Communicating the value of family story time
➤ Launching pads for literacy at home and in the community

# Part *II*

# The Journey With Families:

### OPTIONS FOR FAMILIES AND TEACHERS TO SHARE INFORMATION

➤ Inviting families to join the classroom journey
➤ Providing experiences for family engagement
➤ Representing and celebrating each child's personal journey

## PART I

### Building the Home-School Partnership

Communicating the Value of Family Story Time

"Future education cannot be simply about skills. It must foster the growth of community – of people learning, working, and living together in supportive relationships that enhance dignity, allow for individuality, and share responsibility." –Pearpoint

Family life today is complex and its effect on young children profound. "The village" is needed more than ever to join families in the challenging task of raising their children. As educators, we want to create a genuine relationship with families. Together we seek to understand each child in the context of the classroom and the context of his or her family culture. We need to work together, building on a foundation of trust and encouraging each other to provide the best care and education to the children we share.

A story I once heard about geese gives us a mental picture of what we can do for each other. It is said that when geese fly in their V formation, each goose flaps its wings to create an "uplift" for the birds that follow. By flying in this V formation, the entire flock can fly farther than if each bird flies alone. The geese flying in this formation honk to one another to encourage each other to keep moving forward. When the lead goose tires, it moves back into the existing formation to let another goose lead for a while.

The lesson for us as families and educators might be that if we share a common direction and develop a sense of community, we can move toward common goals for the children in our care. Perhaps by traveling together we can share our unique skills, capacities, dreams, gifts, and resources to keep moving forward while supporting one another for the duration of our "flight" together.

Surveying families early in the school year for their preferred way of communicating is helpful to both families and teachers. We want to express to families how vital their participation is and how aware teachers are of the constraints on their time. Our desire is to know what will work for families in terms of the home-school partnerships and how comfortably and fruitfully they can be involved.

The Storybook Journey process provides a strong bridge between home and school through the development of story extensions beyond the classroom. It welcomes an exchange of ideas, help in developing and collecting materials, suggestions of stories, and communication with each other about the children's reactions to our Journey experiences. The continuity of learning between home and school is fostered by offering many avenues for family engagement and information sharing.

There are helpful articles and books that focus on promoting the home-school relationship. This chapter will focus on tangible ways the Storybook Journey has joined families in making storybook reading, story replay, and literacy learning delicious ways of spending meaningful time with young children. This focus brings families, children, and teachers together as literacy partners.

In a perfect world, many families would like the tempo of their lives to slow down. Oh, to be able to spend more quality time with their little ones…telling stories or reading all those beautifully illustrated books while snuggled down in a big overstuffed chair! Though families may not be able to do this as often as they'd like to, there is much that can be done with the time available. Parents have a major influence on their children's conception of literacy; therefore, it is imperative that teachers conscientiously make every effort to develop home-school connections (DeBruin-Parecki, 2008).

Starting from day one in a child's life…families can read, sing, hum, recite nursery rhymes, make interesting sounds, and respond to their child's voice with gentle reciprocal banter. Reading to young children anywhere and as many times as possible during the day or at bedtime is vital to literacy development. Read while at a bus stop, at a restaurant, in a doctor's office, in the grocery store line…read, read, read! Children's most attentive time, however, is usually before their nap or at bedtime or while eating their lunch or a snack. It is an especially lovely way for a family to end a day together. The dust and dishes can wait while spending this precious time cuddled up close with a book to read, a story to tell, or a song to sing. It is one of the most precious gifts a parent can give to their child – their time and the love of books!

Taking turns choosing the book also allow families to see which subjects and stories the child is drawn to and offers ideas for future book selections. Books can be bought affordably at garage sales, thrift shops, secondhand bookstores, and bookstore closeouts. There are also sale prices in catalogs, especially the Scholastic book catalog. Older siblings receive these catalogs in school. Of course, the local public library is a wonderful alternative to purchasing.

The advantages are great for children who have had the privilege of being read to early in life. They are further enhanced when some of the following extended experiences are offered:

- Children need time to reflect on a story. When the events of the story relate to aspects of the child's own life, they can make personal connections. The adult reader can also pause and study the illustrations with the child, point out meaningful words, or answer questions.

- Adults can listen while children play with interesting ideas or new information offered in the story. They can also inspire deeper pondering by asking questions that start with: "I wonder if…" or "How come…" or "What else…?"

- Just chatting together about the book is very beneficial. These conversations often reveal or ensure whether the child has understood the story.

- Sometimes children like "to read" the story to their parents. This is always a fun way to see what they retain from the story and how they might change ideas and characters that attract or repel them.

- Storybook reading gives children opportunities to hear a more formal, rich book language. In her book, Reading Magic, Mem Fox wrote: "Because words are essential in building the thought connections in the brain, the more language a child experiences – through books and through conversation with others, not passively from television – the more advantaged socially, educationally, and in every way the child will be for the rest of his or her life." Two examples that illustrate this book language are Mem Fox's Tough Boris and Cynthia Rylant's Scarecrow.

- Storybook reading builds a foundation for learning new vocabulary. The words children listen to before they can read become the words with which they will be most familiar as they learn to read. As Jim Trelease said in his book, The Read Along Handbook, "The listening vocabulary is the reservoir of words that feeds the reading vocabulary pool."

- When a child sits next to her parent and the parent moves a finger under the words being read, the child begins to focus her attention on seeing as well as hearing the words. She may begin to realize that print conveys meaning, that all of those funny marks are letters and that letters create words. A wonderful example of this is Josh's dictation experience. Josh drew a picture and dictated a story about it to his teacher. When he got home, he handed the masterpiece to his mother. Mom looked at the picture and ran her fingers along the words as she read his story. Puzzled, Josh looked at her and said: "How did you know my story?" Mom showed Josh the words that were written and explained, "The letters go together to form the words you told your teacher." Josh said, "Wow…it's like magic!" (What joy to be able to observe the outward evidence of an inner involvement. The lights went on for Josh!) The Alphabet Tree by Leo Lionni is a wonderful book to read when it looks like a child has reached this point.

- Children often like to tell stories about their pictures or spontaneously begin telling a story they want you to write down. Vivian Paley, an author and brilliant teacher, has said that dictation helps children organize their thoughts in a story framework. She suggests that we listen to children in our role as active scribes and:
  - Encourage children by your attention and interest.
  - Question children to seek clarification.
  - Reread aloud to make sure you transcribed what "the author" said and meant.

Children also like to write (scribble) their own stories. Sometimes they will "read" what they have written or ask you to read it. A friend said that when her preschooler was about three he wrote a page of wavy lines and things that looked like Ts and asked her to read his "story" to him. Mom asked him if he could tell her the story. "No, Mom, you read it! I can't figure it out!" Mom was very clever. She said she didn't want to make something up. That would be her story – so she said: "I know you love the ocean. Could these marks here be waves in the ocean? Tommy smiled, "Yes." Mom pointed to the Ts. Tommy added: "OK, that's me in the ocean waves! The end!"

This scribble will eventually incorporate more letters. Next come attempts at words. Through this writing process, children can also learn to read. Children usually learn the letters in their own name first, which is why the T was very significant for Tommy.

Many children will start the writing process by drawing a picture and telling a story about where, who, and what is going on in the picture. Ask them if they would like you to write their story on the back or on a separate piece of paper. Say the words as you write them. This helps them see that letters form words and that what they say can be transformed into these written symbols.

Enjoy the bonding power and magic that accompany sharing a book or drawing and writing a story together. The Storybook Journey is based on reading, telling, and replaying the story. The repetition assists the child not only in the area of cognitive development, but also emotionally through identifying with a character, feeling, or situation. You can refer back to characters, feelings, and situations at salient times. You could ask a child if she's having a "Humpty Dumpty" kind of day when everything is falling apart and it's hard to put herself back together. You could relate to a child acting like a "Wild Thing." Maybe a child feels like Corduroy bear when he had that accident knocking over the lamp or when he was left behind at the department store. Children's emotional connection to a storybook character, feeling, or situation gives the adult a meaningful tool for helping children relate to and cope with difficult moments. Remember when Winnie the Pooh was stuck in Rabbit's hole? He began to sigh when he realized he couldn't get out because he was so tightly stuck. A tear rolled down his cheek and he said, "Would you read a sustaining book, such as would help and comfort a wedged bear in great tightness?" A book that can relate to an emotional time in a child's life is a gift indeed!

Perhaps some of the ideas mentioned in this chapter could be incorporated into a newsletter to support what families are already doing or to suggest the importance and benefit of reading stories to children at home. Some schools have a section in their newsletter that focuses on literacy with an idea or suggestion each week for families to ponder. It can also include an experience in the class-room, a particular book the children are interested in, or a book for parents in the lending library.

### Launching Pads for Literacy at Home and in the Community

"Our challenge as educators and families together is to make it possible for <u>all</u> of our children, regardless of ability, experience, or cultural heritage to feel successful in their attempts to be liter-ate." –McCord

Home, school, and the community provide endless opportunities to launch incidental literacy learning. (Incidental literacy is referring to the casual, spontaneous, everyday things we do that expose children to listening, seeing, and talking about what they experience.) In this section of the Journey with families, we will look at some ideas for incidental experiences around the house and out in the community.

The home setting is indeed a marvelous launching pad for incidental literacy learning. Some parents will already be doing much of what is on the following list and hopefully they will gain some new ideas for extensions. Involving children in the tasks of everyday living takes extra time and patience. However, it is a marvelous way to gently ease young children into an awareness of literacy and a sense of responsibility. This list might be a helpful attachment to the newsletter. One idea at a time from the following list could be incorporated into the literacy section of the newsletter. Perhaps a brief paragraph could be written explaining how valuable these experiences are in build-ing strong literacy foundations or launching pads for the years ahead.

Children experience sheer enjoyment when they are invited to participate in these literacy at-tempts. It may be easier for adults to do the tasks on their own…but to miss out on "flying flour" during a cooking experience or strange things "growing" in the garden is to miss a very delightful part of children in the process of learning!

## Incidental Literacy around the House:

Think of all of the possibilities in your house that will build awareness and skills in language development, listening, reading, writing, math, speaking, and rhyming. Here are a few suggestions to get you started:

- Calendars of family activities provide many literacy opportunities: numbers and days of the week in sequence, writing the activities for each day, recording time of dentist appointments, soccer practice, meetings, birthdays, no school days, etc. Talk about what you're doing when you write things on the calendar, such as: "See, this is Dad's birthday. It is on Friday, September 13th." The children can also have their own personal calendar to encourage "writing" important dates for themselves.
- Notes to children (on bed at night, in lunchbox, on refrigerator, on their car seat…). Encourage them to write back. Combine words with pictures or sketches.
- Start a tradition! Turn off the TV for a certain amount of time each week and spend the time "reading" as a family (silently and independently). The reading can be magazines, mail, catalogs, newspapers, and, of course, books!
- Telling stories at dinnertime about family experiences or asking everyone at the table to tell one good thing that happened to them today. Help children to listen to others as well as to talk.
- Job chart for family (feed dog, water plants, clear table, empty garbage, set table…)
- Write thank you notes, birthday invitations, valentines, get well cards, name tags…
- Magnetic words on refrigerator, either homemade or bought. For homemade, use magnetic tape on the back of labels or cut up file cards.
- Photo sequences for replay of a vacation, zoo visit, birthday celebration, etc. Take photos and put them in plastic sleeves, put magnetic tape on the backs, and children can retell the events in sequence using the refrigerator or a file cabinet as their surface.
- Following directions for games, chores, cleanup, errands, or putting a toy together.
- Environmental print reading of cereal boxes, book covers, food labels, mail, coupons, big print ads in newspapers…
- Grocery list writing with child sitting next to you and watching you write as child says "Cheerios," "bananas," etc.

- <u>Coupons</u>: put children in charge of these in the store. They can match product to coupon or use for their own grocery list.

- <u>Listening</u> to tapes, conversations, directions, ideas…

- <u>Lemonade stand setup</u> with directions for mixing lemonade, drawing pictures, and copying words onto sign, counting money…

- <u>Making signs</u> for block/road play, grocery store, doctor's office, restaurant play (writing menus), place cards for table, signs on bedroom doors…

- <u>Planting garden</u> and observing growth and differences in leaves, "reading" seed packets, finding certain words on the seed packet, listening to the directions when read by adult, measuring each week and recording the growth…

- <u>Children "reading" books or telling stories</u> to siblings, parents, dolls, stuffed animals…

- <u>Telephone</u> literacy can begin with finding the first letter of a person's last name in the phone book; follow adult's finger as he or she scans pages for the whole name (which child has on a card); memorize numbers; speak on or answer phone; press buttons on phone to compute numbers. With cell phones, children not only see numbers on the keypad, but also on the screen.

- <u>Newspaper comic reading</u>. Children enjoy the color, brevity, sequence of pictures, and minimal number of words.

- <u>Magazine and newspaper sale ads</u> are good sources of pictures to discuss and can help children create their grocery wish list. Words are usually in big print.

- <u>Catalog "reading"</u> or matching pictures and words for toys on a birthday wish list. Catalogs also encourage interest in numbers, as children check the cost and page number of items.

- <u>Cooking</u> together offers many literacy opportunities. You can use the index to find recipes in a cookbook; the adult reads aloud the ingredients needed and the child gathers them; there's a progression/sequence of steps in preparing a recipe, children get to use various utensils for measurement (i.e., measuring cups and spoons), and help set the oven temperature and timer. Vocabulary includes ounces, pounds, grate, sliver, half, whole, etc.

- <u>Snack and meal preparation</u>: Serve alphabet cereal in a small cup for snack, alphabet noodles in soup, or straight pretzel sticks to form capital letters. Snacks and mealtime are also a fine time to have conversations, tell or read a story, and play with rhyming… I'd like some more cheese, please; I wish this apple of red was purple instead; I'm cutting my bread to look like a _____! Have fun with this.

- <u>Start a tradition</u> of telling family stories at dinner time

- A few ideas to <u>link snacks and/or desserts to a story</u>:
  - ➤ **Nursery Rhyme**<u>: Humpty Dumpty</u> – use eggs in a variety of ways: eggnog, egg boats (half a boiled egg with a cheese sail held in place with a toothpick), or hard-boiled eggs – encourage the children to peel them.
  - ➤ **Story**<u>: Peter Rabbit</u> – take half a pear, place it on a plate, and use half a banana slice lengthwise for the ears, toothpick whiskers, raisin eyes and nose. Put it on a bed of lettuce for a salad.
  - ➤ **Story**<u>: The Snowy Day</u> – cut three circles of whole wheat bread with a round cookie cutter. Spread cream cheese on each piece and create eyes, mouth, nose, and buttons with raisins, carrot rounds, or olives.
  - ➤ **Story**<u>: Mouse Paint</u> or <u>Seven Blind Mice</u> or <u>Give a Mouse a Cookie</u> – the pear works well with this snack too. Just turn it a different way and make little ears and tail with cheese.
  - ➤ **Story**<u>: The Three Bears</u> – make porridge and serve it in three differently sized bowls or cut bread with a bear-shaped cookie cutter and spread with peanut butter. Use a variety of healthy foods for features.
  - ➤ **Story**<u>: The Three Pigs</u> – wrap a hotdog in a piece of cheese and wrap both in a tortilla. Bake long enough for cheese to melt. Cut into three little pigs. The wolf could be a spoonful of black beans; houses could be grated cheese, pretzels, and Jell-O bricks. Literacy also involves listening to and following directions.
  - ➤ <u>A few other things to make together</u>:

    All of these foods require chopping, grinding, peeling, grating, or mixing. Children enjoy doing all of these! Keep it simple so the children can do the tasks as independently as possible.

    | | |
    |---|---|
    | orange juice | making soup |
    | mile shakes | creating sandwiches |
    | scrambled eggs | apple sauce |
    | lemonade | peanut butter |
    | fruit salad | butter |
    | granola | pudding |
    | peeling potatoes | grating cheese or carrots for salad |

An inventory listing other literacy opportunities in the community follows.

## Incidental Literacy Ideas in the Community:

There are a number of opportunities where literacy can be nurtured in the community. Here are locations and things to point out, observe, read, participate in or discuss while out and about.

### Bank
- write on deposit slips (name)
- counting money
- open/close signs in tellers' windows
- bank sign
- checks
- ATM screen "reading"
- letters, words, numbers on money
- calendar on wall or counter

### Doctor's Office
- read magazines in waiting room
- read eye chart
- listen to music
- fill out name on card for next visit
- sign in
- doctor writes symptoms
- prescription pad
- medical supply labels
- appointment book
- clock
- blood pressure numbers
- scales (height and weight)
- stethoscope (count heart beats for 1 min.)

### Supermarket
- find cereal that begins with F, L or Ch or W, etc.
- check out all of the price signs
- sequence of: put things in cart, check out, and pay
- concept of paying money for everything you put in the cart
- organization by categories – fruit, veggies, soup, cereal, meat, cheese...
- all the writing on the itemized receipt
- what is in the refrigerated section
- what can stay on the shelves
- different jobs: shelf stockers, checkers, manager, baggers
- different packages – boxes, bottles, jars, plastic bags...
- weighing items
- words on advertising
- words on items in cart
- child can have own shopping list
- signs for each aisle

### Toy and Department Stores
- labels for categories of toys
- individual names of toys on boxes
- sign/store name
- badges on employees
- prices on shelves
- bathroom signs (men/women)
- book section
- tapes and videos
- computer games
- aisles may be numbered
- check-out lane numbers
- shopping list before you go
- money/check/credit card
- lettering on shopping cart
- directory or map for locations
- receipt – words and numbers
- directions on game boxes
- music and/or talking toys
- categories of toys

## Car

- listening to car radio or tape
- talking about what you see out the car window
- singing songs together
- reading numbers of passing license plates
- keeping score of how many cars you see of one color
- road signs
- symbols for restaurants, gas station, etc.
- street names
- speedometer
- clock
- map reading
- following directions
- any writing in the car (gas gauge, numbers for radio stations...)
- talk about destination

## Airport

- exhibits
- up and down sign on escalators/elevators)
- exit signs
- job labels
- names of various airlines/symbols of airlines
- sizes of suitcases
- luggage tags
- stores, restaurants, menus
- levels of building/concourses
- map in train
- map of airport
- time/clocks/different time zones
- arrival/departure schedules
- talk to people
- women's/men's room (out of order or floor's wet signs)
- parking signs/letters for parking car

## School

- names of teachers on each door
- director's/principal's office sign
- check out books in school library
- conversation at snack/lunch
- writing on packages in lunch boxes
- write child a note for their lunch box
- cubbies/lockers/hooks with children's names
- brochures
- student art (discuss names, colors, shapes, themes)
- mailboxes in office or room
- clocks
- identifying all of the sounds
- license plates in the parking lot
- sign in/out

## Celebrations

- writing invitations
- make a list of items needed
- grocery shopping
- dial number if calling to invite guests
- recipes to prepare food/read
- make party favors
- plan games
- make list of people who RSVP
- name cards – write and put them out
- socializing/communicating
- deciding on theme of party
- music/movement/dancing (learning steps)
- looking at books for ideas/discuss

## Other places to be aware of literacy opportunities:

- walking downtown/mall/neighborhood
- restaurant
- laundromat
- movie theater

# *Chapter Six: Part II*

## THE JOURNEY WITH FAMILIES:
Options for Families and Teachers to Share Information

Inviting families to join the classroom journey

"A child's first source of identity is the family, so making family members part of the program provides both continuity and validation in the form of a child's positive concept."
–Ann S. Epstein

Families come in all sizes and configurations. They come from many different backgrounds and cultures. They have varied interests, ideas, and viewpoints. But they and we share one vital gift in common – the children! Just as it is important to have ways to present stories, it is important to find different ways to invite all families to come along on our Journeys.

Our aim is to engage all children in meaningful learning experiences through the extensive development of each Storybook Journey. Over the years, we have developed supportive ways to help families understand what we do in the classroom to achieve this goal. We have also found ways to ease families into feeling a part of their child's entry experience into the classroom. Some of these ideas may be familiar to you and, hopefully, some will give you a starting point to build upon.

**Home Visits**

Home visits can be one of the first ways to begin to build a relationship with the child and the family. They are especially helpful if they can be completed before the school year begins. In some cases when this is not possible, teachers have gone on home visits during the first couple of weeks after school has started. Children are most comfortable in their own home and enjoy seeing their teacher in this setting. It is fun to see what the children do at this first meeting. Some will want to show you their room, their collections, the dog, and whatever is special to them at the moment. Others will look you over in silence or disappear. For most children the home visit makes the transition from home to school a little easier when the child has had this one-to-one time with you.

Teachers have tried various ways to ease the child's introduction to their school by bringing pictures of the classroom to share, reading a book that they've brought with them from the classroom, or a small jar of bubbles to play with outside. One teacher always brings a finger puppet who tells them the things he loves about school. Bring anything you feel comfortable with to set the child at ease if this is his or her first "sighting" of a new teacher.

When you make your initial call to set up the visit, be aware that some families may not be comfortable having you come to their home. If you sense this hesitation, you will want to suggest an alternative. Some families prefer a neutral place such as a park, playground, school, or another place close to their home. The home visit also provides a good time to collect the required health records and any other paperwork that might be valuable for you to have.

**Transition Book**

Transitions are part of life, and children have their own unique ways of dealing with this process. Teachers and families can play a significant role in preparing children's transitions in advance and supporting them with concrete, meaningful information. Developing a book to introduce incoming children to your classroom can help them with the transition. The welcoming teacher can have a book ready for newcomers that will introduce the children to their future classroom. This book would be an excellent "transitional object" to leave behind on a home visit. (This might be possible with a digital camera and a printer to print multiple copies so each child could have one.) The child could look the book over later and ask her family questions, seek the familiar, and anticipate what to look forward to in the new setting. Photographs are a good way to familiarize children with a new place. Ideas to share might be gathered from the outgoing class. Ask them: "What do you think children coming here for the first time might like to know about this classroom?" Here are a few suggestions of what you might like to photograph:

- Each room in the school (to get the "big picture" of the layout)
- pets that live in the class (gerbils, fish, guinea pig)
- the bathroom
- personal places (i.e., cubbies or a project box for child's ongoing creations)
- water table
- loft
- materials (books, markers, puzzles, Lego, blocks, dolls, cars, easels)
- equipment (mini trampoline, climber, big balls, bikes)
- things to explore (beehives, ants, rocks)
- teachers, assistants, cooks, janitors, director/principal
- picture of school from the outside
- the playground, etc.

**Family Album**

Some schools have created a scrapbook or album that the children can share with one another. It holds pictures of the children's families. Each family is given a colored piece of paper and a plastic sleeve. They can use both sides of the paper for photos of their family, pets, extended family, good friends, or whatever the child and family choose to share. When they have completed their page, it is placed in the album. The album is very popular, especially at the beginning of the school year. The children like to look for their page and to share each other's photos too. Families are free to add to their album page all year long.

**A Space or Place for Families**

Providing a space for families depends on what is available in each school. It would be ideal to have a room where families could meet for a cup of coffee before heading to work or back home. The room could be a place to have a parent library, to hold meetings, have conferences, display children's artwork or projects, and do whatever else the families would find helpful in their pursuit of being informed parents and connected to other families.

When I first started teaching, I was in a struggling rural area of upstate New York. Our families were spread far apart and did not have a chance to get to know one another. I often wished I could have found an empty room where I could provide washing machines, a coffee pot, and a long table for folding laundry. Many of the families didn't have the luxury of a washing machine at home and neither did I. Just think of what the families could have learned from each other while folding their laundry and having a chance to be social. Handouts, books, and other materials could have been available to check out or keep. We could have been open during school hours and maybe one evening a week when I could join them! It is an idea I think about to this day.

Very few preschools have a room available, but many have a space set aside for parents. It could be a corner space, bookshelf, bulletin board, or mobile table or chalkboard to set up outside of the classroom each day. It could also be an empty wall by the sign-in sheet or out in the hall. It is a place to hang an article for parents to read, an announcement of community events for families, a list of places to take children for family activities, story times at the local library, special programs at the museum, medical information, and the like. The secret to creating such a space and having it used is to rotate the information! If the space is ever changing and full of information that is timely, interesting, relevant to families, translated in languages represented in the classroom, and eye-catching, it will succeed. It is extremely helpful if a parent is willing to take on this task.

**The Newsletter**

The newsletter is most effective when it is brief, allowing busy families to quickly review a synopsis of the children's past week at school. Highlight the events of the week to help families grasp the ongoing experiences in which their children are involved. It is particularly helpful before a new Journey starts to attach to the newsletter a write-up on the upcoming story. Some settings have successfully incorporated a translation into the family's first language or a taped version for nonreaders. (Families, libraries, universities, community colleges, volunteer organizations such as Rotary, Kiwanis, and religious organizations can often help locate people who can translate.)

The newsletter can also include the information that is presented on the bulletin board for those families who have children in carpools or who ride a school bus.

In today's world, e-mail will be especially helpful in relating all kinds of information to families

**Providing Experiences for Family Engagement**

"One of the key requirements for sustaining a successful program of family participation is a diversity of offerings that meet the various interests, needs, and aspirations of different families..." –Sergio Spaggiari

Research shows that when families model naturally occurring literacy events at home on a daily basis, their children have a foundation to build on that is a significant advantage when they start school. Children who see their families engaged in reading, writing, and communicating every day will attribute importance to these experiences and are more likely to want to emulate this behavior.

Families that are able to stay abreast of the classroom experiences can relate to the Journey and become involved in the process. The Journey is a voyage that encourages the family's playful adventures with story extensions at home. It inspires parents to feel a creativity they didn't know they had, or perhaps they had forgotten how creative they could really be! Many families have mentioned how story replay at home has brought out their own genuine playfulness and has provided moments of relief from the stresses of a hectic day at home or at work. One parent said she felt sharing the Journey with her child helped her to "reconnect to that child within." Story replay gives families something tangible to rekindle their joy in having meaningful memory-building experiences with their children.

As teachers, it is important to communicate the significance of engaging in activities at home and how they relate to what is happening in school. The family/school connection is vital to fostering a deeper understanding of the developing literacy process. The strength of the partnership between home and school can play a significant role in supporting the children's lifelong learning. For children who need more time to feel comfortable playacting a story character in school, home "practice" in the security of their family is very reassuring.

Teachers who have embraced the idea of living with one story in depth know that the experiences built around each story create a common classroom culture. They want to invite families to feel part of that culture and to join the Storybook Journeys and other literacy experiences.

In the beginning of the school year, you might put out a request through a letter or during the home visit to see if any of the families would like to participate in the classroom. You could list any of the following ideas and solicit other suggestions about how they might like to become involved in the life of the classroom.

Read or Tell a Story

Invite family members to read or tell the Journey story or a story of their choice at group time. Mom, Dad, siblings, or grandparents can make the arrangements to participate.

Tape a Story

- As an alternative, families may want to read or tell a story on tape. This is especially helpful if families have a great storyteller among them, but distance, logistics, or work schedules make it complicated to come into the classroom.
- Some schools have asked parents to tape a story from their own childhood that connects to the story the class is taking on a Journey. When a class was doing Charlie Needs a Cloak by Tomie dePaola, a mother offered to make a short tape on her childhood adventures with weaving. She told this story: Her mother was halfway through a priceless weaving project and left her loom for a lengthy phone call. When she returned, she found her "helpful" little daughter had taken her scissors and cut selected pieces of wool loops that were part of the design. It was a total disaster that was forgiven, but never forgotten.

Share a Hobby or Collection (connected to a story if relevant)

Many families have interesting hobbies or collections that they enjoy sharing with the children. They also have interesting stories of how they started these collections or hobbies.

Some collections that have been shared:

| | |
|---|---|
| shells | teddy bears and dolls |
| rocks | stamps |
| animal bones | buttons |
| coins | model airplanes |

Some hobbies that have been demonstrated:

| | |
|---|---|
| pottery making | pressing flowers |
| glass blowing | tissue collages |
| quilt making | woodworking |
| photography | cake decorating |

Share your Profession with Possible Story Connections

Most classrooms have parents with an interesting array of professions. It's helpful to know what professions are represented in your particular class so you can ask families if they'd be willing to come and share them with the children. If you are doing a story that has any connection to one of the represented professions…what a bonus!

A Colorado preschool classroom had a wonderful experience with a very involved father who was a detective by profession. When he heard the class was doing a Journey on The Gingerbread Boy, he offered to try to help out. He and the teacher decided that the class could place a "missing persons" report. The teacher gathered the class the morning after they baked cookies and told them that all of the gingerbread boys are gone – they were missing. She explained that she would call William's father to file a missing persons report because he was a detective. The children could hardly wait for him to arrive. He interviewed the class – what color eyes did the gingerbread boys have – any hair? What color? Ages? What were they wearing? (When the children said "nothing," he acted shocked). When and where were they last seen? It was a delightful experience for all involved. When the cookies were found, the detective ate one with the children while they asked endless questions about what he did on the job besides finding gingerbread boys!

Other profession/story connection possibilities:

- farmer – Over on the Farm – Christopher Gunson
- auto mechanic – Sheep in a Jeep – Nancy Shaw
- doctor/nurse – Curious George Goes to the Hospital – Margret and H. A. Rey
- veterinarian – Bark, George – Jules Feiffer
- dentist – Where the Sidewalk Ends – Shel Silverstein
- dog trainer – Harry the Dirty Dog – Gene Zion
- chef – In the Night Kitchen – Maurice Sendak

- hairdresser – <u>Dandelion</u> – Don Freeman
- artist – <u>The Legend of the Indian Paint Brush</u> – Tomie DePaola or <u>I Am an Artist</u> – Pat Collins
- teacher – <u>Miss Nelson is Missing</u> – James Marshall
- builder – <u>The Three Little Pigs</u>

If there is no story that relates to a parent's profession, just have the parent come and read to the children. If parents are firefighters, police officers, mail carriers, or in the armed services, suggest they wear their uniforms and explain why they wear or carry certain things. It might be interesting to have them show the children how the ability to read and write affects their jobs no matter what their profession (i.e., forms, reports, instructions, etc.). Imagine the power of this modeling for our youngest children!

<u>Participate at Snack and Group Time:</u>

Some programs invite parents to join the children for snack or lunch. Others have invited families that pick their children up at the end of the school day to join their children during the story and closure experience. It's very informal but gives parents a sense of the children in the class and the story presentation.

<u>Make a Special Snack:</u>

Now and then parents enjoy making a snack that relates to a story. Some ideas for this are:

- making butter with the children to spread on the wheat bread the <u>Little Red Hen</u> just took out of the oven
- making tortillas to go with <u>Big Moon Tortilla</u>, a beautiful story by Joy Cowley
- creating <u>Wild Things</u> with a rice cake, spread with cream cheese, humus, or peanut butter, carrot rounds or raisins for eyes, a red pepper slice for a mouth, and bean sprouts or grated carrots for wild hair. The ingredients are provided by the parent and each child gets to create his or her own. It's an added treat if the parent can stay for the fun!

## Story Replay:

Parents can be extremely helpful in locating certain props that might enhance or encourage creative replay. This might include costume jewelry for <u>Tough Boris'</u> treasure chest or the robbers in <u>Bremen Town Musicians</u>, a tent for <u>Daddy and Me</u> for their camping trip, an old bathtub for <u>King Bidgood's in the Bathtub</u>, or a spinning wheel for <u>Rumplestiltskin</u>.

## Pajama Night at the Library:

Pajama night can be such a fun way for families to get together. The children are in their pj's when they come to the public library for one or two stories. (Of course, this is arranged with the children's librarian ahead of time!) Cookies and milk could be served beforehand, then stories are read and then it's home to bed. Some schools have suggested that parents might want to get library cards for their children at this time.

## Potluck Supper:

Potluck suppers take more planning, but give families a way to combine their need for dinner with socializing with other parents. Many teachers have found that it is helpful to combine a brief meeting with dinner to catch parents up on what is happening in school. If possible, the children can go into a different room and have a short movie or story or sing-along with a staff member or responsible high school "caregivers."

## Ice Cream Social:

This is always a big hit! It's a dessert night at school with ice cream in a variety of flavors, different sauces, sprinkles, and other toppings. After the ice cream, the children sing a few of their favorite songs, act out a story, or show their art projects. Then they all head for home.

## Variation:

After the social gathering, a meeting can take place on a topic parents have chosen ahead of time. A lecturer, facilitator, staff member, or parent leader can lead the discussion. Some popular topics include:

| | |
|---|---|
| guidance of behavior | play date activities |
| bedtime routines | transitions |
| potty training | children's fears |
| healthy eating | books for children |
| sibling rivalry | books on parenting |
| separations and babysitters | unique issues in inclusive settings |

<u>The Following Ideas Can Flow from School to Home or From Home to School:</u>

The important point is that they are delightful ways to continue to engage families and connect us through our literacy pursuits together.

<u>Sally Rose Goes Home on Weekends:</u>

Sally Rose, named by a group of four-year-olds, is a stuffed bear that travels to a different home each weekend. She goes home in a special bag with a journal. The idea is for Sally Rose's "hosts" to record the adventures of Sally Rose while she is visiting the family. The special adventures recorded in the journal are then read to the class during Monday's group. One adventure was told through magazine pictures, as that was Molly's only way to communicate her experience of washing Sally Rose in the washing machine. Molly's mother came to class to assist in telling about the experience from Sally Rose's point of view. The children were intrigued. In other adventures Sally Rose was carried off by the family dog, left at McDonald's all night, and taken shopping for some new pajamas.

<u>Story Retellers:</u>

- Many settings have developed "take home retellers" to be lent out to interested families. The retellers are a collection of props families can use for telling stories the class has taken on a Journey. It can be a miniature world of story characters, a small flannel board with character pieces, puppets, or magnetic characters for replay on the refrigerator door, a cookie sheet, or the side of a metal filing cabinet. These materials can be checked out or sent home.
- Commercial tapes or stories read on tape by parents or teachers can be sent home with the companion book as well.

<u>Suggestions to Think about When Making "Story Retellers"</u>:

Instructions for making the various kinds of story retellers (i.e., flannel boards, miniature worlds, magnetic characters, etc.) can be found in chapter five, entitled Props for the Journey.

- remember to make materials durable and aesthetic
- have "spare parts" available
- losses and breakage are to be anticipated
- cover books that accompany tapes with clear contact paper or take books apart and enclose each page in plastic Baggies. Use rings to hold books together
- explore garage sales, store closures, and end-of-conference/convention closeouts to gather miniature pieces to use for the story retellers
- attach to a <u>strong</u> Baggie full of pieces a list of the items that are to be returned
- encourage families to use what they may have at home e.g., three stuffed bears and a small doll for Goldilocks or three differently sized rocks for bears and jar lids for bowls
- some settings have enclosed paper, crayons, fur scraps, and other materials in a Baggie (relevant to the story) for puppet or book making
- tapes and books can be created in the languages represented in the class. Universities, libraries, and religious organizations often have people who can tap resources necessary to help with translation.

<u>Lending Library</u>:

The lending library is a wonderful resource for parents and children! You can seek donations to buy books or scrounge at garage sales, bookstore closures, and secondhand bookstores. Set up a process for checking books out and alert families about when they are expected to return them. Have every book in a Baggie. It saves wear and tear on the books.

<u>Family Memories</u>:

It might be fun to tape-record or write a story from each family about an interesting incident in the early life of their child. These stories can be listened to or made into a book with photos or drawings to be shared at school. Children can listen to the tape and look at the pictures together. The stories can also be read to the children individually or in small groups.

Children love to hear stories about their beginnings and early years. It's fun to share how children's names were chosen, their first words, favorite stories, and funny incidents. Told at bedtime, these stories are particularly soothing and a wonderful means of sharing a child's family history. Some parents find it helpful to give a tape of these stories to a baby-sitter to play at bedtime.

My children used to love to hear about the time our dog, Josephine, delivered seven puppies between the kitchen and the backyard. After building a special pen for the puppies in a hallway, our three-year-old son decided to be Josephine's eighth puppy. He quietly got up very early one morning, slipped into the pen, curled up in the middle of all the puppies and fell asleep. When our daughter, aged four, decided to join him, the puppies woke up and the wild rumpus began!

Childhood Memories:

Childhood memories of parents, teachers, and other important adults in the children's lives are also fun to record. Memories about pets, friends, siblings, houses, family, playtimes, or experiences growing up in foreign countries or on a farm, ranch, or in the city are also possibilities. (When I was teaching kindergarten, the children loved to hear about my childhood camping trip when a porcupine crawled up on my sleeping bag during the night and stayed there until I let out a loud sneeze in the early morning.)

Video/CD Creation:

- A group of parents gathered one evening in the preschool to produce a videotape of Three Billy Goats Gruff" for their children. They dressed up in makeshift costumes, set up their homemade props, and carried on like their kids. There was much self-conscious laughter at first, but after a trial run, the parents became hams! One mother played the narrator and introduced herself as Laura's mother. Everyone followed suit with the introduction: "I am Billy's father, but today I am also the Biggest Billy Goat Gruff." It was marvelous fun for the parents that night. However, when we showed the tape to their children the next day, the children seemed nonplussed! We think the costumes disguised the parents so well the children couldn't tell which one was their parent. It's probably a good idea to make sure costumes do not obscure faces when creating for very young viewers. If you think the children are ready to comprehend disguises, have parents put on the face paint, mask, and so on in full view of the camera so the children can see the transformation.

- A video camera was also used when a teacher filmed her class acting out story of <u>Corduroy</u> bear. The teacher made a copy of the video and included it in the lending library with a copy of the book. Families could check this out and be able to see their child's class in action. The children loved it because they could show their parents their friends as well as themselves acting out the story. Parents who came to school infrequently could feel more a part of their child's school life. This strategy is another pleasurable chance to embed the story sequence and meaning into a child's experience.

<u>Photo Stories:</u>

Photo albums containing selected pictures from the children's own lives coupled with simple memories and short stories are a beautiful introduction to or extension of their literacy and emotional experiences. One family expanded this idea by coordinating an audiotape with the album. Family members told stories to go along with the photos and sang "turn the page now" when it was time to move on to the next episode. Extensions of such an album would depend on the children's interests and the wonderful ingenuity of parents. Sharing ideas will help families who might need encouragement or inspiration to use simple experiences from their child's unique life as a meaningful literacy adventure.

<u>Songs as Stories:</u>

Songs and music are a universal form of communication. They break down language barriers. Songs are stories set to music and their beat and lilt invite people to participate in a comfortable way. Writing out song lyrics in more than one language and sending home a tape of songs in the various languages represented in the classroom encourage cultural exchange and sharing. Parents, children, teachers, friends, or relatives can draw or collect pictures to accompany the words of various songs, especially if the subject matter is foreign to a particular culture.

I remember that when I was a child, a French friend of my grandmother told me a story about an old man organ grinder and his trick monkey. She sang in French about the monkey's life in the streets of France. I was fascinated. Though I didn't understand a word of French, I loved the song and understood the gist because she told me "the story" first. Joining in to sing the refrain of a song is a wonderful way of learning a few key words (or tunes) in English or another language.

One Word at a Time:

How about a vocabulary section of the newsletter where a new word from the story or from classroom experiences is introduced? Families can work it into their conversations at home and teachers can do the same in school. A list of such words or signs can be kept at school to be worked into our daily lives in the classroom. Building a vocabulary relevant to the children's experiences will be ever so helpful as they learn to read and write.

Checking out books from the lending library

Families join their child for closing circle time

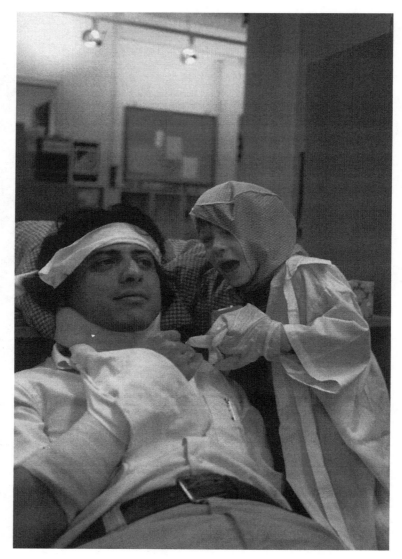

Dr. Dad is now the patient for a few minutes while dropping his child off at school.

Parents creating a literacy box at an evening workshop

Mother coming in at storytime to be goldilocks.

Storybook journey night for fathers

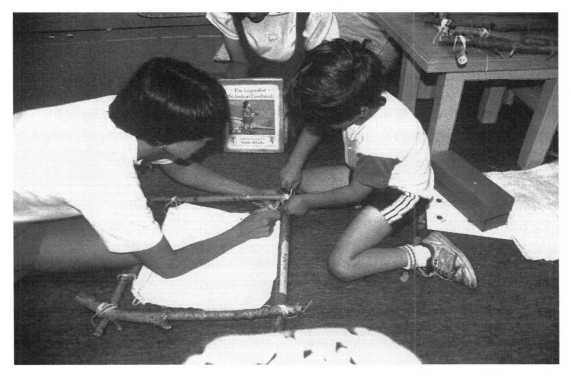

Visiting mother, artist working with child on making a canvas for a painting project.

**Representing and celebrating each child's personal journey**

"Our own knowledge of the individual child, his or her developmental stage, and unique set of strengths and weaknesses, braveries and fears will guide us in our task together…" –Rita M. Warren

Building a curriculum around the interests and play of young children requires carefully developed skills of observing, listening, note taking, and reflecting upon what children are revealing through their words, experiences, and behavior. Our observations and other information gathering guide our understanding of each child, provide the blueprints for constructing our plans for the Journey, direct how we plan the environment and provide raw materials for exploration, and give us the information we want to share and celebrate with each family.

The idea of sharing our documentations of each child as a celebration was a suggestion from a teacher in an inclusive preschool setting. She is a teacher who understands the importance of establishing relationships that are accepting and trusting with the families. Her respect for every child's attempt to learn is shared in her family interactions with a sense of celebration. She observes carefully and can find something joyful to share with each child's family. The relationships that she has built with families over the school year allow for both the celebration and the discussion of any sensitive issues she and the family have to share with each other.

The critical aspect of establishing trust and mutual understanding with families relies on our ability to build sincere relationships with them. This can be a challenge at any time; however, with most parents working and a troubled economy the challenge is even greater to find the quality time to build these relationships. Teachers and families will need to reach out and find ways to support each other. We want to encourage families to participate in their child's learning at school and at home, as this will have positive ramifications all through the children's school years.

In this section, we have gathered a few unique ideas for the collection of important data that might be interesting to include in the conference in celebration of a child's personal journey.

**The Video Journal**

A video journal is an extremely helpful form of a "visual journal." Various moments in each child's life in the classroom over the course of the year are documented on their personal videotape. The videotape is labeled with the child's name and a place to record the dates when the footage was recorded. The tapes and video camera are placed on a shelf in the classroom for easy access. When a child is engaged in working on a project or acting out a story with peers, the camera can capture a bit of the activity. When it feels relevant the person taping can comment while filming (as long as the child isn't speaking) to narrate the significance of the moment. This is an excellent documentation tool for reviewing and discussing a child's development during a staff meeting and for sharing with a parent during the celebration conference.

There are <u>important</u> steps to take before a teacher ventures into this form of documentation:

- Families <u>must be</u> informed that you would like to do this form of documentation.
- Families should be assured that these tapes will be used <u>only</u> for staff review and for the family during the celebration conference.
- Families will sign an agreement to allow the taping of their child with the assurance that the sole copy of the tape is theirs at the end of the year.
- If a particular tape would be beneficial for teaching purposes, i.e., to use as an example of development in an early childhood course or workshop, written permission from the parents will have to be obtained.

Some families will be reluctant to have their child videotaped. Make sure to meet with them and explain the process and value inherent in this form of documentation. Listen to their concerns and respect their feelings if they do not want to participate.

**Wonder Books**

The Wonder Book can be thought of as a mini traveling documentation panel. It has been so named because children have such a beautiful sense of wonder about everything and such magical ways of inviting us into their experiences. It has also been so named because parents wonder what their children have been doing in school all day. The Wonder Book is a meaningful way to capture and document the spontaneous and planned learning experiences of children that occur during the life of a Storybook Journey or any other engaging experiences.

Wonder Books can be made in notebooks with plastic sleeves or any other form as long as the photographs are protected. The photographs are arranged to show the progression of the Journey and the children's engagement with learning. A written text is developed to share the essence of the experiences, and to explain what may not be obvious to families or others who view the book.

Families can check out the Wonder Book over the weekend. It is a tangible way for busy families to share the Journey, as it can be part of the bedtime reading. It is a comfortable closure for the day as the children can revisit the experience and share what holds meaning to them. When parents can share this type of experience with their child the potential for them becoming more interested and invested in their child's learning is obvious.

Children revisit and reflect on their experiences when the book returns to the classroom book nook. It is a popular item long after the class has finished a Journey and a wonderful way to keep the memories alive! It is strongly recommended that you make two copies in the event a Wonder Book gets lost, damaged in transition, or is loved until it is "dog-eared."

**Tell Me a Story**

The teachers in the Child Learning Center tried an experiment that might be interesting for other teachers to experience. It is a unique way to document a specific ability. During the weekly staff meeting, one of the staff members was wondering if the group would like to do a little casual unscientific "research" with the morning class of four-year-olds. She was interested in exploring the children's concept of story. Everyone thought it was worth a try so they brainstormed and devised a plan. The plan was to set up a "bedroom" where each child, one at a time, would tuck the teacher (Marilyn) into bed and tell her a bedtime story. Marilyn would say to each child something along the lines of "Before I go to sleep, could you tell me a story?"

The classroom has a small room that is used for dramatic play and various other things during the year. It was the perfect place to set up for the experiment. The equipment in the room was stored in the hall for a few days while the makeshift bedroom was created and in use. Marilyn told the children about the idea at group time two days before the experiment. In that way the children could think about the idea, ask questions as a group, and take part in preparing the room.

The children were game, and had a grand time moving everything that wasn't needed out of the room and assisting Marilyn in setting up her "bedroom." There was a covered mattress, pillow, quilt, makeshift night table, and lamp. A video camera was also set up on a tripod in the corner of the room. This camera was frequently used in the classroom so the children were oblivious to it when the experiment started.

The following day, Marilyn showed the room to all of the children again and explained that each child would have a chance to come into the room and tell her a bedtime story. She told them she would shut the door and that they could knock…one at a time…and she would invite them in. She slipped a nightgown over her clothes, turned on the camera, crawled in to bed, and waited for the first knock on the door.

The results exceeded our expectations. Some children wanted another child to come along, which worked well. In some cases, it gave the more reluctant child a chance to see what was going on before his or her turn. Most of the children, however, knocked…walked in…shut the door… and sat somewhere on the bed. The stories ranged from various renditions of the storybooks they had taken on a Journey, to the story of one child's scary dream, an original tale about a sad dinosaur, and to a child who came to the door, knocked and left. The final storyteller created a scrambled rambling that combined Red Riding Hood and Papa Bear. This precious child, with significant challenges, told his story:

"Red Hood…she go to woods…she come home! Out bed I said…" (He got up from the bed and with hands on his hips shouted at Marilyn.) "OUT BED SAY PAPA BEAR!"
Marilyn: "Your shouting is scaring me. Are you trying to tell me to get out of this bed?"
Child: "Yes!" He goes over to her and gently pats her on the head and whispers, "The end." They leave the room hand in hand.

Having the stories on videotape, gave the staff a chance to transcribe them and learn what basic components of a story the children might use in this "casual research." They looked for the inclusion of:

- a title
- beginning, middle, end
- semblance of a plot
- named characters
- originality
- creative variations of known stories

They were also interested in vocabulary and sentence structure.

Using the tapes for documentation of this experience helped the staff predict how to support, engage, and extend the evolving process of learning to reach each child's potential.

This was such a delightful way for the teacher to spend time with each child and to gain valuable insights. No test could ever have revealed so much about the uniqueness of each child's physical presence, temperament, confidence, affect, thought process, or charmingly individual personality! Each child's story was a wonderful addition to his or her portfolio or video journal. It was also a memorable moment to share with families during the celebration conference.

It might be interesting at this point to compare the Storybook Journey process to the process of joining families in a yearlong partnership with their child's teacher. In both cases, we want to create a journey that develops over time and provides a variety of meaningful experiences. In school, we share the story as our common thread with the children and provide many choices for them to live and relive each story. With families, we share their child as our common thread. We encourage them to come along and live their child's journey with us by introducing and providing a variety of options for them to be participants. The family's final role is the final conference and celebration over the year.

This celebration can be combined with the Focus observations, Focused portfolio documentations, and the Performance Standards recordings written up in chapter seven. This combination provides the families and teachers with extensive options that will offer families a rich understanding of their child's life at school.

Celebrating A Child's Personal Journey is the culminating event of our documentation gatherings to be shared with families. Time is set aside twice a year to celebrate with each family the growth of their child during the school year. It is an invitation to come and contribute to each other's knowledge of the child we share as the child attempts to navigate life at home as well as at school.

Having the ability to gather, interpret, and share what we believe to be a representation of each child's development in all domains is a skill one learns from experience. Families will appreciate the opportunity to have their child's way of learning at school described through your observations of their child's:

- play schemas
- disposition to learn and style of learning
- ability to regulate emotions
- evolving interests
- pursuit of peer relationships
- experimentation with ideas
- physical capabilities and challenges
- stamina to persist when frustrated

Children also demonstrate their learning through their work, and that work represents what they know or are trying to learn. However, most of the children's work will have traveled home with them long before the celebration meeting with families. Therefore, it is wise for us to take photographs or videotapes of a project in its stages of development whenever possible. We can then discuss the <u>process</u> the child went through to create his or her project. This is important information for families. Many times, they receive the glob of wood scraps, glue, and paint and have no idea what effort went into their "masterpiece" or what learning transpired. Some families will understand this or their child will be able to explain how and what they created. Other families will need help to see the learning process beyond the "globby" product that arrived home in a crumpled paper bag.

The emphasis in the celebration is on the most positive aspects of a child's classroom journey. As in any passage through a child's life, however, there will also be the "bumps." This is where the celebration becomes collaboration. We want to sensitively discuss with families any issues that may be disrupting the child's ability to learn or socialize. At some point in the conversation, it might be wise to build an awareness that a child's disposition and capacity to learn can be deeply affected by his or her emotions and personality. Our aim is not only to celebrate but also to share the more sensitive or difficult information so the children will have whatever support and guidance they need both at home and at school.

It is important for us to be aware of the fact that all families may not share our basic philosophy or beliefs about how children learn best. These differences could be based on cultural perspectives, socioeconomic conditions, and parents' experiences or their educational backgrounds. Some families might be afraid that "play "is not giving their child the tools he or she will need for the schooling that lies ahead. The challenge for teachers is to articulate and demonstrate through the tangible examples they have available, the value and depth of learning through play. Play encourages children to rehearse, practice, and master what they're motivated to learn.

Teachers celebrating with families will want to share verbal examples, videotapes, portfolios, audiotapes, or any other tangible evidence of a child's learning through play in the classroom. Edward Miller (2009), who is Program Director of Alliance for Childhood in New York City, has written: "Engagement in rich dramatic play and make believe play is directly related to the development of literacy as well as social skills, empathy, imagination, self control, and higher levels of thinking. Child-initiated play is where children are more likely to exercise their oral language skills!"

In the Celebration, it is important to emphasize how children will seek out ways to express themselves through their play. Share with families that our task is to provide the environment that encourages the children to sing, dance, draw, paint, sculpt, collect, make friends, move, transform, discover, and build as they playfully search for "the language" that suits their chosen form of expression. Zorba the Greek said it just right: "Oh if you could dance all that you've just said then I'd understand!" This quote is a delightful reminder that if we listen and observe carefully children will reveal the "language" which serves them best.

As teachers and families, we sometimes need to be reminded that children know how to celebrate and learn through the simple things in life, including the everyday wonders that may go unnoticed in our busy lives. Can we remember how to be more playful and spontaneous ourselves and join the children in their curious pursuits? The outdoor world provides one of the richest classrooms on earth. It is so rewarding to be with children as they watch the ants on the dirt mound. Get down with them and see what fascinating discoveries they make. Join them when they walk in someone's footprints in the snow and see where they lead you. Watch the spider weaving her web and marvel how she knows just what to do!

These simple acts are like looking through a kaleidoscope. Ordinary things take on new dimensions when we explore them through a child's eyes. Their sense of wonder is contagious and if we're willing we can "catch it" and learn along with them in their endless playful explorations.

Children demonstrate what they know best only through a process that speaks to them and makes sense to them. They attach something they have experienced to new information in order to scaffold learning to the next level.

As teachers of young children, we can begin to reveal, from our classroom experiences, the nature of these exquisite children in all of their diversity. We can demonstrate and celebrate their individuality, interests, style of learning, creative expression, playful spirit, and personality by gathering our information through a variety of means. These means capture the essence of each child in significant moments. These are the moments we will want to share with each family.

# REFERENCES AND RELATED READINGS

Allen, J. (2007). *Creating Welcoming Schools: A Practical Guide to Home School Partnerships with Diverse Families.* New York, NY: Teachers College Press.

Bergen, D. (1994). *Assessment Methods for Infants and Toddlers: Transdisciplinary Team Approach.* New York, NY: Teachers College Press.

Bredekamp, S. and Rosegrant, T. (Eds). (1995). *Reaching Potentials: Vol. 2 Transforming Early Childhood Curriculum and Assessment.* Washington, DC: National Association for the Education of Young Children.

Brett, D. (1988). *Annie Stories: A Special Kind of Storytelling.* New York, NY: Workman Publishing.

Bromfield, R. (2000). *Handle with Care: Understanding Children and Teachers. A Field Guide for Parents and Educators.* New York, NY: Teachers College Press.

Carini, P. (2001). *Starting Strong: A Different Look at Children, School, and Standards.* New York, NY: Teachers College Press.

Carson, R. (1956). *The Sense of Wonder.* New York, NY: Harper & Row.

Cohen, S. Stern, V., and Balaban, N.(1997). Observing and Recording the Behavior of Young Children, Fourth Edition. New York, NY: Teachers College Press.

Copple, C. and Bredekamp, S. (Eds.) (2009). *Developmentally Appropriate Practice,* Third Edition. Washington, DC: National Association for the Education of Young Children.

Curtis, D. and Carter, M. (2000). The Art of Awareness: How Observation Can Transform your Teaching. St. Paul, MN: Redleaf Press.

DeBruin-Parecki, A. (2008). *Effective Early Literacy Practice: Here's How, Here's Why.* Baltimore, MD: Paul H. Brookes Publishing Co., p. 87.

Edelman, M. W. (1992). *The Measure of Our Success: A Letter to my Children and Yours.* Boston, MA: Beacon Press.

Edwards, P.A. (1995). Combining Parents' and Teachers' Thoughts About Storybook Reading at Home and School. In L.M. Morrow (Ed.). *Family Literacy: Multiple Perspectives to Endorse Literacy Development.* Newark, DE: International Reading Association.

Edwards, C.; Gandini, L.; and Forman, G. (Eds). (1993). *The Hundred Languages of Children.* Norwood, NJ: Ablex.

Fox, M. (2001). *Reading Magic: Why Reading Aloud to our Children Will Change Their Lives Forever.* New York, NY: Harcourt, Inc.

Fox, M. (1993). *Radical Reflections: Passionate Opinions on Teaching, Learning, and Living*. New York, NY: Harcourt Brace & Company.

Gronlund, G. (1998). *Portfolios as an Assessment Tool: Is Collection of Work Enough? Young Children*. May 1988. Washington, DC: National Association for the Education of Young Children.

Gronlund, G. and Engel, B. (2001). *Focused Portfolios: A Complete Assessment for the Young Child*. St. Paul, MN: Redleaf Press.

Gullo, D. (2005). *Understanding Assessment and Evaluation in Early Childhood Education* (2nd Edition). New York, NY: Teachers College Press.

Healy, J. M. (1990). *Endangered Minds: Why Children Don't Think and What We Can Do About It*. New York, NY: Simon & Schuster.

Healy, J. M. (1999). *Failure to Connect: How Computers Affect our Children's Minds and What We Can Do About it*. New York, NY: Simon & Schuster.

Helm, J. H. Beneke, S. and Steinheimer, K. (2007). *Windows on Learning: Documenting Young Children's Work*, Second Edition. New York, NY: Teachers College Press.

Himley, M. (Ed.) with Carini, P. (2000). From *Another Angle: Children's Strengths and School Standards*. New York, NY: Teachers College Press.

Howes, C. and Ritchie, S. (2002). A Matter of Trust: Connecting Teachers and Learners in the Early Childhood Classroom. New York, NY: Teachers College Press.

Martin, W. (1999). *The Parent's Tao Te Ching: Ancient Advice for Modern Parents*. New York, NY: Marlowe and Company.

Miller, E. P. (May/June 2009). Harvard Magazine, Inc., Cambridge, MA, p. 4.

Rogers, C. S. and Sawyers, J. K. (1988). *Play in the Lives of Children*. Washington, DC: National Association for the Education of Young Children.

Trelease, J. (1985). *The Read-Aloud Handbook*. New York, NY: Penguin Books.

Zigler, E. F. (Ed.) (2004). *Children's Play: The Roots of Reading*. Washington, DC: Zero to Three Press.

Let me introduce you to Kathy Stewart, the author of this chapter on the Early Learning Standards. Kathy is the Director of Saint Saviour's Nursery School in Old Greenwich, Connecticut. She has been a devoted advocate for the Storybook Journey for a long time, both as a teacher and currently as a full time administrator. She admits, however, that she will always be a teacher of young children first; she is unable to contain her interest in what is happening in the classroom! This will become obvious as you read this chapter.

Kathy is an educator who caught on quickly to the magic of the Storybook Journey and what it can bring to children and families. She has worked closely with her staff as they developed rich and involved journeys that engage children in extended experiences with an array of wonderful stories.

Kathy has provided community-wide development opportunities which have afforded her the chance to know and consult with inspiring educators such as Vivian Paley and Gaye Gronlund. Kathy and her staff have taken these inspirations and interlaced them with the Journey to further enrich the lives of children. When Kathy told me that she and the teachers had been weaving the Early Childhood Standards into the Journey planning, I immediately asked her if she would write this important chapter. I am eternally grateful to her, as this will give authenticity to your own work with children and families. Your observations of the children's engagement with the stories and their connection with the Journey through all aspects of their development will be well documented with this intentional process.

# Chapter Seven

Weaving Early Learning Standards into the Storybook Journey: The Personal Journey of One Nursery School

# *Weaving Early Learning Standards into the Storybook Journey:*

**THE PERSONAL JOURNEY OF ONE NURSERY SCHOOL**

Kathy Stewart, Director, Saint Saviour's

Wikipedia defines weaving as textile art in which two distinct threads, called the warp and the weft, are interlaced to form a fabric or cloth. We visualize the Storybook Journey as a loom, a framework for and provider of necessary, durable, and quite beautiful fabrics, none identical. In our analogy, the "warp threads" stretching from one end of the loom to the other are the avenues of exploration that we follow. The weft threads, woven in and out of these explorations, are our early learning standards. Weaving these threads together creates an unforgettable tapestry of learning.

**<u>Our experience in weaving early learning standards
into the Storybook Journey curriculum</u>**

**What was in place? The Storybook Journey curriculum and classroom observation**

St. Saviour's Nursery School (SSNS) is an NAEYC-accredited nursery school located in Connecticut. We were fortunate to find the Storybook Journey over ten years ago. It struck an immediate chord and we jumped right in. The richness of the Journey and its results in the classroom have more than justified our initial and continuing enthusiasm. In our first year using this curriculum, my colleagues and I shared thrilling moments as the ideas of children came to life and became community-building, enriching, integrated learning opportunities. These moments remain vivid memories today. One such memory recalls a class of three-year-olds sharing a journey with <u>The Gingerbread Baby</u>. One child had the idea of capturing the gingerbread baby. After much consideration and exploration, a "trap" emerged. Assembled from construction paper, and trailing masses of tape, it was indubitably a mechanism for trapping. Even more important, it was a master creation in the firing of imagination. In the days that followed, traps of all types and designs grew and could be found in the most unlikely corners of the room, trailing string, yarn, colored tape, construction paper, foil, cloth, and other materials. Children cut, measured, attached, tied, considered, and rejected trapping areas, and tried to avoid trapping themselves. It was magic, the magic of real enjoyment coupled with excited, communal learning. The third edition of <u>Developmentally Appropriate Practice</u> reminds us that "learning experiences are integrated and meaningful when children work on projects and other studies in which they can see the connections between concepts and skills they encounter." Like Archimedes, we want to shout, "Eureka!" We have found it, The Storybook Journey, and we want to share it with all teachers of young children.

Recognizing the importance of observation as a foundation skill of our professional practice, about a decade ago we began a comprehensive review of our system of observation. We found that we didn't have an observation process that all staff members used systematically. It was hit or miss in the classroom. We recognized that we needed to restructure observation and that observation needed to be a school-wide pursuit. How to begin? Observation is a skill that must be practiced and cultivated. We became comfortable observing children in different ways throughout the child's program day and recording the observations "in the moment." Observations do not occur in a quiet, peaceful location. They occur in the organized chaos of a classroom. We did not let this deter us from our goal. We soon found that the knowledge gained from our observations was worth the effort.

As we began to make recorded observation an intentional part of our day, each teacher wore a half apron with pockets, one of which held "sticky" Post-it notes and a pen for writing anecdotes. While supervising a classroom, we reached for the pad of Post-it notes and hastily scribbled a short conversation between two children or the details of a dramatic play scenario. Then we slapped the note onto the back of the sticky pad and thrust it back into an apron pocket for later perusal and, with our pad ready for the next observation, our day went on. This became a natural part of our day. Observations became a part of our everyday practice throughout the year and for every child.

Teachers worked to ensure that their observations were meaningful and nonjudgmental. A true observation is what a child says or does, what we see or hear, *and only that*. It was important to remember the maxim, "Is it cute, or does it count?" We want to document the moments that count. To enhance the written observations, we bought a digital camera for each classroom. A digital photo printer placed in the common corridor outside the classrooms was easily accessible. Where possible, photos were taken to illustrate an observation. In prior years, teachers had collected work samples, but now we tried to match them to written and photographic observations.

As our observation skills developed, we focused our attention on a workable system of recording the observations. Our early record-keeping collections were quite simple. We set up a notebook with a section for each child in the class and inserted in each child's section log sheets, formatted to separate the developmental domains. To avoid tedious recopying of our observations, we simply transferred the sticky notes to this form. A sample copy of the form we used is appended to the end of this chapter.

These observations were shared among the teaching team at weekly planning meetings, providing food for ongoing reflection and development of curriculum that would guide the child's next steps. Before we knew it, we found that we could not teach without recording observations; we realized what they added to our practice and to our understanding of the children. Observation became satisfying in a deeply personal way.

*When starting to utilize standards, training for all our staff members was a necessity.*

Rather than design a national framework of early learning standards, the National Association for the Education of Young Children (NAEYC) has supplied guidelines for what effective standards should include. Their guidelines are as follows:

1. Effective early learning standards emphasize significant, developmentally appropriate content and outcomes;

2. Effective early learning standards are developed and reviewed through informed, inclusive processes;

3. Early learning standards gain their effectiveness through implementation and assessment practices that support all children's development in ethical, appropriate ways; and

4. Effective early learning standards require a foundation of support for early childhood programs, professionals, and families.

Each state has had the task of designing a framework of early learning standards. When the State of Connecticut first published the CT Preschool Curriculum Framework in 1999, and followed this publication a couple of years later with the companion CT Preschool Assessment Framework, we did not work to incorporate them into our curriculum immediately. Even with observation in place, our initial, informal, exploration brought an immediate and hesitant reaction, "How will we accomplish all this?" Eventually, we scheduled a training session with a state "trainer," recognizing that it's easy to fall victim to visions of "overload" and do nothing at all.

Training provided a turning point in our understanding of the rationale behind the standards and sparked our willingness to incorporate them into the Storybook Journeys in process in our classrooms. Once we dipped our toes into the material, we found that the basic elements made eminent good sense. As we became increasingly familiar with the standards, and the benchmarks that point out the expected sequence of progress within the standards, our comfort level grew, along with a sense that this direction is "right" for early childhood education.

### Weaving the standards into the Storybook Journey, the threads are chosen

Which comes first, the chicken or the egg, the Storybook Journey or the early learning goals? As coherence and depth of study are key goals in our classrooms, we made the choice of Storybook Journey our initial decision. Our teachers are intentional in the selection of Storybook Journeys, choosing rich stories with multiple avenues of exploration and giving due consideration to the needs and interests of the children. When we started to explore meshing the early learning goals of the curriculum framework with our Storybook Journey plans, we found the early learning standards fit the emerging avenues of the Storybook Journey neatly and easily. Observing the children's response to the story, we discovered the avenues of exploration that interested them. Weaving several standards into the exploration of the story was and is effortless and natural.

When we embark on a Journey, we select three complementary goals or early learning standards that are meaningful in the context of the Journey. These goals join our storybook in the center of our planning web. We plan activities for the classroom centers that allow the children to work toward these goals while exploring the story avenues that interest them. Observations are made; goals are achieved. Early learning standards and the Storybook Journey work together and provide a seamless experience for the children. Because activities are not planned out of context, but are integrated into the discovery that is engaging the children, the child's day makes sense to him or her. This interconnected experience allows the children to build knowledge while being absorbed in the process. At the same time, by working together within the Journey experience, the class grows more cohesive. The sense of community builds even while the Journey simultaneously supports independent ideas of individual children. Children with special needs are engaged and become integrally involved in the community.

### *Vignettes*

The best way to illustrate the process of combining the Storybook Journey with early learning standards is to provide a series of vignettes from the actual classrooms. It is difficult to choose specific Journeys to best illustrate this process, as there are so many successful candidates. However, as the essential point is that early learning standards can be woven into **any** Journey, perhaps it will be most effective to describe the three Journeys currently in process at our school. These Journeys were not chosen or initiated as an illustration for this chapter; there was no "staging" involved. The Journeys were planned and are being implemented by the teaching team, just as any journey they undertake is planned and implemented. This demonstrates that standards are easily incorporated into any Storybook Journey, not just a special few. The Journey remains fluid, following the interests of the children, and exploration is deep and meaningful. Observation of the children, focused on several chosen standards, supplies authentic documentation of the children's growth and the feedback necessary for effective planning as the Journey evolves. Just as we are weaving the early learning standards designed by the State of Connecticut into our curriculum, the early learning standards of any state can be similarly integrated. The Journey makes this possible, sustaining the child's engagement in learning opportunities and providing the backdrop against which learning is measured.

Readers may process how the standards become a natural companion to the curriculum in different ways. For that reason, I will reference the standards differently in each of the classroom / curriculum descriptions that follow.

### A Four-Year-Old Classroom – Never-Never-Land

Never-Never-Land recently began a journey into the beautiful Caldecott Honor Book, <u>A Chair for My Mother</u>, by Vera B. Williams. In this story, a young girl named Rosa, her mother (a waitress), and her grandmother have moved to a new apartment after a fire destroys their old apartment and everything in it. Far from a tragedy, this is a story of the power of kindness and persistence. Neighbors come to their aid with basic necessities; however, they no longer have a comfortable chair in their home. Rosa, her mother, and her grandmother work together, saving their coins in "the biggest jar" they can find at the diner where Rosa's mother works. Eventually the jar fills and they buy "the chair they were dreaming of," a chair in which a mother can find comfort in moments of fatigue and a mother and daughter can find security in each other's love as they snuggle together.

I walked into the classroom yesterday. One child's mother and grandmother stood at the large table near the sink making onigiri, or "rice balls," with the children. At a nearby "snack" table, several children were eating their second rice ball with gusto, chattering about the process of dipping their hands in water, having a bit of salt sprinkled over their hands, and manipulating the rice into a ball.

A thriving restaurant scene was taking place in the dramatic play center. The center was rear-ranged to provide a remarkably effective diner with a narrow galley kitchen and a table set for customers. Props lent by an actual diner (menus in small plastic sleeves, order pads, etc.) added to the realistic effect.

I wandered in and was immediately asked if I'd like to order something in the restaurant. I sat down at the table and was given a menu. The five children in the center at the time were all boys. They were deeply involved in the play and quite serious in their roles. One child told me that I was at "table 20." Another took my order, again very seriously, and quickly scribbled my order onto his order pad. When I asked for toast and eggs, he replied that this was a lunch and dinner restaurant. I changed my order to a cheeseburger. Another child came over with a pad and asked me to write the word cheeseburger on it. Yet another child carefully made a cheeseburger with a plastic burger, cheese, and buns, while another piled all kinds of food in front of me. And so it went.

I was given a child-created apron from the clothesline against the wall and told to put on my "bib." I noticed a number of dishtowels, aprons (child-made paper aprons and cloth aprons), as well as police officer and fire fighter dress-up items, on the clothesline. I enjoyed my cheese-burger, watching the flurry of activity in the diner "kitchen." Upon finishing, I was kindly supplied with a few dollars (having inexplicably wandered into a restaurant without my purse), which were immediately returned to the cash register upon my payment. (I understand that yeasty pizza dough will be placed in the diner soon, a very realistic prop for our chefs.

At the sensory table, which had been filled with flour, children were busily stirring, sifting, using eggbeaters, measuring in measuring cups, and transferring flour to mixing bowls and cupcake tins. One little girl in this area was wearing a chef's cap she had made. Three chain-links of colored construction paper hung on either side of the cap, an unusual decoration. When I asked her about her cap, she told me that these were her "braids."

Two children were nestled into the book nook. It is full of books about families (The Relatives Came), restaurants (including Dinner at the Panda Palace, Restaurant Owners, Frank and Ernest, and The Moon and Riddles Diner and the Sunnyside Café), fire trucks and fire fighters (such as Fire Trucks, Fire Fighters! Smoke Jumpers One to Ten, The Little Fireman, Fire Bears, The Rescue Team, and Machines at Work, Fire Truck), and even a couple of special books about chairs (Peter's Chair and Mrs. Piccolo's Easy Chair).

When it was time to head back to my office, I stopped in the hallway to admire the start of an interesting bulletin board. The bulletin boards in the common hallway of our school are a staging area for the children's emerging ideas. They are large, low, and long, made to measure for three- and four-year-old artists. At the start of a Journey, they are bare. As the Journey takes shape, so does the bulletin board.

The content becomes richer and deeply idiosyncratic as the Journey continues; children's contributions and ideas fill its space. It is not unusual to find children from other classes (on their way to the bathrooms) stopped in front of a bulletin board, giving profound attention to its contents. The children work in the hallway itself, moving in and out of the classroom as they perceive a need for a material they do not have on hand.

As I stepped into the hallway, I passed two large pieces of butcher paper on the floor and a marvelous assortment of materials, glue, paste, fabric scissors, paint, and children, of course, kneeling or sitting on the floor as they worked. It was too soon to say what would emerge from the tumble of paper and fabric scraps that were being worked, but great determination was evident in the children's purposeful activity. A week later, two bulletin boards have emerged. One is a large pouf of a chair, highly decorated and surrounded by photos and stories of the children in their "favorite chair" at home; the other is a fascinating, charcoal-dark "smokestack," conceptualized by two children and brought to life with great interest and persistence by those children, with the help of others.

The children are completely engaged in the current "diner" phase of the Journey and this will continue for a bit longer. The teachers have initiated a class "savings jar." At clean-up time, the teams of children working in each center have the capacity to earn up to five pennies for the jar. The focus during clean up is on putting things where they belong, sorting things out, and working as a team, rather than on how fast the children can clean the center. The pennies are awarded and counted during small-group time and are also used for estimating purposes as the jar fills. The children have been hugely excited by this project. Every day, while they are cleaning, we hear them tell each other that they are going to earn five pennies. They have been working hard and encouraging each other so that every member of the team is productive. A crescendo of excitement was heard throughout the school yesterday, as they earned an all-time record of 43 pennies! The children will vote (charting the results) to decide on what special item their pennies will "buy."

We have also seen that some children have been greatly interested in "the fire" and a time when this family had nothing. We live in an affluent town. Can the children appreciate a time when a family has so little? If this becomes a future direction of the Journey, the children will arrive in their classroom to find that the dramatic play center is completely empty. It has been destroyed by "fire" and there is nothing left. Lists will need to be made of what needs to be replaced. Large sheets of paper covering the doors will be available for the children to illustrate or write the names of items of importance. The children will visit other classes in the school to tell "their story" and ask if there is anything the other children can give them that will help them rebuild their "home."

Families become involved in a Journey in different ways. In this particular Journey, families provided a photo of their child in a chair that they loved, while the children provided the stories of the chair's importance. Extra copies of <u>A Chair for My Mother</u> were also available to be taken home on a rotating basis, giving opportunities for the children to share their experiences at school in a relaxed familial setting.

Community involvement is natural extension of this Journey, so we started a food drive for a local food bank. The food drive has been a natural way for us to talk about how to help people who don't have as much. The children illustrated pages in their journals of what they would give to a family who lost everything. The children practice a fire drill each month, but we now have a *meaningful* opportunity to have a firefighter visit us and answer the children's questions.

The three early learning standards that were chosen for the start of the Journey were Physical 2 – uses coordinated small muscle movements, Cognitive 6 – relates number to quantity, and Creative 1 – ability to represent experiences, thoughts, and ideas, through various art forms. They were woven into the plan by incorporating the following activities. For Physical 2 and Creative 1, the children have been involved in a lot of cutting and pasting as they make aprons, hats, and other props for the dramatic play center. The children's efforts at the bulletin boards are a testament to emerging concepts and skills. Charcoal drawings, working with dough, making menus by cutting foods out of magazines and gluing them to construction paper, among other activities, provide many opportunities to observe these standards. The saving jar and its related counting and voting activities, use of the cash register in the restaurant (which is stocked with small bills and coins) during dramatic play in the "diner," graphing "heads and tails" at the activity table, and a sorting-and-counting-coins activity give us opportunities to observe the children within the cognitive standard. Future standards that the teachers expect to incorporate into the Journey as their dramatic play center is devastated and rebuilt include Personal and Social 5 – uses words to express emotions or feelings, Personal and Social 6 – shows empathy and caring for others, and Cognitive 2 – uses a variety of strategies to solve problems. This Journey has just gotten under way, but you can see how easily standards can fit with activities that are meaningful to the story and the children's experience.

### Our Second Four-Year-Old Classroom named the Pooh Bears

Our Pooh Bears have been exploring Mem Fox's moving <u>Wilfrid Gordon</u> *McDonald Partridge* for several weeks. In this story, a little boy named Wilfrid feels a special bond with a resident of the nursing home next door. Miss Nancy Alison Delacourt Cooper has four names, just like him. Wilfrid hears his parents talking and learns that Miss Nancy has lost her memory. He doesn't know what a memory is, so he goes on a quest to find out. He asks everyone he knows and then searches for items that make sense given the explanations he has received. As he gives the items to Miss Nancy, each prompts a memory. Miss Nancy has found her memory again. This wonderful story of love and friendship provides a fascinating journey into memory – what is it, how can we make memories, and how do we preserve them?

One little boy in our class lost his grandmother a few months ago and his grandfather just before this Journey began. He has been deeply connected to this exploration, which has also been meaningful for every child in the classroom.

Initially, small-group discussions focused on what is a memory. Teachers charted the responses of the children. At home, families explored memory "treasures" and each child brought in a photograph or object and described a special memory that accompanied it. They illustrated this "memory." (We assessed Creative 2 – Draws and paints to represent our own ideas.)

> when he gives them to Miss Nancy she gets her memory back. In small group time we asked the children what is memory? This is Leo's response.
>
> "When I went to France a long time ago I can remember my cousin who speaks French gave me a matching game. He is still alive. When I look at the game I think of him. He is 4½."

A photo of the item and the child's thoughts in presenting it were placed in a special class-made memory box installed on the bulletin board. The children's illustrations surrounded the memory box. The discussions that took place during small-group time were as meaningful to the children listening as they were to the child sharing. We witnessed how one person's "memory item" can spark a wonderful memory for another, just as they did for Miss Nancy. (We assessed Cognitive 5 – Compares and orders objects and events, and Cognitive 8-Uses complex sentences and vocabulary to describe ideas and experiences.)

As this class had recently experienced some children excluding others from play, the teachers came up with a new concept for the children, "making a friendship memory." After a discussion of how memories are made in general, and friendship memories in particular, the children were ready to begin a class-wide project. They were asked to "make a friendship memory" during their day. They shared their memories and charted the results with stickers daily during an end-of-day reflective small-group time. When they were ready to tally them at the end of the week, each child counted out special "treasures" (beads) equivalent to the number of stickers he or she had accumulated during the week. The beads were placed in a special cup with the child's name on it. (We assessed Cognitive 6 – Relates number to quantity and Personal & Social 3-Participates in teacher-led group activities.) While this strategy was introduced only last week, it has shown considerable promise. Children have invited others into their play and sustained their engagement with each other. They have excitedly recounted their shared experience to their small group. (We had many examples that allowed us to assess Personal & Social 7 – Interacts cooperatively with peers.) When this project is complete, the children will make a special treasure with their beads, perhaps a concrete reminder (like those found by Wilfrid) of happy friendship memories.

In the sensory table, a remarkable collection of dried beans is growing. Children have brought in their favorite dried beans (or the most intriguing ones they found while visiting the grocery store with a parent). A chart on the wall near the sensory table identifies each bean by its name and by its contributor. The children are eager to sift through the mixture of beans, find their bean, and show it to their friends. Occasionally, a group of children can be observed wide-eyed at the chart blurting out, "Look, there's my bean!" while comparing one he or she has located in the table to the identical bean on the chart. (We assessed Physical 2 – Uses co-ordinated small muscle movements.) Some remarkably sophisticated sorting activities have oc-curred without any suggestion from a teacher. One parent, a native of Italy, sent in a wondrous gift, twelve remarkable Italian beans of different sizes and colors (many of which we had never seen before), each marked with its Italian name, a phonetic pronunciation, and English trans-lation (where translation was possible). These beans have been pored over, but not added to the sensory table.

This is a wonderful time for classroom planting activities. These beans will be planted and, hopefully, transplanted to our school garden in April. This will give us wonderful opportunities for comparison, including measurement comparisons. (Will the sprout sizes correspond to the bean sizes? How will the sprouts differ from one another?)

The children are also interested in cooking and tasting some of these beans. This project will take some research, but a "bean tasting" lies ahead. (We anticipate assessing Cognitive 1 – Engages in scientific inquiry during these activities.)

In a recent e-mail sent home, parents were asked to reply with their children's full names and any stories about how these names were chosen. The children have been talking about their middle names. This is an excellent opportunity to discuss and chart the number of names they enjoy, as well as the concepts of more than, less than, and equal to as they compare their names to those of Wilfrid and Miss Nancy. (This gives us another opportunity to assess Cognitive 6 – Relates number to quantity. We can also assess Personal & Social 9 – Recognizes similarities and appreciates differences.)

The story of Wilfrid and Miss Nancy is also a wonderful introduction to the idea of relationships with older people. The ongoing class discussions of memories, which have evolved from what is a memory, to significant memories of our past, to how we make a memory, may now move to special memories of older family members.

The class is about to move from this Journey to a new Storybook Journey, Miss Tizzy, which will extend and enrich this concept while providing rich new avenues of exploration.

I did not fully describe all of the centers in this classroom, but with this small window into the curriculum, you will observe that the children are learning about themselves and about each other. They are recognizing connections they previously did not know existed as they explore memories they find that they hold in common. These bonds are drawing this community of children closer. In the process, without stress or strain, they have simultaneously explored learning goals in the cognitive, language, creative, physical, and social emotional domains. The natural progression of the Journey effortlessly provides the framework for these explorations in a manner that has engaged every child's interest and is developmentally appropriate. Taking observations of the children as they participate in these activities, sharing these observations as planning for the Journey continues, and using them as the basis of portfolio sheets that assess the child's ongoing learning requires effort, but it is worthwhile and incredibly rewarding as our understanding of each child is significantly enhanced in the process.

## The Puddleducks and the Cottontails

Two classes of three-year-olds share this classroom. They have been involved in an exploration of six classic nursery rhymes that has spanned the last two and a half months. Time is our ally during the Journey. Each of these nursery rhymes represents at least two weeks of beehive-like activity, but there is no scheduled ending.

We know when it's time to move on, as the children's interest wanes. When we relax into the Journey, unfazed by the passage of time, the children do as well. In this case, as the weeks have passed the children have started to playfully change the rhymes, taking characters from one rhyme on a journey into another or into an entirely new story, with utterly delightful results. Suddenly, "the cow (from Hey Diddle Diddle) is eating curds and whey when a tiger comes along." New characters are introduced, new endings make surprising entrances, and the fertile imaginations of young children are enthusiastically supported. This can be seen in the children's bulletin board as well. It was fascinating to find a cow thoughtfully placed by its creator on the roof of the house "that Jack built," well situated for jumping over the moon!

The "house that Jack built" on children's bulletin board

The classic rhymes as well as the children's versions are dramatized frequently. We use Vivian Paley's story acting method for this purpose. A portfolio observation follows. When the children are dramatizing <u>Wee Willie Winkie</u>, one child announces that he wants to be "the lock." The child who is taking the role of Willie says, "I just have to pretend you are in the door and yell, "Children are you in bed?" This is agreed between them. The "lock" stands perfectly still as "Willie" comes right up to him and pretends to call to the children. When the children, playing themselves, hear William calling, they all lie down and pretend to fall asleep. The "lock" laughs. At the end of the day, as we share our favorite part of the day, the child responds, "I liked being the lock best."

Let's take a quick look at the early learning standards that were woven into this Journey, and the goals the teaching team chose to use in their observation and planning. Rather than describe a classroom scenario, I have chosen to represent this information in a table. It makes clear how naturally the complementary threads of activity and standard or learning goal weave together into a well-crafted fabric while supported by the solid framework of the Storybook Journey.

All of the activities outlined on this table were included in the class plans. However, it would not be possible to document all of the standards that could sensibly be assessed during this Journey. The teaching team chose the standards that they wished to assess. Those standards are highlighted in bold in the table. A standard is frequently explored through multiple activities and might be explored over the course of two nursery rhymes.

| Nursery Rhyme | Planned Activities | Early Learning Standards |
|---|---|---|
| Humpty Dumpty | Hard boiled egg painting, Textured painting (shells added to paint) | Coordinated small muscle activities Draws and paints to represent own ideas |
| | Rubber egg experiment | Engages in scientific inquiry |
| | Building walls with different materials Things falling off the walls Dramatizing the rhyme | Uses coordinated large-muscle activities Uses a variety of strategies to solve a problem **Interacts cooperatively with peers** **Demonstrates spatial awareness** Builds and constructs to convey meaning Represents experiences and fantasies in pretend play |
| | Humpty Dumpty's rhyming wall, visual illustration wall. Printed word | **Recognizes similar sounds in speech.** Identifies printed words Uses writing to convey meaning |

| Nursery Rhyme | Planned Activities | Early Learning Standards |
|---|---|---|
| | Making scrambled eggs | Participates in teacher-led activities<br><br>**Interacts cooperatively with peers** |
| Hey Diddle, Diddle | Playful rhyming | **Recognizes similar sounds in speech**<br><br>Identifies printed words<br><br>Uses writing to convey meaning |
| | Puppets are introduced, popsicle stick and other materials<br><br>Making puppets in different ways | Understands and participates in conversations<br><br>Uses writing to convey meaning<br><br>Builds and constructs to convey meaning<br><br>Draws and paints to represent own ideas<br><br>**Represents experiences and fantasies in pretend play** |
| | Puppet shows<br><br>Making a puppet theatre | **Demonstrates spatial awareness**<br><br>**Interacts cooperatively**<br><br>Uses coordinated large muscle activities<br><br>Uses complex sentences and vocabulary to describe ideas and |

| Nursery Rhyme | Planned Activities | Early Learning Standards |
|---|---|---|
| | | experiences<br><br>Shows understanding of stories<br><br>**Represents experiences and fantasies in pretend play** |
| | Fiddle player performs and children sing | Sings and responds to music |
| Little Miss Muffet | Dramatization<br><br>Story dictation (encouraging playful stories incorporating other nursery rhyme characters) | Manages transitions, follows routines and rules<br><br>**Uses complex sentences and vocabulary to describe ideas and experiences**<br><br>**Interacts cooperatively**<br><br>Shows understanding of stories |
| | Curds and whey – making butter, pouring off the whey, tasting | Engages in scientific inquiry |

| Nursery Rhyme | Planned Activities | Early Learning Standards |
|---|---|---|
| | Making sock (and other) puppets<br><br>Puppet shows, making tickets, etc. | Understands and participates in conversations<br><br>Uses writing to convey meaning<br><br>Builds and constructs to convey meaning<br><br>Draws and paints to represent own ideas<br><br>**Represents experiences and fantasies in pretend play** |
| | Feeling afraid – discussions<br><br>Use of 'Feelings Chart' | **Uses words to express emotions or feelings** |

| Nursery Rhyme | Planned Activities | Early Learning Standards |
|---|---|---|
| Wee Willie Winkie | Story Acting | Demonstrates spatial awareness<br><br>Uses coordinated large muscle activities<br><br>**Uses complex sentences and vocabulary to describe ideas and experiences**<br><br>Shows understanding of stories<br><br>**Represents experiences and fantasies in pretend play** |
|  | Making puppets of any nursery rhyme characters | Coordinated small muscle activities<br><br>Builds and constructs to convey meaning<br><br>Draws and paints to represent own ideas |
|  | Making oatmeal<br><br>Pancakes in our pajamas | Interacts cooperatively with peers |
| Sing a Song of Sixpence | Dough, pizza dough, muffins with raisins, etc.<br><br>Play dough with small wooden blackbirds | Shows self-direction with a range of materials<br><br>**Coordinated small muscle activities**<br><br>**Relates number (small blackbirds) to** |

| Nursery Rhyme | Planned Activities | Early Learning Standards |
|---|---|---|
| | | **quantity**<br>Demonstrates spatial awareness |
| | Counting House – sorting coins | Sustains attention to task<br>**Coordinated small muscle activities**<br>Sorts objects<br>**Relates number to quantity** |
| | Cleaning pennies experiment | Engages in scientific inquiry |
| | Planting birdseed, 'what will grow' predictions | Engages in scientific inquiry |
| | What do we know about birds? Charting birds we see outside, tallying<br>Making binoculars, magnify | Engages in scientific inquiry<br><br>Sorts objects<br>**Relates number to quantity**<br>Uses writing to convey meaning |
| The House that Jack Built | Building a house with hollow blocks (playground)<br><br>Children's bulletin board house, door sized to children, measurement | Uses coordinated large muscle movements<br>**Uses a variety of strategies to solve a problem**<br>Builds and constructs to convey meaning |

| Nursery Rhyme | Planned Activities | Early Learning Standards |
|---|---|---|
| | | Represents experiences and fantasies in pretend play |
| | Sequencing the order of the rhyme, sequence cards | Participates in teacher led activity<br>**Uses a variety of strategies to solve a problem**<br>**Compares and orders objects and events**<br>Shows understanding of story |
| | Sensory table, flour, rye, malt | **Uses coordinated small muscle movements** |
| | Building a story, each child repeating the previous pattern and adding to it | Understands and participates in conversations<br>**Compares and orders objects and events** |
| | Woodworking table | **Uses coordinated small muscle movements**<br>Engages in scientific inquiry |

This is only a sampling of activities that occurred during this Journey. Even in this incomplete sample, six of the nine personal/social early learning standards, two of the three physical early learning standards, twelve of the fourteen cognitive early learning standards, and all four creative learning standards could have been assessed using the activities listed. Almost all of Connecticut's learning goals from its preschool curriculum and assessment frameworks could be assessed in this one Storybook Journey. The teaching team, therefore, chose standards that were not previously assessed or ones they wanted to reassess at this time.

This table demonstrates the remarkable ability of the Storybook Journey to provide a framework that easily and flexibly provides meaningful context for early learning standards. It also demonstrates that the teaching team can continue to assess development, using this broad array of learning standards over an even greater period of time should the children's engagement warrant it.

### How do we document early learning standards for assessment and ongoing planning?

Our documentation grows out of the everyday experiences of the children as they explore within the context of the Journey. These experiences accurately reveal what each child has learned and the progress he or she has made.

### Observation with a focus on early learning standards

We know that each child is unique. How do we find and follow each child's developmental path? How do we support and guide each child's next steps? We wish to refine our curriculum in such a way that it follows the interests and needs of the children and allows us to reach learning goals (early learning standards). Meaningful observation and a system of documentation allied to our standards are essential.

So what, when, and how do we observe? At SSNS, teachers have observed the children, planned a Journey, chosen three learning goals (from the CT Preschool Curriculum Framework) to accompany the Journey, and then implemented their plan. Teachers take careful observation notes during the week. They observe moments in which a child's development, interest, or need for support or guidance is revealed. They also observe the children to document the benchmark they have achieved within the learning standards or goals currently complementing the Journey. These "focused" or directed observations, made by rotating members of the team, occur during a period of twenty or thirty minutes set aside for this purpose during the program day.

While we still use individual sticky Post-it notes to capture observations that appear relevant to a child's growth as they occur, we designed a specific set of forms, each linked to a specific early learning goal to provide the organizational structure for "focused" observation time. The forms were designed to match each of Connecticut's early learning standards. Our teachers find it helpful to have the benchmarks outlined directly on the form for handy reference. The forms also give the teacher a means to ensure that no child is forgotten; each child has a designated box on the form. The box is small, so if the observation requires a full anecdote, it's written on a sticky Post-it and attached to this form. (Examples of the forms we developed are appended to this chapter.) At the start of the year, each classroom is given a full set of forms, one for each of the standards to be observed.

Once the observations have been gathered, what happens next? The teachers' observations of each child are shared weekly during planning, providing substantial food for thought in terms of how the children are reaching different benchmarks in the standard or goal and the ongoing direction of the Journey. This reflection guides our planning. Do we need to spend more time with these goals? Should we replace one goal with another? What interests are paramount in the classroom? Are the children showing a strong interest in nocturnal animals during a Journey with <u>Owl Moon</u>? What activities would support this interest? And so it goes, in a cycle of planning, implementation and observation, reflection and assessment, and back to planning, that continues as the Journey continues. A productive Journey will take six weeks or more, and over the course of this time, we will have embedded six to nine early learning standards from several different developmental domains into the curriculum. Attainment of these standards will be assessed from the children's explorations of activities that were meaningful to them, connected through the storyline, and interconnected with other children who shared their interest.

### *Portfolio development with a focus on early learning standards*

Over the last couple of years, we have significantly changed the nature of our children's individual portfolios, which began as collections of children's work. Gaye Gronlund and Bev Engel's book, <u>Focused Portfolios</u>, made tremendous sense to us. In a "Focused Portfolio," each child's progress is followed along numerous developmental goals, in our case the CT early learning standards. This ongoing assessment takes the form of individual portfolios into which teachers put evidence of each child's learning and accomplishments. The portfolio therefore reflects each child's interests and strengths. In addition, documenting a child's achievement of accepted developmental benchmarks helps us assess and reflect on a child's growth in relation to age-appropriate expectations. Thus, we started creating portfolios, which worked seamlessly with the standards and the Storybook Journey.

Currently, observations are shared during planning sessions; decisions are made at that time as to which observations should be included in a child's individual portfolio. Observations not needed in the portfolio are put in the child's section of the class observation book. Those anecdotes needed for the portfolio are transcribed onto portfolio sheets and put into the child's portfolio. A face page, on the cover of the portfolio, handily references the dates on which observations were made and in which developmental domain. A face page is appended to this chapter.

Staff members have some paid time each week to write up and file their portfolio sheets. Examples of these sheets (adapted from portfolio sheets included in <u>Focused Portfolios</u>, Gaye Gronlund and Bev Engel, 2001) are also appended. As observations are taken on the observation sheets, it's possible to document which benchmark is being met. This information is put onto the portfolio sheet along with the anecdote and occasionally a digital photograph illustrating the moment. If a particular group activity, such as a science experiment, is being observed and documented, staff members have found it helpful to type a description of the experiment and follow it by a given child's personal response to it. In this way, it's possible to re-use the form for all of the children who participated, pasting the copied description onto the page and adding the individual child's response and the benchmark achieved to his or her page, and saving the busy staff member valuable time.

Work samples can be collected and form a very meaningful part of the child's portfolio. Charted children's responses during small-group time, as they respond to open-ended questions, and bulletin boards created by the children also provide insight into a child's understanding and reflect their growing abilities. Rich bulletin boards emerge naturally during the course of a Journey, as the child's imaginative exploration of the story unfolds. Photos of portions of bulletin boards on which a child worked or photocopies of work can also be useful in portfolios.

### How do we use the documentation?

There are two purposes of our documentation, reflection and sharing. When our observations are systemically used in ongoing planning, this is a **reflective** process. Observation informs the path of the continuing Storybook Journey and the ongoing choice of early learning standards. The resulting documentation, in our case the child's portfolio, is a confidential document that provides timely snapshots of development that are **shared** with families, consultants involved with children that have a special need, and, with permission, as an illuminating way to flesh out a child's profile for a kindergarten teacher or a child's private school recommendation.

Collaborative conferences keep families up-to-date and provide opportunities for family input. The portfolio guides the conference, telling the story of the child and his or her personal journey. Documentation also benefits the transition of a child to a new school or to kindergarten. With the information in hand, the kindergarten teacher will know how to prepare a smooth transition. For children identified with special needs, once the requirement for confidentiality is met, consultants performing diagnostic screening can be fully informed, thus assisting in early intervention when necessary.

Three times a year, the teachers pull together what they have collected and prepare a conference report which evaluates the child's accomplishments and progress. The conference report and the portfolio are shared with each child's family in the fall and in the spring. A written update goes home at the end of January addressing how the child has responded to strategies that were discussed at the fall conference and implemented in the months since to help the child reach various individual goals. Teachers and family members confer to set goals and make plans to support each child's growth, both at home and in school. The conference forms include an area that invites family input about the child. Opportunities for family involvement are essential, as our role is one of partnership, helping this child to thrive during the period of time we are together. At the end of the year, the portfolio belongs to the child and his or her family.

### Conclusion - Where are we now?

Early childhood educators frequently meet state standards with resistance, often due to fear that substantial change may be required. However, combining early learning standards with the Storybook Journey is accomplished simply, without a sense of a burden undertaken. The weaving of the meaningful exploration of aspects of the story and the selected goals for learning is a harmonious process. The educator finds it natural to work with these combinations and the resulting experience is durable and meaningful to the children. The activities that the children undertake occur within this coherent structure, supporting their acquisition of knowledge and a strong sense of community. Progress can be observed and documented within a recognized framework of goals.

**As we have seen, the Storybook Journey is a remarkable vehicle for the delivery of early learning standards.** The addition of early learning standards provides a level of intent in ongoing assessment and reflection that empowers teachers. The Storybook Journey encourages the child's deep exploration, while the early learning standards concomitantly permit the establishment of goals for learning. Choosing the threads of story explorations and learning goals allows the teacher and children enormous flexibility; a unique design is woven with every story. The ease we have experienced with this process compels us to believe that this will be true regardless of the educational setting. The results in the classroom are compelling. Every child is deeply engaged and every child is building on prior knowledge. At the same time, through shared exploration within a common journey, the sense of community is strengthened.

**Attachment A**

The first attachment is a simple form used for methodically filing classroom observations. A class observation notebook is prepared with a section for each child that includes copies of this form. A typical form is used for a period of two weeks. Post-it note observations, written in the classroom, are placed in the appropriate area of the form. As observations are discussed in planning sessions, particular goals or strategies for the child may be noted at the bottom of the form.

| NAME: | WEEKS: |
|---|---|
| **SOCIAL/EMOTIONAL DEVELOPMENT** | **PHYSICAL DEVELOPMENT** |
| **COGNITIVE/LANGUAGE DEVELOPMENT** | **CREATIVE DEVELOPMENT** |

**Reflections on observations and current goals for the child:**

_____

_____

_____

_____

**Attachment B**

Several forms are appended that are examples of those we use during directed or focused observation time in the classroom, a period of approximately 20 minutes during the program day. One of the three standards chosen by the teaching team will be observed during this period. The form for a particular standard is filled out, each child's name is printed in a square, and the form is placed on a clipboard, ready for action. If longer observations are needed, Post-its are used and placed in an overlapping fashion over the squares. Each class is given a full set of these forms – in our case, there is one for each standard in the CT Preschool Assessment Framework. Additional copies can be made if needed. Providing the benchmarks on the form has been quite helpful to the teachers. As they write observations, they refer back to the benchmarks and make a quick correlation to what they have noted.

**EXAMPLE**

**Focused Observation: Performance Standard- PHY 3 Cares for self independently**

Activity: __Observing children manage their snack process or lunch process__

Date: _____October 4, 2008____ Teacher observing: ____MB_____

Benchmark 1- Performs self-care tasks with teacher's help

Benchmark 2- Attempts to dress, eat, and toilet independently with some success

Benchmark 3- Manages most aspects of dressing, eating, and toileting independently

Benchmark 4- Dresses, eats, and toilets independently

| Kimmy 4 Photo K washed hands, found placemat, placed it. Counted her 5 crackers, poured water. K ate and drank, talking w. Sophia re dog @ home. Cleaned up and on to block center. | Mark 1-2 M needs direction to retrieve lunchbox and wash hands. Process of hand washing fine. Cannot open sandwich bag. Forgets lunchbox under seat. Leaves the table, throws away his trash. | | |
|---|---|---|---|
| | | | |
| | | | |
| | | | |

**Focused Observation: Performance Standard- COG 1, Engages in scientific inquiry**

Activity: _____

Date: _____ Teacher observing: _____

**Benchmark 1-Observes or explores and notices effects**
**Benchmark 2-Experiments, observes, and comments**
**Benchmark 3-Experiments, observes purposefully and describes how effects vary**
**Benchmark 4-Describes, predicts, and plans for purposeful exploration or observation**

| | | | |
|---|---|---|---|
| | | | |
| | | | |
| | | | |
| | | | |

**Focused Observation:  Performance Standard- CRE 1 Builds and constructs to represent own ideas**

Activity: _____

Date: _____ Teacher observing: _____

**Benchmark 1-Explores with sensory and building materials in repetitive manner**
**Benchmark 2-Uses sensory and building materials with purpose**
**Benchmark 3-Creates simple constructions to represent own ideas**
**Benchmark 4-Creates elaborate constructions to represent own experiences, thoughts, and ideas**

| | | | |
|---|---|---|---|
| | | | |
| | | | |
| | | | |
| | | | |

**Focused Observation: Performance Standard- P&S 1 Shows self-direction with range of materials**

Activity: _____

Date: _____ Teacher observing: _____

**Benchmark 1-**Selects and uses a limited range of familiar materials; uses some new materials with direction and encouragement

**Benchmark 2-**Selects familiar materials; participates in unfamiliar activities with teacher support

**Benchmark 3-**Usually participates in both familiar and unfamiliar activities

**Benchmark 4-**Independently selects and participates in a wide variety of activities; requests additional materials to extend work

|  |  |  |  |
|---|---|---|---|
|  |  |  |  |
|  |  |  |  |
|  |  |  |  |
|  |  |  |  |

**Attachment C**

Our portfolio sheets have been adapted from those devised by Gaye Gronlund and Bev Engel (Focused Portfolios, Gronlund and Engel, 2001). Portfolios are created for each child and segmented into domains, including additional sections for family, friends, and interests. The forms were adapted for the CT Preschool Assessment Framework, listing the learning standards in a particular domain and including a space for the benchmark that was observed. These forms ingeniously include quite a bit of information that can be quickly checked off at the top of the form, to which are added the anecdote, photo, work sample, etc.

The face page is also helpful, giving the teacher a handy reference of which standards have been assessed and what information has been collected and when.

## Focused Portfolio Collection Form
## Preschooler – Physical Development

Child's Name _____ Age _____

Observer _____ Date _____

| Check off the areas of development that apply:<br>o Fine Motor<br>o Gross Motor | This photo, work sample, and/or anecdote illustrates the following **Physical** performance standard(s):<br>o Uses large muscles - (PHY 1)<br>o Uses small muscles – (PHY 2)<br>o Cares for self – (PHY 3) |
|---|---|
| Within the performance standard, the following benchmark is met: | |

Check off whatever applies to the context of this observation:

| |
|---|
| o Child-initiated activity<br>o Teacher-initiated activity |
| o New task for this child<br>o Familiar task for this child |
| o Done independently<br>o Done with adult guidance<br>o Done with peer(s) |
| o Time spent (1-5 mins.)<br>o Time spent (5-15 mins.)<br>o Time spent (15+ mins.) |

**Anecdotal Note:** Describe what you saw the child do and/or heard the child say.

Adapted from © Gaye Gronlund and Bev Engel.

# Focused Portfolio Collection Form

## Preschooler – Social/Emotional Development

Child's Name _____ Age _____

Observer _____ Date _____

| Check off the areas of development that apply: | This photo, work sample, and/or anecdote illustrates the following **Personal and Social** performance standard(s): |
|---|---|
| o Social Competency<br>o Emotional Competency | o Shows self-direction - (P & S 1)<br>o Sustains attention - (P & S 2)<br>o Participates in groups - (P & S 3)<br>o Manages transitions - (P & S 4)<br>o Expresses emotions - (P & S 5)<br>o Shows empathy - (P & S 6)<br>o Cooperates with peers - (P & S 7)<br>o Resolves conflicts - (P & S 8)<br>o Appreciates differences - (P & S 9) |
| Within the performance standard, the following benchmark is met: | |

Check off whatever applies to the context of this observation:

| |
|---|
| o Child-initiated activity<br>o Teacher-initiated activity |
| o New task for this child<br>o Familiar task for this child |
| o Done independently<br>o Done with adult guidance<br>o Done with peer(s) |
| o Time spent (1-5 mins.)<br>o Time spent (5-15 mins.)<br>o Time spent (15+ mins.) |

**Anecdotal Note**: Describe what you saw the child do and/or heard the child say.

| |
|---|
| |

Adapted from © Gaye Gronlund and Bev Engel.

# Focused Portfolios
## Recording Individual Child Observations by Date
## Utilizing the CT Preschool Assessment Framework

Child's Name_____ Date of Birth _____

### Knowing the Child

| Documentation Collected | Date(s) Collected |
|---|---|
| Family | |
| Favorites/Interests | |
| Friends | |

### Cognitive Development

| Documentation Collected | Date(s) Collected | Documentation Collected | Date(s) Collected |
|---|---|---|---|
| Engages in inquiry | | Compares and orders | |
| Solves problems | | Quantifies | |
| Sorts objects | | Shows spatial awareness | |
| Makes patterns | | | |

### Language Development

| Documentation Collected | Date(s) Collected | Documentation Collected | Date(s) Collected |
|---|---|---|---|
| Uses sentences | | Recognizes sounds | |
| Understands conversations | | Identifies words | |
| Understands stories | | Writes for meaning | |
| Understands books | | | |

### Physical Development

| Documentation Collected | Date(s) Collected | Documentation Collected | Date(s) Collected |
|---|---|---|---|
| Uses large muscles | | Cares for self | |
| Uses small muscles | | | |

### Personal and Social Development

| Documentation Collected | Date(s) Collected | Documentation Collected | Date(s) Collected |
|---|---|---|---|
| Shows self direction | | Expresses emotions | |
| Sustains attention | | Shows empathy | |
| Participates in groups | | Cooperates with peers | |
| Manages transitions | | Appreciates differences | |
| | | Resolves conflicts | |

### Creative Development

| Documentation Collected | Date(s) Collected | Documentation Collected | Date(s) Collected |
|---|---|---|---|
| Builds and constructs | | Pretends in play | |
| Draws and paints | | Responds to music | |

Adapted © 2001 Gaye Gronlund and Bev Engel

## REFERENCES AND RELATED READINGS

Copple, C., and Bredekamp, S. (2006). *Basics Of Developmentally Appropriate Practice: An Introduction For Teachers Of Children 3 To 6.* Washington, DC: National Association for the Education of Young Children.

Copple, C., and Bredekamp, S. (Eds.). (2009). *Developmentally Appropriate Practice In Early Childhood Programs Serving Children From Birth Through Age 8.* Rev. ed. Washington, DC: National Association for the Education of Young Children.

Gronlund, G. (2006). *Make Early Learning Standards Come Alive: Connecting Your Practice And Curriculum To State Guidelines.* St. Paul, MN: Redleaf Press and Washington, DC: National Association for the Education of Young Children.

Gronlund, G. and Engel, B. (2001). *Focused Portfolios: A Complete Assessment for the Young Child.* St. Paul, MN: Redleaf Press.

NAEYC and NAECS/SDE. (2002). *Early Learning Standards: Creating The Conditions For Success.* Joint Position Statement, adopted November 2002. Washington, DC. Online: www.naeyc.org/about/positions/learning_standards.asp.

NAEYC and NAECS/SDE. (2003). *Early Childhood Curriculum, Assessment, And Program Evaluation: Building An Effective, Accountable System In Programs For Children Birth Through Age 8.* Joint Position Statement, adopted November 2003. Washington, DC. Online: www.naeyc.org/about/positions/pdf/pscape.pdf.

Amy Thrasher is the author of chapter eight. I met Amy when she first entered the graduate program in speech-language pathology at the University of Colorado at Boulder. I was one of Amy's faculty mentors as she began her practica in early childhood development. At the heart of the early childhood program is the Child Learning Center, a vibrant, inclusive learning community of toddlers, preschoolers, families, teachers, graduate students, and faculty. Amy understood the essence of the Storybook Journey approach immediately, on a very deep level, and developed outstanding and meaningful experiences with each story for our classroom of diverse learners. Children with a range of learning abilities, including advanced learners and children with learning and communication challenges, actively participated together in joyful interactions and projects to explore the ideas presented in each story. From her strong foundation in child development and her sincere compassion for all children, Amy seamlessly wove the strengths, interests, and needs of all learners into the shared experiences of the storybook Journey.

Amy has been asked to present the Storybook Journey approach to many early childhood programs and consult in their implementation of the approach. In 2008, she co-presented the Storybook Journey to a large audience at the national conference of the American Speech-Language and Hearing Association with Donna Boudreau. I am eternally grateful to Amy for being so willing to share her talent and knowledge in explaining how the Storybook Journey represents evidence-based practice in terms of the integration of child and family priorities, professional experience, and current theory and research. The information Amy has gathered for this chapter will be a valuable resource for early childhood professionals, administrators, and students pursuing a career in teaching our youngest children.

# *Chapter Eight*

## The Storybook Journey as an Evidence-Based Practice

➢      An invitation to a story

➢      For what learning contexts is the Storybook Journey appropriate?

➢      How is the Storybook Journey compatible with local and national early childhood standards and other curricula?

➢      How is the Storybook Journey supported by the evidence base in early childhood development?

➢      Conclusion

## AN INVITATION TO A STORY
### Amy Thrasher, MA, CCC-SLP

Stories are a medium for learning about our world, for sharing experiences, and for exploring both the familiar and the fantastic. Stories can transmit the values of a culture and stories can inspire. Stories can be personal, while some stories are universal. The Storybook Journey has inspired thousands of early childhood professionals in their own quest to provide a rich, culturally relevant, and engaging learning context for children. I feel enormously fortunate that I encountered the Storybook Journey and Sue McCord during my own graduate education in speech-language pathology, for the experience was a profound one. And now I am excited to be a part of sharing the "story" of the Storybook Journey here with a wider audience of readers who can in turn share the exploration of a story as the medium for meaningful, integrated learning with children and families.

Along my own journey as a professional in early childhood services, I've continued to use the Storybook Journey in a variety of contexts. As a developer of a toddler child-care program, I used the Journey to provide continuity and familiarity for these very young children and their working families during their long separations across the week. Families read the Little Red Hen at home and we continued the story at school, baking bread together and including favorite family recipes in our cooking at childcare. As a preschool teacher, the Storybook Journey brought families and children, interventionists, teaching assistants, and teachers together as learners. On a twist on The Three Little Pigs, we read The Three Javelinas, enhancing our background knowledge about javelinas with the book, Don't Call Me Pig! Did you know that javelinas have poor eyesight? It was a wonderful introduction to the sense of sight, our different perceptions of the world around us, and thus the celebration of differences among us.

As a speech-language consultant in preschool classrooms using the Storybook Journey approach, I find that my interventions are seamlessly incorporated into the curriculum, because language and literacy experiences are so integral to the children's explorations of the story at school and at home. Leading my own inclusive intervention groups of toddlers, preschoolers, and children with social communication challenges such as Autism, the Storybook Journey has been an invaluable resource for children's greatest task: making meaning out of their world. For example, another favorite storybook for a Journey was *Bear* Feels Scared in which the familiar but frightening childhood experience of being lost is sensitively overcome as the bear's friends go on a search for him and find him not 10 feet from his cave. This Journey gave us innumerable opportunities to learn about our own feelings, empathy for others, friendship, and working together to solve a problem. I've also found that while providing individual intervention services, exploring one story in depth is one of the most effective and positive means of supporting a child's communication challenges. Even what seems like a relatively simple storybook can have a deep impact, such as Machines at Work. By exploring this story of construction in action across multiple sessions, exposing the child to the basic building blocks of language, children come to internalize the message that their communication is working too.

**FOR WHAT LEARNING CONTEXTS IS THE STORYBOOK JOURNEY APPROPRIATE?**

The Storybook Journey is appropriate for early childhood programs, including infant-toddler and preschool programs, as well as individual and group intervention programs. This approach to curriculum may also be used in kindergarten through early school age programs, although the focus of this guide will be early childhood programs, with an emphasis on the preschool population. While the term "early childhood professional" is most accurate to describe the variety of early childhood educators, special educators, and interventionists from all disciplines that the Storybook Journey approach is recommended for, the term "teacher" will be used to apply to all. Similarly, while the Storybook Journey is also used in the contexts of therapeutic interventions, the term "classroom" will be used in place of "classrooms, individual therapy, and group intervention sessions."

**HOW IS THE STORYBOOK JOURNEY COMPATIBLE WITH LOCAL AND NATIONAL EARLY CHILDHOOD STANDARDS AND OTHER CURRICULA?**

The Storybook Journey is a responsive approach to curriculum that addresses families' priorities and children's learning styles, interests, abilities, and needs. Teachers can use this approach to provide learning experiences and teacher-child interactions required by other curricula and by local and national early childhood standards. While standards, and many other curricula, suggest developmentally appropriate learning experiences and teacher-child interactions, the Storybook Journey approach serves to set those experiences and interactions in a meaningful context for the children and families: the context of exploring the story in depth.

The Storybook Journey may be thought of as an enveloping framework for other early childhood curricula, an enveloping framework that connects the children's learning experiences together in an integrated manner. For example, the Storybook Journey has been the approach to curriculum used for many years in the Child Learning Center for an inclusive preschool classroom and an inclusive toddler group at the University of Colorado at Boulder. Teachers have combined family priorities with their observations of the children and their knowledge of child development to determine next steps for each child. Recent changes in the national, and thus state, requirements for outcomes measurement created the demand for a more unified system of reporting children's progress. School districts in Colorado were given the option of choosing one of four systems of outcome measurement for preschool. These requirements led to the local school district's adoption of the Creative Curriculum (Dodge, Colker & Heroman, 2002). Teachers in the Child Learning Center, along with other early childhood programs across the country, have found the Creative Curriculum highly compatible within the Storybook Journey approach.

Three significant areas of compatibility between the Creative Curriculum and the Storybook Journey exist, while using the Storybook Journey as the enveloping framework will provide further benefits for children, families, and teachers. First, the objectives identified within the Creative Curriculum Developmental Continuum are based on current understanding of child development, and thus compatible with the next steps that teachers using the Storybook Journey approach identify for children based on their observations of children and knowledge of child development. Still, the Storybook Journey approach can extend the cultural appropriateness and individualization of goal setting for children through the practices of meeting with families to identify their priorities as well. Another area of compatibility is the consistent use of observation to document children's progress. The Storybook Journey approach goes beyond the entry of observations to meet Creative Curriculum checkpoints for data collection and measurement of progress. Through the Storybook Journey approach, teachers use their observations, combined with input from the families, to then expand on children's learning experiences by making responsive changes in the environment, materials, and interactions. These observations lead children, families, and teachers to deeper investigations of concepts along with the further exploration of the story.

Finally, the Creative Curriculum provides suggestions for developmentally appropriate activities in eleven interest areas for children. The activities in eleven areas may be separate in focus or loosely connected within a theme. In the Storybook Journey approach, teachers design learning experiences that integrate developmental domains and build upon one another within the meaningful context of the story. These meaningful experiences are developmentally appropriate since they are based on the teachers' observations of children and input from the families. Teachers consider the individual child's level of development as well as the range of development within the classroom community, and design experiences that are accessible at various levels of development. This consideration of multiple levels of access to the learning experience allows children of varying abilities to engage in learning together, strengthening the classroom community, and providing rich opportunities for social development.

In a similar manner, other systems of outcome measurement, sets of standards, and developmentally appropriate curricula can be used with the Storybook Journey approach as the enveloping framework for children's learning experiences. Also at the Child Learning Center, the Work Sampling System (Harrington et al., 1997) was considered at one time for documentation purposes. Similarly to coupling the Creative Curriculum within the Storybook Journey, the Work Sampling System would be compatible in that the Developmental Guidelines are based on current research in child development and documentation is based on teachers' observations of children engaged in learning. Chapter Seven will further detail how one preschool in Connecticut addressed state early childhood standards using the Storybook Journey approach and supported children's learning in an integrated, cohesive manner. The philosophy and practices of the High Scope Curriculum (Hohmann &Weikart, 1995) would be another example of a developmentally appropriate, observation-based curriculum for which the Storybook Journey approach could provide the enveloping framework that connects children's learning experiences in a meaningful way. Project approach curricula, such as the investigations of the Reggio Emilia approach (Katz & Chard, 2000), are also compatible with the Storybook Journey approach, in that the narrative sequence of the Storybook Journey itself could be the project that the children, families, and teachers develop. Another way to use the Storybook Journey approach with project approach curricula would be to choose smaller projects related to concepts within the context of the story exploration.

## HOW IS THE STORYBOOK JOURNEY SUPPORTED BY THE EVIDENCE BASE IN EARLY CHILDHOOD DEVELOPMENT?

Evidence-based practice refers to the integration of current theory and research, professional experience, and the unique values, preferences, and needs of the child and family being served (Sackett et al., 2000). The figure below from the American Speech-Language-Hearing Association's Evidence-based Practice Introduction (ASHA, 1998) illustrates the dynamic integration of these three core components when providing services for individuals. The model of evidence-based practice originated in the medical community and the figure below represents the adoption of this method of developing appropriate practices by related services providers. By adjusting the terms "client/patient" and "clinical" of the figure below to "child and family" and "professional expertise," the figure can represent how all early childhood professionals, including teachers, can support children and families through evidence-based practice.

The Storybook Journey approach to curriculum embraces this model of evidence-based practice through the consideration of child and family's values and priorities, teacher's professional experience, and sound theory and current research in early childhood development.

In the Storybook Journey approach, children and families are at the center of curriculum development. Teachers intentionally seek to understand families' unique values and preferences and then incorporate families' priorities for their children into culturally relevant experiences along the Storybook Journey. Family priorities and teacher observations of children's strengths, interests, and needs are the propelling force behind the curriculum design.

Teachers' professional experience is a critical factor in the Storybook Journey approach. A significant component of the teachers' professional experience is the actual professional learning experience that goes on within each Journey. Teachers are viewed simultaneously as guides and learners, alongside the children and families, who are engaged in learning explorations with each story. Teachers are participants in learning as the classroom community explores the story concepts, vocabulary, and narrative sequence as well as the many potential meanings and associations that can be discovered through the story. Through extended exploration of the story over time, teachers can learn about the cultural context and setting of the story, and the author's motivations and process in creating a story. Just as children make connections to their own life experiences when exploring a story over time, the story may evoke teachers' own life experiences to share with the children. Through engaging in the learning process along with the child, teachers provide a positive example of learning and engagement. In this approach, children learn within the context of the interactions with others, including the teachers who are active learners themselves.

Teachers' knowledge of child development and developmentally appropriate practice is critical within the Storybook Journey approach. Teachers continue to hone their observation skills and, based on these observations and input from the families, scaffold the children's learning to the next level of development. Other elements of teachers' professional expertise that are critical to the Storybook Journey include planning a day that provides a variety of large-group, small-group, and individual learning experiences and thoughtful transitions between these types of experiences, as well as a balance of physically active and quieter learning experiences. Teachers' skills in establishing relationships with families and communicating with them in a reciprocal manner are essential to the process of the Storybook Journey. In short, all of the teachers' professional knowledge and skills are utilized within the Storybook Journey approach. At the same time, given the perspective of the teacher-as-learner alongside the children and families, both new and experienced teachers gain considerable professional experience while engaging in this approach.

Finally, the third component of the evidence base necessary for the adoption of a professional practice is the support of sound theory and research. Throughout the surrounding chapters, Sue McCord details the theoretical underpinnings of the Storybook Journey approach based on the integration of seminal childhood development and learning theories including the works of Erickson, Piaget, and Vygotsky among many others, and references research as it applies to each stage of the Journey. Provided here is a brief introduction to the accumulating wealth of research that exploring a story over time in an in-depth manner supports young children's overall development.

A significant focus of current research in early childhood development is the consideration of the method of instruction. With a specific focus on emergent literacy, Justice and Kaderavek (2004) use the terms "embedded" and "explicit" to describe methods of instruction in early childhood that are frequently seen as opposing and are the subject of much debate. The Storybook Journey approach allows teachers to integrate both explicit and embedded learning experiences into meaningful and engaging contexts. Following a discussion of explicit and embedded learning experiences within the Storybook Journey approach, five of the most integral elements of this approach will be considered with supporting research: following the children's lead, narrative development, the exploration of story narrative through play, the exploration of the story through multiple developmental domains, and repeated exposure to concepts within meaningful contexts.

Justice and Kaderavek describe embedded approaches to instruction as having a focus on providing "naturalistic exposure" to concepts throughout the day within meaningful socially interactive experiences. The Storybook Journey is grounded in this embedded approach to instruction and learning, in that the classroom community's exploration of a story together provides learning experiences within a meaningful social context. The emphasis on adult facilitation of children's discoveries within this specific context of the shared story exploration places the Storybook Journey along the continuum of holistic, embedded approaches to instruction. Explicit approaches, Justice and Kaderavek go on to explain, refer to approaches that rely on decontextualized, regularly scheduled, systematically sequenced direct instruction of specific, discrete skills. According to their review of the research, both embedded and explicit approaches have been found to have benefits to children's emergent literacy development. The author's note that it is not necessary to consider these two approaches, embedded and explicit, in polar opposition. Rather, Justice and Kaderavek recommend an integrated approach, which they refer to as the "embedded-explicit model." The

Storybook Journey allows for this type of integrated approach, not only in regards to emergent literacy but to all domains of child development. Through the Storybook Journey, explicit, targeted focus on specific skills and concepts may be addressed with the whole classroom community within the meaningful context of the story exploration while children's individual needs for instruction can be addressed as well.

One of the essential elements of the Storybook Journey approach is the consideration of the needs and interests of the individual learner and the classroom as a community of learners. The Journey follows the children's lead through the story, as an emergent curriculum. Teachers engage families and children in conversation to elicit their own background knowledge about the story as well as in direct experiences through investigation of story content. Activating background knowledge and enriching content knowledge to increase comprehension is a practice supported by conceptual frameworks proposed by Kintsch (1998), arguments by Hirsch (2003) developed from scientific findings, and studies such as MacNamara et al. (1996). Along the journey, through repeated readings and retellings of the story, children and teachers make connections between the text and their lives, a practice in dialogic reading strategies (Whitehurst et al., 1988) that has been supported through numerous studies (Valdez-Menchaca & Whitehurst, 1992; Lonigan, 1993; Bus et al., 1995; Dickinson & Tabors, 1991).

The value of following the child's focus of attention and engaging in joint attention through the Storybook Journey approach is supported scientifically as well. For example, Tomasello & Farrar (1986) found that contexts utilizing child-directed attention facilitate children's word learning. Following children's focus of attention can also be examined in light of supporting curiosity and motivation. In the National Resource Council of the Institute of Medicine's review of research in early childhood development, From Neurons to Neighborhoods (Shonkoff & Phillips, 2000), the council identified motivational dimensions of early learning as a significant consideration in children's development, including the motivation to explore, manipulate, and persist in problem solving toward mastery, engagement in activity without external pressure or reward (also referred to as intrinsic motivation), and challenge seeking and self-perceptions of competence (p. 152). The Storybook Journey actively promotes children's curiosity by choosing a story and developing the curriculum in direct response to the children's interests.

Early childhood programs that emphasize child initiation in the curriculum have been found to have better outcomes for children in terms of basic skills and longitudinal academic outcomes compared to programs that emphasize academic skill instruction (Marcon, 1999). Further, curricula that support child initiations are consistent with recommendations for developmentally appropriate practice (Bredekamp & Rosengrant, 1992). Regarding early learning environments that foster children's curiosity and exploration, the National Research Council (Shonkoff & Phillips, 2000) concludes that "the elements that support early learning revolve around relationships and the resources they provide for children," emphasizing parent, teacher, and peer group interactions (p.156). The council stipulates, "Specifically, highly didactic, performance-oriented early childhood classrooms have been found to depress children's motivation," citing Stipek et al. (1995). In terms of fostering language development and early learning, the council recommends "talking to children more and using more elaborate talk, taking advantage of everyday interactions to introduce number concepts, and not only spending more time reading but also exploring the words and pictures in the book" (p. 162). The Storybook Journey, as it engages children, families, and teachers in interaction through the exploration of stories across the day based on children's interests, is an exemplar of the National Research Council's recommendations for evidence-based practices in early childhood education and intervention.

A second integral element of the Storybook Journey is the use of narrative as the backbone of the curriculum. One significant aspect of children's cognitive development is their expanding capacity to recognize and carry out sequences. From early discoveries of cause-effect, to means-end thinking, to early sequencing of "first, then" activities and tasks following the progressive pattern of "1, 2, 3," children explore the relationships and connections between events within their world. Later, children develop the ability to recognize greater meaning within sequences such as the pattern of a beginning, middle, and end, as in most narratives. For a review of the development of narrative, please see Nelson, (1998). Longitudinal research has explored the positive relationship between narrative development and academic and social success (Boudreau, 2008).

The power of narrative is that it can connect one's experiences within a coherent, logical progression. Polkinghorne (1988) considers narrative as "the primary experience by which human experience is made meaningful. Narrative meaning is a cognitive process that organizes human experiences into temporally meaningful episodes" (p. 1). Children can begin to internalize narrative structure in order to sequence their own actions and regulate their activity within their environment. The National Research Council (2000) identifies self-regulation as "a cornerstone of early childhood development that cuts across all domains of behavior" (p. 3), a conclusion that will certainly resonate with early childhood professionals and families alike when considering young children's development.

In two complementary findings, research supports the practices of repeated readings and story retelling that are essential in the narrative exploration of the Storybook Journey approach. On the one hand, repeated readings have been found to facilitate narrative development (Boudreau, 1997; Zevenbergen, Whitehurst & Zevenbergen, 2003). On the other hand, story retelling facilitates narrative comprehension (Morrow, Sisco & Smith, 1992). The two practices in combination then may have a reciprocal effect, in which narrative comprehension and narrative development are supported in a mutually scaffolding manner.

The third central element in the Storybook Journey to be discussed here is the practice of exploring a story narrative through play as a vehicle for learning. Recently, the topic of play in itself has been the subject of great concern to early childhood professionals and researchers, as the recent focus on pre-academics and early childhood outcomes measurement has overwhelmed many early childhood programs whose reaction has been to focus on pre-academics at the expense of play (Zigler, Zigler & Bishop-Josef, 2004). However, in actuality, current theory and research point to best practice as addressing pre-academics through the medium of play. For a full review of developmental research demonstrating how play facilitates children's development including opportunities to maximize their attention spans, to learn to get along with peers, to cultivate their creativity, to work through their emotions, to engage in physical activity and to gain foundational academic skills with pervasive and long-term effects, please see Singer, Golinkoff, and Hirsh-Pasek (2006).

Within the Storybook Journey, play is an important vehicle for exploring story concepts and ideas, as well as the sequencing of events within the narrative. With repeated exposure to the story, children engage in highly complex interactions through guided or spontaneous play reenactments and extensions of the story schema. Decades of research underscore the conclusion that children use language that is more complex when engaged in pretend play (Galda & Pelligrini, 1985). Vedeler (1997) found that children used significantly more advanced language, including greater syntactical complexity and explicit and elaborated references, when engaged in sociodramatic play than in other activities. For children with language challenges, sociodramatic play was found to support greater conversational success with their peers than other contexts (DeKroon, Kyte & Johnson, 2002).

Benson (2003) reviewed the literature regarding the relationship between pretend play and narrative development, beginning with the ability to take on roles emerging for some children as early as two years of age, then through the subsequent study of preschoolers found that children produced narratives that were more sophisticated within pretend play contexts than when asked to tell a story. Ilgaz & Aksu-Koc (2005) concurred, summarizing that children are able to construct narratives with greater competence when action and objects are available to scaffold their conceptual organization and expression. Baumer and colleagues (2005) found that children developed greater narrative length, coherence, and comprehension through engagement in joint adult-child pretense. Ways for children to further explore the narrative in the Storybook Journey approach using action and manipulatives include reenactments with figurines in a miniature environment in the sand table, dictation of their own story to a teacher while using a flannel board of the story characters, or puppet play with their peers.

The fourth essential element of the Storybook Journey is the exploration of the story across all of the developmental domains. Various systems of categorization of the developmental domains exist across authors and researchers in early childhood development. The National Research Council (2000) identified self-regulation as the cornerstone of the following developmental domains: linguistic, cognitive, emotional, social, and moral. Other systems of categorization would add sensorimotor, and fine and gross motor domains. Still others might divide linguistic and cognitive domains into language, literacy, numeracy, music, problem solving, and further divisions. Regardless of the system of categorization for the developmental domains used by an early childhood program, the Storybook Journey can address the myriad aspects of child development. Children engage in integrated learning experiences as they explore the story:

- through song and movement
- through the physical construction of the environment of the story
- through conversation and story retellings using a variety of manipulatives
- through their own representations in art mediums and early writing
- through experiences with sensory materials related to the story
- through related children's literature and factual books

Because this element of addressing all the developmental domains through the exploration of the story is so broad a topic, the following selected examples, including oral and written language and motor development, will be presented as a brief introduction to the supporting research.

The use of abstract language across contexts has been found to support the development of expressive language (Dickinson & Tabors, 1991). The use of abstract language and making connections between the story and the child's life is inherent in the exploration of the story across multiple domains. For example, a child who participates in large-group interactive storybook readings of The Very Busy Spider, retells the story with a friend as she draws a spider, goes on a spider web hunt in her family's backyard, makes a spider web of yarn on the playground climbing structure, and sings alternate versions of <u>The Itsy-Bitsy Spider</u> including <u>The GREAT BIG Spider</u>, will have rich opportunities to make connections across her experiences in multiple developmental domains.

The Storybook Journey places a strong emphasis on incorporating literacy, including print awareness and early writing, throughout the children's experiences. Children engage in meaningful print and writing experiences, such as looking for the repeated words "Good night" in <u>Good Night, Gorilla</u> or using invented spelling for the animal cages while constructing their own zoo. Another example would be to include a mailbox on the dramatic playhouse of *The Three Bears*, to invite children to write letters to the bears and take on the roles of the bears reading the letters. These practices used within the Storybook Journey approach are supported by early literacy intervention research. For example, Roskos & Christie (2001) found that including the support of writing skills in play resulted in improved overall literacy skills when compared to storybook reading alone. Nicolopoulo, McDowell, and Brockmeyer (2006) describe how play serves as a language experience that can build connections between oral and written modes of expression and provide opportunities to teach and learn literacy. Combining literacy-rich play settings with active adult assistance has been found to positively impact skills such as reading environmental print and labeling the function of print (Neuman & Roskos, 1993).

Through physical reenactments of the story and related sensorimotor, fine and gross motor experiences, children actively engage in motor learning through the Storybook Journey. Quite literally, children are "actively engaged" in physical learning. According to motor-learning research, the nature of the environment and demands of a task are essential for the expression of a motor behavior (Thelen, 1995). Emerging motor skills are assembled within the context of the action and sensory perception of the educational experience itself, and not replicable in simulated tasks. (Thelen, 1989; Thelen & Fogel, 1989). The Storybook Journey provides exploration of the story through active, contextual learning experiences, allowing children to integrate their emerging motor skills within meaningful tasks as opposed to arbitrary tasks or discrete skill drills.

The last element to be considered here as part of an introduction to the supporting research for the Storybook Journey approach to curriculum is the element of repetition, or repeated exposure. The benefits of repeated exposure through the Storybook Journey approach will be illustrated through considerations of the impact on social-emotional features of classrooms with a variety of diverse learners, language development, and sensorimotor development.

By using a variety of interactive reading strategies, teachers can support participation of children with a variety of ability levels through repeated readings. For example, greater child participation can be facilitated through the use of predictable storybooks. Children with advanced cognitive and linguistic skills who are confident in their skills will be able to answer teachers' open-ended questions with their own complex answers. At the same time, children who are less competent or confident in their abilities may be able to fill in words within repeated lines from the story when the teacher uses the cloze technique. The Storybook Journey not only provides explicit and embedded learning experiences in meaningful and engaging contexts as discussed throughout this chapter, but does so in a way that allows children repeated exposure to concepts, vocabulary, sequences, and events. By providing materials and experiences in an open-ended manner that allows children to return to their investigations and further their own explorations, the Journey provides repeated exposure at a deeper level than many commercially available curricula allow for.

Research makes a strong case for repetition, practice at the child's pace, and repeated exposure. Across repeated readings, children begin to shift their attention to word meanings (Justice, Meier & Walpole, 2005; Hargrave & Sénéchal, 2000). Further, repeated exposure to target words improves vocabulary acquisition (Justice, Meier & Walpole, 2005; Penno, Wilkinson & Moore, 2002; Rice et al., 1994). Research also supports targeting words by experiencing the concepts tangibly, through conversations in which children use the vocabulary as well as hear it, and by making associations to other known words within their vocabulary (Wasik & Bond, 2001) and through teacher elaborations (Justice, Meier & Walpole, 2005; Penno, Wilkinson & Moore, 2002). The Storybook Journey provides these experiences through the exploration of the story across multiple developmental domains and through repeated exposure.

The second domain to be considered here as an example is motor learning. By exploring a story narrative over time, learners have the opportunity for repeated motor-learning experiences in meaningful contexts. The primary mechanism in motor learning in children is practice (Schmidt & Wrisberg, 2004), and the amount of practice has been identified as the most important variable in motor-skill development. Further, practice across the day and practice across natural environments are identified as essential elements in learning, retaining and applying motor skills (Schmidt & Wrisberg, 2004). Along the Storybook Journey, repeated exposures to integrated learning experiences across the day, across environments, and across time provide children with essential practice opportunities for motor learning. For example, children exploring the story of The Wide Mouth Frog may practice the motor skill of transitioning from wide-open mouth postures to lip-rounding in the contexts of reading the story through the use of the pictures and sight words and in play ("WOW! You don't see many of those around here, do you?" said the frog to the crocodile who eats wide-mouth frogs,) and in the contexts of pretending to eat like the wide-mouth frog at school with friends and at home with family. Large motor movements such as hopping like a frog can be repeated in the context of reenacting the story with the large group as the frog hops from lily pad to lily pad in the large group, in indoor "obstacle course" setups with mats representing lily pads, or in outdoor play with leaves representing lily pads.

While the above discussion is certainly not an exhaustive review of the research that supports the practices within the Storybook Journey, it introduces how this approach is in line with current research and recommended practice in early childhood development and learning. Combining this discussion of the research with the other components of evidence-based practice, family- and child-centered practices, and professional experience, the Storybook Journey is an evidence-based approach to curriculum that can address a wide range of developmental abilities within a classroom community.

## CONCLUSION

The Storybook Journey is an approach to curriculum that joins children, family, and early childhood professionals in the pursuit of meaningful, learning experiences through the in-depth exploration of a story across the developmental domains. It provides culturally relevant, developmentally appropriate learning experiences at the individual child's own pace within the social context of the classroom community. The Storybook Journey can be considered evidence-based practice in the context of the integration of professional experience, the child- and family-centered approach, and the current theoretical and research evidence. It is with great pleasure and anticipation that I invite you the reader to explore the process of developing a journey with children and families. You will enter into a whole new world of teaching and learning.

Amy Thrasher, MA, CCC-SLP

(A.K.A. "Teacher Amy" to children and families, students, and colleagues)

Clinical Assistant Professor

Department of Speech, Language, and Hearing Sciences

University of Colorado at Boulder

## REFERENCES

ASHA (1998). Evidenced-based practice introduction. http://www.asha.org/members/ebp/intro.htm

Baumer, S., Ferholt, B., Lecusay, R. (2005). *Promoting Narrative Competence Through Adult Child Pretense: Lessons From The Scandinavian Educational Practice Of Playworld,* Cognitive Development, 20(4), 576-590.

Benson, M.S. (1993). The Structure Of Four- And Five-Year-Olds' Narratives In Pretend Play And Storytelling. *First Language*, 13, 203-223.

Berk, L. E., Mann, T. D., and Ogan, A. T. (2006). Make-believe play: Wellspring for development of self-regulation. In D. G. Singer, R. M. Golinkoff, and K. Hirsh-Pasek *Play=Learning* (pp. 74-100). New York, NY: Oxford University Press.

Boudreau, D.M. (2007). Supporting The Development Of Spoken Narrative Skills In Children With Language Impairment. In A.G. Kamhi, J.J. Mastterson, and K. Apel (Eds), *Clinical Decision Making In Developmental Language Disorders* (pp. 203-221). Baltimore, MD: Paul H Brookes Publishing.

Boudreau, D.M. (2008). Narrative Abilities: Advances in Research and Implications for Clinical Practice. *Topics in Language Disorders*, 28(2), 99-114.

Bredekamp, S., and Rosegrant, T. (1992). *Reaching Potentials: Appropriate Curriculum And Assessment For Young Children* (Vol. 1). Washington, DC: National Association for the Education of Young Children.

Bus, A.G., van Iizendoorn, M.H., and Pelligrini, A.D. (1995). Joint Book Reading Makes For Success In Learning To Read: A Meta-Analysis On Intergenerational Transmission Of Literacy. *Review of Educational Research*, 65, 1-21.

DeKroon, D.M.A., Kyte, C.S., Johnson C.J. (2002). Partner Influences On The Social Pretend Play Of Children With Language Impairments. Language, Speech and Hearing Services in Schools, 33(4), 253-267.

Dickinson, D. K., and Tabors, P. O. (1991). Early literacy: Linkages between home, school and literacy achievement at age five. Journal of Research in Childhood Education, 6(1), 30-46. Edn, 6(1), 30-46.

Dodge, D.T., Colker, L.J., and Heroman, C. (2002). The Creative Curriculum for Preschool. Fourth Edition. Washington, DC: Teaching Strategies, Inc.

Galda, L. and. Pellegrini, A.D. (Eds.) (1985). *Play, Language, and Stories*. Norwood, NJ: Ablex.

Katz, L. G., Chard, S.C., (2000). *Engaging Children's Minds: The Project Approach.* 2nd Edition. Stamford, CT: JAI Press, Inc.

Hargrave, A.C., and Sénéchal, M. (2000). A Book Reading Intervention With Preschool Children Who Have Limited Vocabularies: The Benefits Of Regular Reading And Dialogic Reading. *Early Childhood Research Quarterly*, 15, 75–90.

Harrington, H.L., Meisels, S.J., McMahon, P., Dichtelmiller, M.L., and Jablon, J.R. (1997). Observing, Documenting, and Assessing Learning. The *Work Sampling System:* A Handbook for Teacher Educators. Ann Arbor: Rebus, Inc.

Hohmann, M., and Weikart, D.P. (1995). *Educating Young Children: Active Learning Practices for Preschool and Child Care Programs A Study Guide to Educating Young Children: Exercises for Adult Learners.* 2nd Edition. Ypsilanti, MI: High/Scope Press.

Hirsch, E. D. (2003). Reading Comprehension Requires Knowledge—of Words and the World. *American Educator,* v27 n1 p10-13,16-22,28-29,48

Hirsch, E.D. (2003). *Insights into the Fourth-Grade Slump and the Nation's Stagnant Reading Comprehension Scores.* American Educator, 27(1), 10–22, 28–29, 48.

Ilgaz, H. and Aksu-Koc (2005). Episodic Development In Preschool Children's Play-Prompted And Direct-Elicited Narratives, *Cognitive Development,* 20(4), 526-544.

Justice, L.M., and Kaderavek, J.N. (2004). Embedded-Explicit Emergent Literacy Intervention I: Background and Description of Approach. *Language, Speech, and Hearing Services in Schools,* 35(3), 201-211.

Justice, L.M.; Meier, J., and Walpole, S. (2005). Learning New Words From Storybooks: An Efficacy Study With At-Risk Kindergartners. *Language, Speech, and Hearing Services in Schools,* 36, 17-3.

Katz, L. G., Chard, S.C., (2000). *Engaging Children's Minds: The Project Approach.* 2nd Edition. Stamford, CT: JAI Press, Inc.

Kintsch, W. (1998). *Comprehension: A Paradigm for Cognition.* New York, NY: Cambridge University Press.

Lonigan, C. (1993). Somebody read me a story: Evaluation of a shared reading program in low-income daycare. *Society for Research in Child Development Abstracts,* 9, 219.

Marcon, R. (1999). Differential impact of preschool models on development and early learning of inner-city children: A three-cohort study. *Developmental Psychology,* 35(2), 358-375.

McGee, L., and Schickedanz, J. (2007). Repeated Interactive Read-Alouds In Preschool And Kindergarten. *The Reading Teacher,* 60(8), 742-751.

McNamara, D.S., Kintsch, E., Songer, N.B., and Kintsch, W. (1996). Are Good Texts Always Better? Interactions of Text Coherence, Background Knowledge and Levels of Understanding in Learning from Text. *Cognition and Instruction, 14*(1), 1-43.

Morrow, L.M., Sisco, L.J., and Smith, J.K (1992). The Effect Of Mediated Story Retelling On Listening Comprehension, Story Structure, And Oral Language Development In Children With Learning Disabilities. *National Reading Conference Yearbook, 41,* 435-443.

Nelson, K. (1996). *Language in Cognitive Development: The Emergence of the Mediated Mind.* New York, NY: Cambridge University Press.

Neuman, S. B., and Roskos, K. (1993). Access To Print For Children Of Poverty: Differential Effects Of Adult Mediation And Literacy-Enriched Play Settings On Environmental And Functional Print Tasks. *American Educational Research Journal, 30,* 95-122.

Nicolopoulo, A., McDowell, J., and Brockmeyer, C. (2006). Narrative Play And Emergent Literacy: Storytelling And Story-Acting Meet Journal Writing. In D. Singer, R.M. Golinkoff, and K. Hirsh-Pasek (Eds). *Play=learning: How play motivates and enhances children's cognitive and social-emotional growth* (pp. 124-144). New York, NY: Oxford University Press.

Penno, J.F., Wilkinson, I.A.G., and Moore, D.W. (2002). Vocabulary Acquisition From Teacher Explanation And Repeated Listening To Stories: Do They Overcome The Matthew Effect? *Journal of Educational Psychology,* 94 (1), 23-33.

Polkinghorne, D.E. (1988*). Narrative Knowing and the Human Sciences.* Albany, NY: State University of New York Press.

Rice, M. L., Oetting, J. B., Marquis, J., Bode, J., and Pae, S. (1994). Frequency Of Input Effects On Word Comprehension Of Children With Specific Language Impairment. *Journal of Speech and Hearing Research,* 37, 106–122.

Roskos, K., and Christie, J. (2001). Examining the Play–Literacy Interface: A Critical Review and Future Directions. *Journal Of Early Childhood Literacy,* 1(1),59-89.

Sackett, D. L., Straus, S. E., Richardson, W. S., Rosenberg, W., and Haynes, R. B. (2000). *Evidence-Based Medicine: How To Practice And Teach EBM.* Edinburgh: Churchill Livingstone.

Singer, D., Golinkoff, R.M., and Hirsh-Pasek, K. (Eds.) (2006). *Play=Learning: How Play Motivates And Enhances Children's Cognitive And Social-Emotional Growth.* New York, NY: Oxford University Press.

Schmidt, R. A., and Wrisberg, C.A. (2004). *Motor Learning And Performance, A Problem-Based Approach* (3rd ed.). Champaign, IL: Human Kinetics.

Shonkoff, J.P., and Phillips, D.A. (2000). *From Neurons to Neighborhoods: The Science of Early Childhood Development.* Washington, DC: National Academy Press.

Stipek, D., Feiler, R., Daniels, D., and Milburn, S. (1995). Effects Of Different Instructional Approaches On Young Children's Achievement And Motivation. *Child Development, 66,* 209-223.

Thelen, E. (1989). The (Re)Discovery Of Motor Development: Learning New Things From An Old Field. *Developmental Psychology,* 25(6), 946–949.

Thelen, E., and Smith, L. B. (1994). *A Dynamic Systems Approach To The Development Of Cognition And Action.* Cambridge, MA: MIT Press.

Thelen, E. (1995). Motor Development: A New Synthesis. *American Psychologist,* 50(2), 79–95.

Thelen, E., and Fogel, A. (1989). Toward An Action Based Theory Of Infant Development. In M. Gunnar and N. Hazen (Eds.). *Action in social context* (pp. 23–62). New York, NY: Plenum.

Tomasello, M., and Farrar, M.J. (1986). Joint Attention And Early Language. *Child Development,* 57, 1454-1463.

Valdez-Menchaca, M.C. and Whitehurst, G.J. (1992). Accelerating Language Development Through Picture Book Reading: A Systematic Extension To Mexican Daycare. *Developmental Psychology,* 28, 1106-1114.

van Kleeck, A., Gillam, R.B., Hamilton, L., and McGrath, C. (1997). The Relationship Between Middle-Class Parents' Book-Sharing Discussion And Their Preschoolers' Abstract Language Development. *Journal of Speech, Language, and Hearing Research,* 40, 1261-1271.

Vedeler, L. (1997). Dramatic Play: A Format For 'Literate' Language. *British Journal of Educational Psychology,* 67, 153-167.

Wasik, B.A., and Bond, M.A. (2001). Beyond The Pages Of A Book: Interactive Reading And Language Development In Preschool Classrooms. *Journal of Education Psychology,* 93, 243-250.

Whitehurst, G.J., Falco, F.L., Lonigan, C.J., Fischel, J.E., Debaryshe, B.D., Valdez-Menchaca, M.C., and Caulfield, M. (1988). Accelerating Language Development Through Picture Book Reading. *Developmental Psychology,* 24, 552-559.

Zevenbergen, A.A., Whitehurst, G., and Zevenbergen, J.A. (2003). Effects Of Shared Reading-Intervention On The Inclusion Of Evaluative Devices In Narratives Of Children From Low-Income Families. *Journal of Applied Developmental Psychology,* 24, 115.

Zigler, E.F., Zigler, D.G., and Bishop-Josef, S.J. (Eds.) (2004). *Children's Play: The Roots of Reading.* Washington, DC: Zero to Three.

## CHILDREN'S STORYBOOKS IN THE ORDER IN WHICH THEY APPEAREDABOVE

- ➤ *The Three Javelinas* by Susan Lowell
- ➤ *Don't Call Me Pig! A javelina story* by Conrad J. Storad
- ➤ *Machines at Work* by Byron Barton
- ➤ *Bear Feels Scared* by Karma Wilson
- ➤ *The Very Busy Spider* by Eric Carle
- ➤ *Good Night, Gorilla* by Peggy Rathmann
- ➤ *The Three Bears* by Byron Barton (along with multiple versions of this classic tale)

# Field Testing The Storybook Journey

The Storybook Journey has been extensively field-tested in a wide spectrum of schools. The diversity of programs in which the Storybook Journey has been successfully implemented will inspire confidence in the reader that similar results can be achieved elsewhere. I have asked several schools to share a brief synopsis of who they are and an aspect of the Journey's implementation that has brought about critically important results for their children.

## The Center for Hearing Impaired Children
### Tucson, Arizona

**The Center for Hearing Impaired Children** is an NAEYC-accredited preschool program for children with hearing loss. The children who attend the program come from diverse cultural, ethnic, and socioeconomic backgrounds, to form a cohesive community of families with a significant, similar experience. Typically, the children come into the preschool program with extremely limited language skills in sign language, spoken English, or spoken Spanish skills. Often, children have newly identified hearing loss, and their families have the overwhelming responsibility of learning about hearing loss and wondering about their child's future. It is widely documented that 90% of children with hearing loss are born to hearing parents, so this world of "hearing loss" is completely new. For most families, there has been no previous experience with a person with hearing loss. These parents are overwhelmed by the decisions that they must make, which will impact their child's life path.

Some of our classrooms provide intensive, intentional teaching of the prerequisites for language learning…learning to listen or learning interaction skills such as eye contact and turn taking. As they acquire these building blocks, they are ready to learn language through listening and spoken language or American Sign Language, with the stories as the central anchor for development.

As an alumnus of the Child Language Center at the University of Colorado, Boulder's Department of Speech, Language, and Hearing Sciences, I learned that we were able to receive an in-service and training by Sue McCord in 2002, as part of a privately funded program to provide outreach and support in implementation of The Storybook Journey into "the real world." After the preschool staff attended the workshop, the SBJ was enthusiastically started at the center. We have been using an adaptation of the Journey for the past seven years. During these years, we have found ways to incorporate the highly specialized intervention our children need, within the meaningful and motivating framework of the Journey. We have seen the ways that the Journey has provided a means for the preschoolers to develop the building blocks for language learning, language skills, theory of mind, and play skills, through a shared context. We have also seen the ways that the Journey has provided parents with an anchor to their child.

The Journey provides a way that they can truly share a meaningful and enjoyable experience through a shared topic: the story. This shared experience allows them to feel secure in their communication with their child, and secure in their child's communication with them. It has become a way for the children to connect with, and access, their world.

I remember when one little girl, "M," came to our preschool program. She had been identified with a moderately severe hearing loss at age four, and had recently moved to Tucson with her family. She had been a failure to thrive baby and had other motor and sensory delays. She was a very interactive child, who clearly loved to learn. When she was around the other children, perhaps because she knew her own frailty, she participated as an observer and would usually choose to play independently. Her occupational therapist would struggle with her to help her learn to climb steps; a scary notion for a child with balance issues (often associated with hearing loss). At the time, we were using a "theme-based" approach to teaching language. M would actively participate in the developmentally appropriate, language learning activities in the classroom. Her educational team was frustrated with her difficulties in generalizing her skills, or internalizing meaning – especially for concepts, such as prepositions. She only had one preposition: "in." Then, began the Storybook Journey approach in her classroom. And what a change!

Her first journey was The Three Billy Goats Gruff, by Paul Galdone. She seemed to latch on to this story with an intensive hold. She initiated playing and replaying it during center activities, outside playtime, class time, and even during snack. She lived The Three Billy Goats Gruff! Incidentally, children with hearing loss, who have not yet learned to "listen to learn," do not learn in the way that hearing children do. The teachers were nervous about implementing Storybook Journey…would it be successful for our children? M answered that question! Within one week of introducing this story, M was spontaneously using "on," "under" AND "over," in her spontaneous conversations – even when NOT related to the Three Billy Goats Gruff! There were other changes, as well. She began to take more physical risks. She was so driven to replay the story, that she began climbing up and down the steps to our "bridge," first by asking for help, and then, on her own. She began celebrating each aspect of her independence, saying, "I can do it myself!" with a huge grin.

M grew socially as well. She inspired the other children to play with her, through her enthusiastic approach to replaying each story. She found her inner big, strong self in the Biggest Billy Goat character. She began taking more social risks and became a leader, with a following! The miniature worlds were especially treasured by M. She would patiently wait her turn to participate. She became more flexible in taking on each of the character roles and learned to verbally negotiate with her peers. She developed a greater sense of others and demonstrated empathy. She smiled more and anticipated the stories to come. She continued to embrace each story with the same approach… LIVE IT! Her family was able to use the shared context of the story to connect and converse. They were so happy to see all of the changes in their little girl!

Before using Storybook Journey, we would read a different book every day, based on our "theme." Themes changed often, but we thought that exposure to many books led to providing more vocabulary and a greater number of concepts. We had breadth, but not enough depth. We realized that our students were unable to retell the stories or use expressions found in the language of the story. Our students had some of the basic vocabulary in the "greenhouse" of the classroom, but they didn't use it meaningfully in conversations. We saw how the children learned best through the repetition, re-tell, and immersion in one story over time.

After implementing the Storybook Journey, we saw a generalized increase in our students' language and vocabulary use across conversational contexts. There was increased motivation to actively participate in learning, development in our students' play and social skills, and a marked increase in our students' passion for books. Literacy development for children with hearing loss is so crucial, especially as "the average reading level for a deaf, American, high school graduate, has been reported as being at a third- or fourth-grade level (Paul, 1998; 2001). Passion for literacy is SO important! We experienced more parent involvement in our preschool program as well as in their children's language/learning lives. They appeared more confident in their ability to teach their child as well. They were able to meaningfully learn signs through the shared stories, and the repetition allowed them to learn more easily. We saw our students confidently "reading" to each other, to themselves, and to their families.

A further benefit to our program was the way that the Storybook Journey encouraged team building for our staff, which greatly benefited our students. The preschool team planned together. The concepts and language were incorporated in therapy, and more "therapy activities" were incorporated into classrooms. We created a section, in our planning pages, for development of the listening hierarchy for detection, pattern perception, segmental identification, and finally, comprehension (Chute and Nevins, 2002). We were able to incorporate listening into our classrooms with greater ease.

Team members felt valued and we began asking each other for ideas and input. Storybook Journey built community in every aspect of our preschool program.

We chose the Storybook Journey process to guide our teaching because we experienced the success it provided on so many levels. Our preschoolers at different developmental levels had various, meaningful ways to absorb and experiment with new ideas and concepts. They became comfortable and confident with new vocabulary and concepts. And they were able to choose their own, most comfortable means to internalize and master the elements of the stories. We recognized that immersion in a story leads to a deeper understanding. It provided our children with varied, salient learning opportunities, and provided the adults with opportunities for following the child's lead to facilitate development of the whole child. We have had to adapt many aspects, due to our limited time with our students and their high, specific needs. We strongly encourage using Storybook Journey as a guide in program development, as it provides a developmentally appropriate, highly motivating scaffold for building a confident community of learners and teachers.

Patti Sorkow, MA, CCC-SLP
Speech-Language Pathologist
The Center for Hearing Impaired Children
Tucson, Arizona

### Talking and Listening Program
University of Northern Colorado

The Talking and Listening Program (TALP) at the University of Northern Colorado is a literature-based classroom program designed to support speech, language, and early literacy skills in at-risk children or those experiencing difficulties in communication development. In this program, we adopted the Storybook Journey as the philosophical framework from which we developed our curriculum. Speech-language pathologists are increasingly being asked to utilize evidence-based practice, and to choose intervention approaches that are well grounded in empirical research. Integrating key findings from research, the storybook approach to curriculum provides an authentic and meaningful context to facilitate the development of language and literacy skills using an evidence-based approach.

Each week, a children's story that meets the developmental level and interest of the children who participate in the program is identified. This story provides the context for supporting the development of vocabulary, syntax, narrative abilities, and early literacy skills for the children who participate in the program. Explicit instruction in the contexts of stories and repeated readings of stories provide an opportunity for children to learn new vocabulary (Art & Beverly, 2004; Justice, Meier, Walpole, 2005; Roberts, 2004; Walsh & Blewitt, 2006). Additionally, the repeated readings of a story over time facilitate children's development of narrative abilities (Dryden, 2004; Isbell, Sobol, Lindauer & Lowrance, 2004), critical skills for support later reading comprehension (Morrow, 1988; Kamhi & Catts, 1998). An important contribution that SJB makes to the children's experiences is allowing each child to participate at his or her individual developmental level. For example, some children are able to fully engage in retelling of the story, an activity we complete frequently using props such as flannel boards or miniature worlds to foster the development of story comprehension. However, children with more limited speech and language skills may participate by only limitedly sharing in the repeated reading of the story initially. The opportunity to return to the same story repeatedly enables children to understand the story at a deeper level, and strengthens their knowledge of targeted vocabulary and syntactic structure used in the story.

The SBJ also guides our planning for center-time/free play activities. By connecting ideas from the story to various learning activities and centers throughout the duration of our program, we provide continued opportunities for children to experience relevant vocabulary and concepts presented in the context of the story. These multiple learning opportunities allow children with varied learning styles and rates to learn at their own pace, and in their own way, learning concepts that support developmentally appropriate practice (NAEYC, 2004). The Storybook Journey has provided a wonderfully rich context for supporting language and literacy development for children with varied language and cognitive abilities.

Donna Boudreau, Ph.D., CCC-SP
Ft. Collins, Colorado

### **Louisville Preschool**
Louisville, Colorado

Louisville Preschool is a private, nonprofit, part-day preschool nestled in a neighborhood just outside of the downtown area. We serve children ages 2 ½ to 5, in small classes with a 1 to 6 ratio. Most of our families live nearby and many come to us through subsidized programs, with approximately 30% of our population considered at-risk. As a co-founder, I have been teaching and journeying with children for over 16 years. Here is one journey that brought two special children together.

Aidan and Cooper couldn't have been more polar opposites when they first met in our four-year-old program. "Met" is used loosely, as it was more of a collision – Aidan, entering the room with a loud announcement of "I'm here!" ran right into Cooper, who was standing on the edge of the circle rug. Aidan continued on his way, oblivious of the body he had just had significant contact with. As one teacher helped the stunned, but unhurt, Cooper regain his footing, another drew Aidan's attention to what had just happened. "Aidan, did you realize that your body just ran into another child as you came to the circle rug?" "Oh!" was his response, and he turned to meet Cooper face-to-face. "Are you OK?"

This pro-social, empathic response was a long way from the boy who walked through our doors two years before, bursting with energy but not knowing how to channel that energy into productive interactions with others. He did everything BIG – in a loud voice, with large movements, and through intensely felt emotions. Life was there for the taking, and take he did – with gusto! These exaggerated behaviors often made other children avoid Aidan and he was often seen wandering the room, stopping for a moment but never really engaging in play with others. Our team worked with the support of the parents and, eventually, the school district to help Aidan find strategies to help him temper his impulsive behavior without impacting the enthusiasm he brought to everything he encountered.

Cooper, on the other hand, was in his first year with us and was what we would call a "perimeter player." His tendency was to watch from the sidelines, keenly observing what was going on around him but, again, rarely joining in with others. He could often be found at the art table, engaging in the same activity as others, but not interacting. Areas that typically had groups of children involved in shared activities – dramatic play, blocks – were physically avoided but, we noticed, never outside his field of observation.

It was our journey with the book <u>Tacky the Penguin</u> that brought these two together. As is typical with our school, we were into our sixth week of this journey and the classroom had taken on an arctic look, reflecting various pages of the story in all of the learning centers. Dramatic Play had become especially frozen looking, with icebergs to climb onto and jump off of, stuffed penguin friends, and clothing for those who liked to look exactly like the characters of the story – in this case, brightly flowered shirts and fabrics for Tacky and vests for the hunters.

Aidan was the first of our duo to enter the area, attracted by the energy that burst forth with the largely physical activity that abounded. A group of children were climbing and jumping, shouting for help when they were in the frozen "waters" of the floor, and extending a helping hand so that all penguins could be safely out of harm's way on the bergs. After a couple of jumps, however, something else caught his eye and the jumping was replaced with focused attention on the stuffed penguins. He would gently lift one up, examine it closely, and then just as gently lay it down. "My favorite one is Lovely (one of the penguins in the story),"he'd say.

At the same time, Cooper had sidled up to the area, averting his eyes from the fray of active jumping and bound directly toward the vibrant clothing. He gingerly tried on a piece or two of the fabric lengths until he had several on at once. Standing taller, he made his way to one of the icebergs, climbed up, and simply sat amid the activity for a bit. The game had turned to one of power play and, as children leapt, they would exclaim their power. Cooper, still sitting, merely watched and listened. Aidan was soon drawn back to the iceberg and, "Lovely" in hand, joined Cooper as a watcher. When the larger group tired of the game and moved on to another area, Cooper cautiously stood, looked all around, and then burst into the song we had made up while reading the story. Seemingly getting his power from song, he jumped from the berg with a wide grin on his face. As if on cue, Aidan stood up, gave the penguin a gentle squeeze, said, "I get my power from softness," and stepped down beside Cooper.

Two dynamic players began to blossom that day in a role reversal that could only happen with shared experiences and extended time with materials. The shared experience was, of course, the tale of Tacky the Penguin and his friends. Over the course of six weeks, we had read and retold the story in a variety of fashions. While some of the children had used this time to extend their learning through the vocabulary and situations of the story itself, Cooper's anxiety and Aidan's impulsivity often got in the way of their learning. They had to first allow their outer shells to relax some of the protective factors that had built up to help them through their days before they could truly use the story to make connections with others. This is what The Storybook Journey teaches us to do with children – spend time with the story, allowing each child to take from it what he or she needs to make those next leaps of learning. For those who struggle every day to simply walk through the doors of the classroom, yearning to belong to the group, the Storybook Journey can gently move them from passive listeners to active and engaged learners.

Kathy Krajewski
Director and Lead Teacher
Louisville Preschool
Louisville, Colorado

## The Storybook Journey as a Foundation for Intervention in the
### *Children with Autism Group*: A Story of Friendship
Speech Language Hearing Center, University of Colorado at Boulder

Introduction:

Story of Friendship is a social communication intervention group for young children with autism spectrum disorders and their typical peers. This intervention is recommended for children between the ages of 2 to 8 years. The Storybook Journey (McCord, 1995) approach to curriculum provides the foundation for the children's peer interactions.

History:

In 2004, the Autism Society of Boulder County made a request to the Speech Language Hearing Center of CU Boulder for increased availability of services for children with autism spectrum disorder (ASD) with a particular emphasis on social communication and peer interaction. While families with children with ASD seek out and may receive services in schools, through private providers, or in hospitals and clinics; many of these services are in one-on-one, isolated therapeutic settings or in social skills groups with other children with ASD. Interventions for children that support children with ASD in interaction with typical peers are difficult for families to find. In response to this request, Story of Friendship was developed.

Since 2004, Story of Friendship has been offered as an intensive intervention in a "summer camp" format for two hours per day, four days per week, for two weeks. Beginning in the spring of 2005, the Child Learning Center began offering Story of Friendship in a once a week "playdate" format during the fall and spring semesters. In the fall of 2007, due to the generous funding of scholarships for families through the Scottish Rite Foundation, we were able to hold Story of Friendship as an after-school program at Creekside Elementary School at Martin Park in Boulder. This move to the children's natural environment has increased the potential for children to carry over skills and friendships outside of the intervention itself into their daily life at school.

Program Description:

The groups in Story of Friendship are made up of eight to ten children of a similar age range. Each child with ASD brings a typically developing peer to the group. Our intention in asking families to identify a potential friend to bring is to encourage the extension of interactions within the intervention to a friendship outside of the intervention, and to make an impact on the children's actual social lives. Although initially this may seem like a challenge for families whose children don't make friends easily by the nature of their disability, families have reported that play dates and friendships have continued outside of the intervention. For families with limited access to other typical children, we have arranged for their typical peer buddies, and sometimes have paired typical siblings with another child with needs rather than with his or her own sibling as a "buddy."

Each of the eight to ten sessions follows a predictable routine, including an outdoor playtime, a large-group story circle, "buddy time" in which a graduate clinician in speech-language pathology supports reciprocal interactions based on the story between a child with ASD and the child's typical peer "buddy," free play time, and a closing large-group song circle.

Within the Story of Friendship intervention, children are seen as individuals, regardless of diagnosis or label, and we seek to understand them within the context of their families and everyday lives through home visits, ongoing communication with families, and observations of the children working with other service providers. The children with needs benefit from the social communication modeled by their typical peers, while typical peers develop flexibility in their interactions with peers of varying communication and play abilities. Throughout Story of Friendship, clinicians intentionally use evidence-based practices to promote attention, learning, and social communication derived from the research literature (Odom et al, 2003, National Research Council, 2001, ASHA, 2006) including family involvement, visual supports, social stories/scripts, and peer-mediated intervention.

The Storybook Journey as a Foundation for a Story of Friendship:

Each Story of Friendship intervention group of eight to ten sessions is based around a single storybook. During the large-group story circle of the initial sessions, the story is read in its entirety so that children are exposed to the whole narrative sequence. With each subsequent session, the children participate more fully in repeated retellings. Planning ensures that although children benefit from the predictable routine of the repetition of the story, manageable amounts of novelty are incorporated into each retelling. Children are supported to participate in a variety of ways, such as by performing single actions or taking on full character roles with multiple actions, depending on the child's ability at that moment.

During "buddy time," a clinician supports a child with ASD and the child's typical peer "buddy" in reciprocal interactions based on the actions in the story that the child with ASD is able to participate in.

The environment is set up with experiences and activities related to the story, for children to explore and interact with during free playtime. By providing experiences that the children become familiar with through the story play, there is a greater likelihood that children will be able to interact with each other outside of the structured story circle and buddy time.

The Evidence Base for using the Storybook Journey as a foundation for social communication intervention for children with Autism:

Children with ASD are unique individuals, each with their own strengths, abilities, interests, and needs; hence, the term "spectrum." However, children with ASD typically share some common characteristics. In terms of their learning style, children with ASD tend to be stronger at visual learning (National Research Council, 2001, p.58). They are usually more likely to remember information in "chunks" or as a whole, such as scripts, rather than discreet pieces of information or single words (Klin & Shepard, 1994), and they tend to focus on a select set of interests or objects (DSM-IV, Diagnostic Criteria for Autistic Disorder). Story of Friendship is designed to build on the strengths the child with ASD already has in order to support him or her toward social communication with peers.

One of the challenges that children with ASD share, often described as a "core deficit" of the disorder, is the difficulty in developing and maintaining joint attention. Joint attention refers to the ability to share awareness of an object or an event with another person. This difficulty coordinating joint attention has a significant impact on peer interaction, as shared eye gaze, shared emotional states, and communicative acts such as pointing, showing, and giving are all affected. A second challenge shared by children with ASD is the difficulty in engaging in symbolic play, which may further impact peer interactions. Frequently children with ASD have a limited repertoire of pretend play behaviors and often engage in repetitive behaviors with favorite objects (DSM-IV, Diagnostic Criteria for Autistic Disorder).

Children's individual goals related to joint attention and peer interaction in Story of Friendship are based on their families' priorities discussed at home visit. Through observation and ongoing communication with families, we seek to understand what likes and interests motivate a child in order to incorporate these likes and interests into the story play and peer interactions.

The Storybook Journey approach to curriculum is particularly supportive of children with ASD in relation to their strengths and their needs. By reading the same story over the course of the intervention, children with ASD are repeatedly exposed to the story script and the visual cues of the storybook pictures. This story script then becomes the framework for children's peer interactions.

Frankie and the Story of Friendship:

When we first met five-year-old Frankie, he spoke in a somewhat monotone and pressed voice and made eye contact only occasionally during communication exchanges. Like many children with autism, he had restricted interests and at that time his particular restricted interest was with doors. If allowed, he would stare at the frames of doors and open and close them for long periods, fixated on the angles of the structures coming apart and together again. Although he had been receiving services since his diagnosis a year earlier, and was enrolled in kindergarten and doing well academically, he still had limited ability to interact with other children. He frequently became upset and angered when he misunderstood children's intentions, interpreting them as aggressive even if other children were crying, and in turn, he would push them back. Frankie's family enrolled him in Story of Friendship in order to support his ability to relate to other children.

We began to see Frankie's progress through our first Storybook Journey of <u>What Baby Wants</u> as the group of children tried to figure out why the baby is crying along with the family and animals of the story. At last the brother solves the problem of what baby wants. This Storybook Journey provided a way for us to begin to explore the connections between needs and emotions, a challenging concept for Frankie and children with ASD. It also allowed us to address why people act the way they do, which was helpful for Frankie to see that people don't always intend to do harm to others. The approach to problem solving in the story schema appealed to Frankie's learning style. He liked to figure out mechanical objects, and we told this story in a trial-and-error problem-solving manner.

Frankie participated in this story play schema during story circle, and during "buddy time" he was supported to have reciprocal interactions with a peer based on the story play in which he and his peer took turns trying to solve a mechanical problem. He experienced success in these supported interactions, and we began to observe a slight shift in the monotone, pressed quality of his voice toward a more relaxed, fluid quality.

Across another semester of Story of Friendship, Frankie joined us as we used the elegantly simple story of <u>Sitting in My Box</u> by Dee Lillegard for our Storybook Journey, in which more and more animals join a child in a box until a flea comes in and disperses them all except the child.

Many of the children with autism had an affinity for animals, and also enjoyed wearing the masks that the teachers had made up with durable-weight felt, elastic for a headband, and a glue gun. Although Frankie liked the animal figurines we used during some of the participatory retellings of the story, he did not like the feeling of the mask and did not wear one. The children painted the box the colors of the safari, and Frankie was particularly pleased that we included a door in our box for the animals to go in and out of.

During our retellings of the story, we changed the part about the flea "biting" the animals to "tickling," to make sure that we weren't encouraging any inappropriate behavior. The tickle that we modeled was even an "air-tickle," to further ensure appropriate interactions. Many of the children in the group had social communication objectives revolving around initiation and response, in greeting or otherwise. Also, when the box got "too much in it," it allowed us to explore concepts of personal space, which can be challenging for children with ASD.

During buddy time, the pairs of children would play reciprocal interactions games based on this story, supported by a clinician.

During the course of this Storybook Journey, Frankie became fixated on fire extinguishers. He was still fascinated by doors, but now his attention could also become riveted by these red canisters of fire-dousing foam. At home, his family happened to have an actual small and already used-up fire extinguisher. We found out that Frankie had become fixated on fire extinguishers the day he brought it to the session.

That day was the first session that Frankie refused to participate in the story with the other children. This was unusual for him in our experience, since he usually participated in major roles with gusto. However, his family explained that sometimes when he gets fixated on an object it is difficult to engage him in anything else, even other preferred activities or interactions with people. This is certainly what is suggested by the literature about children with restricted interests as well.

In order to re-engage Frankie, we planned for a new twist in the now familiar story of <u>Sitting in My Box</u>. Although you have probably guessed the bit of novelty that we included into the familiar routine of the story, the children were surprised and delighted when we invited Firefighter Frankie to save the day, because the box was too crowded; it was against "fire code."

The flexibility of the Storybook Journey approach allowed us to incorporate his restricted interest and re-engage him in interaction with his peers. It also provided him a way to extend his symbolic play schemas in that we merged the routine of <u>Sitting in My Box</u> with the new schema of firefighter play. This play allowed Frankie to experience flexibility in his play and his thinking. Children with autism spectrum disorders have significant challenges with cognitive rigidity and inflexible thinking. While routines are a safe, predictable, and effective tool for learning, it is critical that novelty and flexibility be included in the children's routines, to prevent the children from becoming insistent on a routine being performed exactly the same way each time. The Storybook Journey is a supportive intervention tool for children with autism, as the story provides the routine, while subsequent retellings include manageable forms of novelty and build flexibility.

Conclusions: The Storybook Journey as a foundation for Story of Friendship

Individual children have made gains in their social communication skills in the context of the intervention according to the baseline and treatment phase data recorded by clinicians. Clinicians and families have also observed more generalized social orientation outside of the context of "buddy time." Family response has been extremely positive, and families frequently recommend the Story of Friendship to their friends who have children with ASD.

Currently, Story of Friendship has a waiting list of children with ASD. As the numbers of children with ASD has climbed recently to an estimated 1/150 children (Centers for Disease Control and Prevention, 2007), the need for interventions that address children's social communication and peer interaction has intensified dramatically. The Storybook Journey approach to curriculum provides a foundation for intervention consistent with evidence-based practices.

Amy Thrasher, MA, CCC-SLP
Clinical Assistant Professor
Speech Language Hearing Center
CU Boulder

References:

American Speech-Language-Hearing Association (2006). *Guidelines for Speech-Language Pathologists in Diagnosis, Assessment, and Treatment of Autism Spectrum Disorders Across the Life Span* <Guidelines>. Available from www.asha.org/policy.

1994 *Diagnostic and Statistical Manual of Mental Disorders* (Fourth edition). Washington, DC: American Psychiatric Association.

Klin, A., and B.A. Shepard (1994). Psychological assessment of autistic children. *Child and Adolescent Psychiatry Clinics of North America* 3:131–148.

McCord, S. (1995). *The Storybook Journey: Pathways to Literacy Through Story and Play.* Englewood, NJ: Merrill.

National Research Council (2001). *Educating Children with Autism.* Committee on Educational Interventions for Children with Autism, Catherine Lord and James P. McGee, eds. Division of Behavioral Social Sciences and Education. Washington, DC: National Academy Press.

Odom, S. L., Brown, W.H., Frey, T., Karasu, N., Smith-Canter, L.L. and Strain, P.S. (2003). Evidence-Based Practices for Young Children with Autism: Contributions for Single-Subject Design Research. *Focus On Autism and Other Developmental Disabilities.* 18(3), 166-175.

### St. Saviour's Church Nursery School
Old Greenwich, Connecticut

St. Saviour's Church Nursery School is an NAEYC-accredited nursery school, located in an affluent, internationally diverse community. Typically, our classrooms contain several children for whom English is a second language, often with three or four different languages represented. Children with special needs are welcome in our classrooms.

As the lead teacher in a four-year-old class at St. Saviour's, I have been using the Journey for the past ten years. During these years, I have had the opportunity to work with children who have started the school year feeling isolated from the community of the classroom, either deliberately isolating themselves or unintentionally isolated by their anxiety or frustration in communicating with others. In every case, the Journey has unlocked the door to communication, friendship, and a sense of belonging in a cohesive classroom community that encompasses every child.

This past year three girls whose families had moved to our community from Mexico entered my classroom, already very good friends. They had strong bonds with each other and with each other's families. They spoke Spanish and some limited English. While their parents had specified that an important goal for the girls was to improve their English language skills (as they spoke Spanish exclusively at home, but would be entering local public elementary schools in a year), this was not a goal shared by the three children. They chattered happily with each other in Spanish and ignored the attempts of classmates to infiltrate their closely guarded friendship. One of the three girls, an ardent supporter of exclusivity, expended most of her energy in keeping the trio together. She zealously countered any efforts to encourage new groupings of children and worked passionately to keep her friends from becoming involved with others or others from becoming involved with them. This was the challenge to be met and overcome. We chose Wilfrid Gordon McDonald Partridge by Mem Fox, to act as the catalyst for the much-hoped-for breakthrough. As part of this Journey, we focused on important memories, both of family and of friendship, underlining the memories that numerous children held in common. As one revelation succeeded another, the children came face-to-face with children whose memories were surprisingly similar to their own. Connections were acknowledged. As the Journey continued, we focused our attention on how to make a "friendship memory," a class-wide goal. (See chapter eight for a lengthier description of the journey.) The façade of indifference cracked as children told stories of "friendship memories" made, of how they had initiated an activity with another child, drawn another a picture, asked to sit next to another at lunch. Exciting new friendships emerged throughout our classroom. Reluctance to integrate was changed into rich new patterns of engagement. The three children demonstrated their delight, rushing into the classroom in the morning, settling into their small group with smiles and words – lots of words. English flourished, as did Spanish, for the girls became enthusiastic teachers of their new friends. Vocabulary from the story was requested and shared in Spanish. Word cards for vocabulary words, both in English and Spanish, had been located in the Writing Center for our previous journeys, but now children were crafting them. At lunchtime, you could overhear children asking one another how to say different words in Spanish, and then as other children got excited at the prospect of sharing their home language, additional translations were offered in Swiss-German, and Italian. The puppet theater, used for dramatic play during this journey was a joyful place of storytelling and dramatizations, all of which contributed to new and spontaneous partnerships. The children were no longer fearful that they would lose something precious; they felt empowered in their emerging friendships.

In discussing the Storybook Journey as a rich resource for the English language learner, I recognize that we could include many other factors. There is comfort in the embrace of the Journey, the familiarity the child gains as the story is told and retold in multiple ways. The pace of the Journey allows for comprehension development, as the story and a rich array of vocabulary words are fully explored. As the story extends into related activities in the classroom centers, interconnected communal investigations (within the context of the story) give greater understanding to the child who is also learning language. Repetition, vocabulary development, and activities occurring within the storybook framework result in a common language, the language of the Journey. However, the children's inner response, the moment when they wholeheartedly "give in" to the Journey, has less to do with repetition and understanding of words and more to do with a response to others, a sharing of themselves.

The Storybook Journey reaches out to ALL children and pulls them into the life of the classroom community, strengthening that community for all. My focus, in discussing how the Storybook Journey has impacted my classroom, is on the Journey's effects on the isolated child. There is a point at which you, the teacher, will know this child, his or her temperament, interests, and challenges. It is at this point that you can choose a Journey that will change his or her school experience. It is deeply moving to watch the child progress from resistant to nonresistant in a matter of weeks. Feel confident that the right story will unlock the most unwilling child and you will make a dramatic difference in the lives of some special children while benefiting your entire class.

Laurie Tischler, Lead Teacher
The Pooh Bear Classroom
Kathy Stewart, Director
St. Saviour's Church Nursery School
Old Greenwich, Connecticut.

Made in the USA
Charleston, SC
06 July 2011